DICTIONARY OF
THIRD WORLD THEOLOGIES

DICTIONARY OF

THIRD WORLD

THEOLOGIES

Virginia Fabella, MM
and
R. S. Sugirtharajah,
editors

ORBIS BOOKS

Maryknoll, New York 10545

The Catholic Foreign Mission Society of America (Maryknoll) recruits and trains people for overseas missionary service. Through Orbis Books, Maryknoll aims to foster the international dialogue that is essential to mission. The books published, however, reflect the opinions of their authors and are not meant to represent the official position of the society. To obtain more information about Maryknoll and Orbis Books, please visit our website at www.maryknoll.org.

Published by Orbis Books, Maryknoll, NY 10545-0308
Manufactured in the United States of America

Library of Congress Cataloging-in-Publication Data

Dictionary of third world theologies / Virginia Fabella and R.S. Sugirtharajah, editors.
    p. cm.
Includes bibliographical references.
ISBN 1-57075-234-6 (cloth)   1-57075-405-5 (paper)
      1. Christianity—Dictionaries.   2. Christianity—Developing countries—Dictionaries.
  3. Theology—Dictionaries. I. Fabella, Virginia.   II. Sugirtharajah, R.S. (Rasiah S.)

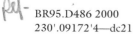 BR95.D486 2000
   230'.09172'4—dc21

                                   00-021887

CONTENTS

EDITORS' NOTE

This volume would not have seen the light of the day without the encouragement and active support of Susan Perry of Orbis Books. When Sugirtharajah first raised with her the idea of a dictionary, at the 1996 New Orleans Meeting of the AAR/SBL, she not only enthusiastically supported the project, but got herself actively involved in all stages of production, from the choice of entries and contributors to the scrupulous rewrites of various submissions. She had the difficult task of not only gathering the entries from all over the world and keeping the contributors in good humor, but also coordinating the work of the editors. More important, whatever Susan did, she did it with humor, care, and energy, and she did it because of her commitment to the peoples of the Third World and their theological concerns. Sue, we owe you a lot and thank you genuinely for all your hard work, and especially for your friendship.

Virginia Fabella, MM
R. S. Sugirtharajah

ACKNOWLEDGMENTS

A publishing venture like this, involving many people spread across the globe, would not have been possible without the help and encouragement of so many people. We would like to express our sincere thanks to many who made this project a reality. First and foremost, to the contributors, especially those who responded to our requests and kept deadlines when their countries were going through political turmoil or were faced with natural disasters of some kind or another; the members of our International Advisory Committee for their counsel and help whenever we approached them; the Orbis staff at Maryknoll—Robert Ellsberg, Michael Leach, and Doris Goodnough—for its hospitality in June 1999, which made the tedious process of editing an enjoyable venture; Catherine Costello, for her efficiency in managing the production process from the copyedited stage to the final publication; and Charles Gillett of the Edward Cadbury Trust for his generous financial help.

Virginia Fabella would like to thank the faculty of the Institute of Formation and Religious Studies and members of the Ecumenical Association of Third World Theologians (EATWOT) for their helpful suggestions; the administration of José Rizal College for use of its technical facilities and the assistance of its secretarial staff; and, above all, the Maryknoll Sisters for their understanding and support during this long-term project.

Sugirtharajah would like to thank the staff at the Orchard Learning Resources Centre—Grieselda Larty, Nigel Mosely, Deborah Dury, Rachel Hayhaw, Robert Card, Pauline Hartley, Jane Sanders, Janet Bushnel, Michael Gale, Meline Nielson, and Gordon Harris—for their professionalism and the friendly manner with which they dealt with the many queries; Lorraine Smith, for her time and help; Dan O'Connor for his extensive involvement and critical interest; and his wife, Sharada, for her unfailing support and constant encouragement in all his work.

Virginia Fabella, MM
R. S. Sugirtharajah

INTERNATIONAL ADVISORY COMMITTEE

Michael Amaladoss, SJ
Delhi, India

Patrick Anthony
Schoelcher, Martinique

Maurice Assad
Cairo, Egypt

James H. Conc
New York, United States

Diego Irarrázaval, CSC
Puno, Peru

Ada María Isasi-Díaz
New York, United States

Kwok Pui-lan
Cambridge, United States

Mercy Amba Oduyoye
Legon, Ghana

Elsa Tamez
San José, Costa Rica

Elochuwu E. Uzukwu, CSSP
Enugu, Nigeria

LIST OF ENTRIES

INTRODUCTION

The book that you hold in your hands is unique. It is unique in the sense that it is probably the first time that a dictionary has been devoted to issues specifically related to the Third World and its theological concerns, and also the first time it has been written solely by the people normally relegated to the periphery. The contributors are men and women of the Third World, including indigenous peoples from different continents, diasporans who find homes outside their native lands, and marginalized people who inhabit the so-called First World. A quick glance at the current lexicographical works on theological and biblical disciplines shows that they tend to be Western-oriented and written from a Eurocentric perspective. The Third World concerns listed in them are either added as an afterthought or tailored to suit Western protocols and expectations. This dictionary, in a way, redresses the balance, viewing everything through the prism of a Third World lens.

There is another justification for calling this volume unparalleled. Until now, dictionary production was seen as a European enterprise. European colonialists—imperial administrators and Christian missionaries—as part of the Enlightenment project, engaged in the task of producing lexicons, grammars, glossaries, and maps as a way of educating the hapless natives, and also in the process gaining control of indigenous knowledge. This dictionary inhabits a transitional moment, a moment in which the former recipients turn into dispensers of their own knowledge. In this sense, it is worth noting that no theological dictionary of this kind exists. We celebrate this significant historical phase. While we subscribe to the view that the experience of oppression is the source of Third World theology, we acknowledge that neither oppression nor the task of doing Third World theology is limited to the Third World.

Definition of "Third World"

This brings us to the use of "Third World" in the title, and it warrants an explanation. Ever since the term gained currency in the public domain, invigorating discussions have been going on regarding the value and limitations of such a term. At a time when the world is becoming a single place, and with the collapse of the socialist project and the apparent success of the market economy, a place for the Third World may seem redundant. However, the naming of the peoples of Africa, Asia, Latin America, the Caribbean, and the Pacific has been problematic and has gone through different processes. In the earlier days, when European countries were carving up the continents of these peoples, words such as "primitives," "savages," "backward," or "inferior" were freely applied. Later, after these countries gained independence, a new vocabulary was introduced: "underdeveloped," "developing," and "low-income group nations." What such descriptions suggest is that these countries had been civilized and developed in order to emulate and measure up to the expectations of the West. At the time of the Cold War, Mao Zedong, the late Chinese leader, came up with his own hierarchy of world order. For him, the First World included the superpowers of the United States and Russia. The Second World consisted of NATO and Warsaw Pact countries. The Third World consisted of economically poor countries. In certain circles the term "Two-Thirds World" is moot as a possible option. The trouble with this usage is that it gives the impression that these people occupy a vast amount of space, but it does not disclose the fact that they neither own nor have access to its resources. More important, it does not highlight their helplessness or vulnerability.

Any definition has its limitations. For our part, as the entry on the term explains, we decided to adopt Third World because it still encapsulates a particular way of existence and experience. We find it a suitable semantic metaphor to convey a relationship, especially the unequal relationship that exists between strong and weak. It is about a people who have been left out and do not have the power to shape their future. It describes a relationship marked, in the past, by power and mediated through old colonial ties and, currently, through the cultural and economic presence of neocolonialism. Such iniquitous relationships exist both globally and locally. In this sense, there is already a Third World in the First World, just as there is a First World in the Third World—the world of the economic and political elite who are in collusion with the world powers. Ultimately, what is important is not the nomenclature but the idea it conveys and the analysis it provides. We believe that the redefined term, Third World, does that.

Format of the Volume

The aim of the volume is to bring to the fore key theological concerns and issues that affect the Third World. It tries to be inclusive and to bring out the plurality of views that exists within the Third World theological discourse. The entries enable the readers to consider the differing ways a particular theological thought has been articulated within the Third World. It tries to root the entries in the historical, social, and theological context of these theological concerns and, more important, to indicate how they differ from Western usage.

In such a project as this, it is inevitable that one has to make decisions as to what to include and what to exclude. The readers will notice gaps and omissions. The length of the entries, too, varies. It is not always easy to get these things right, however vigilant one is. The selection of the entries and the space allocated to them, in our view, reflect their importance in, and relevance for, Third World theologies. Suggestions for further reading appear at the end of the entries. They are listed because they provide significant information about the topic or because they extend the debate. For reasons of space the list is restricted and priority is given to materials written by Third World peoples that are generally accessible.

Contour of the Volume

The production of dictionaries became an important political and cultural activity in nineteenth-century Europe with the emergence of nation-states. Along with national anthems and flags, dictionaries helped to redefine national identity, reshape national images, and cleanse history of its unsavory aspects. The present volume distances itself from such modernistic agendas and sees itself as self-exploratory, seeking clarity at a theological moment that itself is marked by diversity, heterogeneity, and ambiguity.

Dictionaries traditionally act as adjudicators and become authoritative tools in settling disputes among colleagues. These entries make no claim to such definitiveness. They are exploratory and critical rather than definitive or apologetic. Dictionaries are not innocent narratives, and this one is no exception. The views of readers will differ about the relative importance of entries, their length, and even more about their content. Such differences are inevitable, and we see them as positive in the sense that they enable readers to enter into critical conversations. Let the conversation begin.

Virginia Fabella, MM
R. S. Sugirtharajah

ABORIGINAL THEOLOGY

Aboriginal comes from the Latin *ab origine*, or "from the beginning," and means indigenous. In some countries, such as Australia, instead of being used as an adjective, it is used as a proper noun and refers to the Indigenous (or First) Peoples. Thus, aboriginal theology refers to the theology of the Indigenous (or First) Peoples.

In Australia, for example, aboriginal theology begins with the hermeneutical engagement with our historical ancestral narratives (dreaming), which set the foundation of the Creator's actions and interactions with our ancestors, encompassing our identity. Our dreaming is the beginning of everything: the beginning of time, the creation of life, the birth of humanity, and the ordering of all things. It is the remote past of the spirit ancestors, living on in ceremonies that have been passed down by word of mouth from generation to generation, since the beginning. Our dreaming explains the origin of the universe, the workings of nature, the nature of humanity, the cycle of life and death. It shapes and structures aboriginal life by regulating kinship, ceremonial life, and relationships between males and females. It establishes a network of obligations to people, land, and spirits and even affects the rights of aboriginal people to land, through sacred sites.

The West, through colonization and "missionization," tried to destroy our understanding of God and our identity. Two centuries of oppression followed: genocide, slavery, exploitation, stolen generations. In response, aboriginal people reclaimed their heritage in the Creator God, through Jesus Christ, embracing the Holy Spirit. When fully embraced, aboriginal theology can stand against the dehumanizing racist oppression of the West. Aboriginal theology claims Jesus Christ as an ancestor, continuing the relationship with the Creator that has been nurtured and reinforced through the Holy Spirit.

Aboriginal theology is a radical movement in theology, drawing strength from biblical justice. It is autonomous (post-Western, post-denominational) and emphasizes liberation, prophetic obedience, and action.

In our move to interpret and formulate theology for ourselves, aboriginal theology preserves the age-old wisdom of indigenous culture and religion and utilizes more recent critical, exegetical work to deconstruct

1

Western theological concepts that sustain racism, sexism, classism, and imperialism.

Anne Pattel-Gray

See also: INDIGENOUS THEOLOGIES, LAND, TRIBAL THEOLOGIES.

Bibliography
Anne Pattel-Gray, *The Great White Flood: Racism in Australia* (Atlanta, Ga.: Scholars Press, 1998).
Anne Pattel-Gray, ed., *Aboriginal Spirituality: Past, Present, Future* (Melbourne: HarperCollins, 1996).
The Rainbow Spirit Elders, ed., *Towards an Australian Aboriginal Theology* (Blackburn, Victoria: HarperCollins, 1997).

ACCOMPANIMENT

During the last months of his life, Archbishop Oscar Romero of San Salvador spoke and wrote often on the theme of "pastoral accompaniment." The church, he insisted, has a responsibility to accompany those Christians "who have made a political option that they conscientiously see as their faith commitment in history. . . . We must follow them, but according to the church's way, following as pastors, so that these Christians may know that wherever they go they carry the germ, the word, the seed of salvation, the light of the gospel."

More recently, the term "accompaniment" has been used to refer, in a broader sense, to an active solidarity with the poor. In the face of intransigent political obstacles to liberation, the process of accompanying the poor in their everyday struggles is seen as the foundation of more expressly or overtly sociopolitical forms of liberation.

In U.S. Latino theology, the methodological and theological significance of the term is elaborated systematically. Here, the *locus*, or context of theological reflection, is the act of accompanying, or "walking with" the poor in everyday life (*lo cotidiano*). And central to that everyday life is popular religion, the lived faith of the poor, in and through which their dignity as children of God is affirmed. A praxis of accompaniment is a necessary component of an authentic preferential option for the poor.

Roberto S. Goizueta

See also: OPTION FOR THE POOR, PASTORAL THEOLOGY, POPULAR RELIGION.

Bibliography
James R. Brockman, *Romero: A Life* (Maryknoll, N.Y.: Orbis Books, 1989).
Roberto S. Goizueta, *Caminemos con Jesús: Toward a Hispanic/Latino Theology of Accompaniment* (Maryknoll, N.Y.: Orbis Books, 1995).

AFRICAN INDEPENDENT CHURCHES

African independent churches (also known as African initiated churches and African indigenous churches) have many definitions, depending on the motive of the writer and the discipline from which he or she is writing. An African independent church has been defined as "a church that has been founded in Africa, by Africans and primarily for Africans." This definition has solid support among scholars of African independent churches because it indicates that the African continent provides the roots of the churches. At the same time, although the major concern of the churches is Africans, it describes the membership as open to other races. As pointed out by Inus Daneel, the churches are a result of "interaction between a tribal community and its religion on one hand, and a heterogeneous foreign culture intruding with its (Christian) religion on the other. . . . Elements of both traditions are renewed, modified and embodied in a new religious system."

Recent statistics on the growth rate of these churches are hard to come by. However, it is generally agreed among scholars of religion in Africa that the African independent churches are growing faster than the mission churches, both in terms of numbers of churches and numbers of members. This is particularly true in the rural areas. Many reasons are given for this growth, but the major one is that the type of Christianity that they offer appeals to the spiritual needs of African Christians.

African independent churches have been classified into pre-Christian, Christian, and post-Christian based on their doctrines. The *pre-Christian* churches do not believe in Jesus Christ but call themselves churches. This group is further divided into those that advocate African traditional beliefs and practices and those that believe in one God and follow only the Old Testament.

The *Christian* churches are also divided into two groups. The older group includes the "Ethiopian" or "African" churches, which originated between 1890 and 1920 after breaking away from racist European mission churches. They understand that the Bible carries a message of God's plan for salvation for Africans without the influence of white people.

These churches welcome Africans only, although their form of worship is similar to the mission churches from which they originated.

The second group of Christian churches, constituting the majority, includes the "spiritual" or prophetic churches with their origins mainly in the twentieth century. They evolve around a prophet whose teachings emphasize the gifts of the Holy Spirit and usually baptism by immersion. The program of the church and the daily lives of the members are controlled by revelations of the Holy Spirit. These churches practice divine healing through prayer and the use of holy substances like water or candles. Spiritual churches are known by many names in different parts of Africa. In Southern Africa the majority are called Zion and Apostle churches. The Congo, formerly Zaire, has the Kimbanguist, and Nigeria the Aladura churches. Although membership is not restricted by political borders, some do have ethnic followings. A number of these churches have been founded by women.

The *post-Christian* churches are similar to the spiritual churches. The major difference, though, is that the leader or founder is elevated by the members so that he or she replaces Jesus Christ. An example of these "black messiahs" is Frederick Modise of the International Pentecostal Church of South Africa.

Isabel Apawo Phiri

See also: AFRICAN TRADITIONAL RELIGION, ECCLESIOLOGIES: AFRICAN, PENTECOSTALISM.

Bibliography

A. Anderson, "Frederick Modise and the International Pentecostal Church: A Modern African Messianic Movement," *Missionalia* 20, 3 (November 1992).

Inus Daneel, *Quest for Belonging* (Gweru, Zimbabwe: Mambo Press, 1987).

D. A. Shank, ed., *African Independent Churches* (Elkhart, Ind.: Mennonite Board, 1991).

AFRICAN TRADITIONAL RELIGION

Lived predominantly by black Africans south of the Sahara, African traditional religion (ATR) is the sum total of their beliefs, wisdom, ritual practices, and institutions. ATR's basic worldview is that everything in existence has actual or potential religious significance and that there is no dichotomy between sacred and profane, religious and secular, spiritual and material realities. John Mbiti's *African Religions and Philosophy* (1969) was one of the first comprehensive descriptions of this worldview.

ATR is community-based in its origin and orientation. It has no founder, except perhaps in the loose sense of the community's primordial ancestors, who are regarded, under God, as the originators of its customs and traditions. Consequently, ATR feels no need to convert foreigners because its members are born and incorporated naturally into it through marriage and migration. Thus ATR considers all religions equally valid, though some may appear stronger or weaker than others, depending on the energies of the spiritual powers underlying them.

Two spheres comprise ATR's universe, the visible and invisible worlds. Both are intimately linked and constantly interact with and influence each other. Ancestral religion is the principle of order and integration that gives rise to a spirituality of deep respect for tradition. The word for religion in black Africa is simply "custom," the way a given community, bound together by blood, land, and common possessions, ought to live, according to the guidelines handed down by the ancestors. Although modifiable by time and circumstances, ancestral tradition is fundamentally inviolable and the entire community is subject to it.

Insofar as they share a similar worldview, peoples of African origin elsewhere can be said to share African traditional religiosity as well. Therefore scholars speak of Afro-Brazilian and Afro-Caribbean religions, as well as traces of African traditional spirituality in African American Christianity. African traditional religious heritage is also found in cities of the world with a significant number of people of African descent.

Four main beliefs characterize ATR: a belief in the existence of a Supreme Being, referred to by different names, but seen as the source of all life and its resources; God alone is to be worshiped; God's concern and care for humanity are unquestionable even when God punishes; and divine punishment corrects errant humanity.

The dead live on as ancestors when remembered on earth by name. Ancestors are closest to both God and humanity and are the most important influence over the latter. God has invested in the ancestors the energy of universal life, which they dispense or withhold from people as they morally deserve. Unremembered dead live on as spirits and ghosts who are invariably malevolent unless constantly placated through sacrifices, offerings, and libations.

Human beings are the central element in the created order, and human behavior determines the dynamic of life of the entire universe. Good behavior, in accordance with ancestral tradition, stabilizes life and order whereas divergent behavior disturbs them. To restore universal balance and human prosperity, rituals, prescribed by tradition, are required.

The universe is an interconnected whole through the dynamic agency of each being's vital energy. This relationship is hierarchical: the more senior the being in status or age, the more powerful and influential its energy over others. God, ancestors, human beings, animate creatures, and inanimate beings all possess vital energy and influence in that descending but relational order.

The human person can exist only by belonging to a visible and an ancestral community. Conversely, any community values itself in terms of its individual members. There exists an intimate relationship between the two, often expressed in such maxims as "I am because we are, and since we are therefore I am."

Since religion and life are coextensive in ATR, all life is marked by ritual acts. The most common rituals include formal and informal prayers, sacrifices, offerings, and libations. These are most often addressed to the ancestors and other spiritual powers, but occasionally also to God. Important moments in life such as birth, puberty, marriage, investiture, and death are marked by intense rituals during which vital energy is transmitted from a lower to a higher level and from a less to a more fulfilled state. Some of the more prominent symbols in such rituals are the meal and dance. Others include shrines to ancestors, other spiritual forces, and everything reminiscent of the majesty and awesomeness of God.

ATR remained autochthonous until the advent of the religious and cultural expansionism of Middle Eastern Islam and Christianity. While Christianity entered northern Africa at the beginning of the Christian era, it had no impact at all in sub-Saharan Africa until the missionary and colonial movement of the nineteenth century. Islam made inroads into black Africa almost from its founding in the seventh century C.E.

Both faiths have influenced ATR. Whereas Islam is more tolerant of the values and practices of ATR, Christianity has aggressively campaigned against them through organized instruction, education, and the provision of social services.

With the globalization movement today and the fundamentalist, centralizing attitude of much of Islam and Christianity, ATR is under unprecedented pressure to conform to the thought forms, symbol systems, and values of the outside world. Yet, while embracing many elements of these movements, most African peoples remain attached to African traditional religiosity. Converts to Islam simply continue practicing ATR under the guise of Islam. In Christianity, traditional beliefs manifest themselves in thousands of locally initiated churches throughout the continent.

Laurenti Magesa

See also: AFRICAN INDEPENDENT CHURCHES, COSMIC/METACOSMIC RELIGIONS, INDIGENOUS THEOLOGIES, POPULAR RELIGION, SYNCRETISM.

Bibliography
Laurenti Magesa, *African Religion: The Moral Traditions of Abundant Life* (Maryknoll, N.Y.: Orbis Books, 1997).
John S. Mbiti, *African Religions and Philosophy*, 2nd rev. ed. (Oxford/New Hampshire: Heinemann, 1990).

APARTHEID

Apartheid is an Afrikaans term coined as an election slogan for the Afrikaner-led National Party that won the 1948 general election in South Africa. It comes from two Afrikaans words, *apart*, meaning "separate," and *heid*, meaning "ness," and implies racial segregation in all aspects of life. The Nationalists systematized previously enacted land laws (the Land Act of 1913 and 1936) and racial discrimination laws (the Pass Law). The former restricted the lands available to blacks, and the latter inhibited their freedom of movement. As a way of tightening their hold on the blacks, the Nationalist government passed the Population Registration Act, the Mixed Amenities Act, the Group Act, and the Immorality Act, as well as establishing *bantustans* (homelands) for them.

The apartheid system depended upon classifying people according to their race and color. The classification determined where people might live, what jobs they might hold, whom they might marry, and what schools their children might attend. The Nationalists felt that each group in South Africa should have separate "freedoms" in the *bantustans*. From the outset, the majority of black people were against the *bantustan* system. They regarded themselves as South Africans and entitled to citizenship. As a result of the struggle against apartheid, South Africa became a police state, with informers, detentions without trial, and unexplained deaths in police cells with strong evidence of torture. The cases of Steve Biko (1977) and Neil Aggett (1981) are well-known examples of torture and death.

In many towns shopkeepers served black people at a separate counter. It was commonly assumed that a white customer should not have to queue behind black customers, even when their needs were the same. The Afrikan Reformed churches provided the theological legitimation for such practices, and different church buildings were used by different races. Churches based on denominational lines established different branches of the same church to minister to the different color groups.

In 1948 the legislation to enforce the apartheid policy was drafted. Liberation from apartheid came on April 27, 1994. On that day democratic South Africa was born constitutionally, and all its people were reborn. The act of waiting in line together to vote—regardless of race—conclusively affirmed their common humanity.

Luke Lungile Pato

See also: BLACK CONSCIOUSNESS, IDEOLOGY, KAIROS DOCUMENT, RACISM.

Bibliography
Mark Shula and Trapido Stanley, eds., *The Politics of Race, Class and Nationalism in Twentieth Century South Africa* (London and New York: Longman Group, 1987).
Charles Villa-Vicencio, *Trapped in Apartheid: A Socio-theological History of the English-Speaking Churches* (Maryknoll, N.Y.: Orbis Books, 1988).

ART, CHRISTIAN

Even though Christianity was born in Asia, the expression of Christian faith in the Third World through art is a recent phenomenon because, until the twentieth century, Christianity developed primarily in Western countries. To be sure, ancient examples of Christian art exist in some countries of the Third World. At the Hanging Church in old Cairo, Egypt, for example, there is a Madonna with large eyes that dates from the fifth century, and an image of three wise men returning by boat, a popular theme of Ethiopian Orthodox churches, which believe Christianity was brought by a shipwrecked youth from Tyre early in the fourth century.

Pioneers in exploring Christian art in the Third World include Daniel J. Fleming, who published *Each with His Own Brush: Contemporary Christian Art in Asia and Africa* (1938). Fascinating developments in Christian art took place in many Third World countries in the period following World War II after they gained independence. Today, together with music and dance, the visual arts are a vital arena not only for a particular cultural expression of the universal gospel but also for making creative contributions to the whole *oikoumene*. In the words of Engelbert Mveng, SJ, an artist and theologian from Cameroon, "Every rite, dance, piece of music, and work of plastic art is a cosmic celebration of life's victory over death. It is a cosmic liturgy."

Christian art in the Third World can be grouped in five categories, with a certain degree of overlap and intermingling. The first type uses indigenous raw materials or cultural resources. For example, powerful wooden sculptures portray biblical dramas in Africa and New Guinea, such as *Crucifix* by Samuel Wanjan of Kenya. The wood, readily at hand, presents a strong medium to express the suffering and redemption of Jesus Christ. The South African artist Azariah Mbatha utilizes in his woodcuts the African concept of *ubuntu* to appropriate the story of Joseph, not as an individual but as a member of a community.

The second category is the use of traditional media and techniques, both those inherited by people in the Third World and those that are indigenous. Jamini Roy, an outstanding Indian folk artist, expresses himself in the village folk art of Bengal, known as the *pat* technique. The Japanese artist Sadao Watanabe uses a technique of paper stencil print as a unique expression of his Christian faith. The method, with its Japanese roots, has attained universal popularity. Another example of the use of traditional methods is shown in the Nestorian tablet of Hsi-An. This tablet, which shows the oldest Chinese Christian cross, commemorates in calligraphy the arrival of Christianity to China in 781. Calligraphy is widely used by contemporary Christian artists in China, Korea, and Japan. Creative uses of *ikebana* (flower arrangements) in Japan, *batik* in Malaysia and Indonesia, and the art of paper cutting in China are also examples of Christian art using traditional indigenous forms.

A third category of Christian art in the Third World is art that interprets a gospel story in the context of the artist's ordinary life. The fresco painting of the marriage of Cana on the wall of the Cathedral of the Holy Trinity in Port-au-Prince, Haiti, locates the wedding feast in a typical West Indian setting. The bride and groom are surrounded by a drummer, a man rocking in a chair and smoking, and children watching a pig roasting while chickens and a dog are on the floor.

The fourth category of Christian art flows from concerns for social justice and human freedom. During the period of martial law under President Marcos, for example, many Filipino artists depicted the social and political realities of their country through biblical scenes, such as Ang Ku Kok's representation of the extreme agony of the crucifixion. Similarly, vigorous *minjung* artworks surfaced during the struggles for liberation in Korea during the 1970s and the middle 1980s. At the Nairobi assembly of the World Council of Churches in 1975, one striking work of art challenged many people. *The Tortured Christ*, by the Brazilian sculptor Guido Rocha, vividly depicted the agonizing cry of captive, oppressed people. Tadao Tanaka's large painting *Exodus* reflects the agonizing leaders of the national self-determination movement.

The peasants of Solentiname (Nicaragua) used both verbal and visual hermeneutics to describe the oppressive rule of General Anastasio Somoza. Just as with their verbal commentaries, the peasants' visual representation of biblical narratives showed their sense of oneness with the peasants of Palestine in similar contexts of exploitation and redemption. Their depictions of Herod's men carrying automatic weapons marked the historical parallels between Roman-occupied Palestine and Somoza-ruled Nicaragua.

A fifth category is Christian art that represents interfaith dialogue. This refers not to the syncretistic amalgamation of Christianity and other religions but to the artist's efforts to interpret and express Christ in his or her own cultural and religious context. For example, Jyoti Sahi of India works to portray Christ in a Hindu context, and Nalini Jayasuriya, a Sri Lankan woman artist, has created a Christ mandala. Also, many outstanding artists who are non-Christian have produced creative images of Christ. K. C. S. Paniker, a distinguished Hindu artist, composed the face of Christ titled *Sorrow of Christ*, which depicts Christ suffering from leprosy.

Masao Takenaka

See also: INCULTURATION, INDIGENIZATION, MASK DANCE, SYNCRETISM.

Bibliography
Rebecca Lozada and Alison O'Grady, eds., *Creation and Spiritualities: Asian Women Expressing Christian Faith through Art* (Hong Kong: Christian Conference of Asia, 1995).
Philip Scharper and Sally Scharper, eds., *The Gospel in Art by the Peasants of Solentiname* (Maryknoll, N.Y.: Orbis Books, 1980).
Masao Takenaka and Ron O'Grady, *The Bible through Asian Eyes* (Auckland, New Zealand: ACAA and Pace Publishing, 1991).
Masao Takenaka and Godwin R. Singh, eds., *Mission and Art* (n.p.: Christian Council of Asia, 1994).

ATONEMENT

The term indicates a decisive action to bring together or make one (at-one-ment) two estranged parties. It reestablishes a broken relationship. In biblical and theological terms it is the miracle of bringing humanity back to God after the estrangement caused by the Fall. This is first and foremost the effect of the superabundant love or grace of God (John 3:15; Rom. 5-8) revealed in the sacrifice of God's only Son, Jesus, sent into the world by God. Jesus Christ, the Lamb of God, innocent and without sin, was made man and died for us sinners so that we might become the righteousness of God (2 Cor. 5:21; cf. John 1:29; Isa. 51-53). His death on Calvary (and his resurrection) was the sacrifice of atonement that achieved our redemption (Rom. 3:24-25).

Atonement or redemption focuses on the obedient suffering of Christ (Heb. 5:7-10) that made him victorious over sin, death, the law, and the wrath of God (Rom. 5-8). The result is the creation of new relationships between humans and God, among humans, and in the universe as a whole. Consequently, our sins are forgiven and we become the children of our common Father in the church our Mother. The redeemed participate in Jesus' victory by overcoming the negative forces of sin and death, the culture of death and oppression that have become structural to our world. With Christ we present to God a humanity and a world reconciled (cf. 2 Cor. 5:19).

This mystery of atonement has been proposed in the history of theology in a variety of ways. But the victory of Christ over sin and death, which reveals the immensity of God's love and empowers humans to overcome evil in themselves and the world, should remain the central focus.

Third World theologians who have found the Western juridical images difficult to grasp have used local cultural insights to appropriate the atonement. In Africa, where theologians have sometimes used initiatory rites to convey the teaching of atonement, initiation is seen as a continuing process that starts with childhood and progresses to ancestorhood. In this process, a person gradually becomes human. Jesus is seen as the master initiator. In Irian Jaya, similarly, the work of Christ is explained by the Asmat practice of giving a child of a chief as hostage to a feuding group as a way of ensuring peace and harmony. In a somewhat different example, American Indians have used the annual Sun Dance, especially its sacrificing aspect, to understand the mystery in which one assumes personal sacrifice for the health of others. Some Christians in India arrive at an understanding of the work of Christ by drawing on their Hindu heritage of God releasing precious life to make people disciples.

Elochukwu Eugene Uzukwu, CSSP

See also: CHRISTOLOGIES.

B

BASIC ECCLESIAL COMMUNITIES

In the 1960s a new ecclesial phenomenon arose in Latin America and afterward spread to Asia and Africa, Europe, and North America. Small groups of Christian lay people, particularly among the poor living in rural areas and in the peripheries of cities, began to meet weekly to reflect on the word of God. Meeting in houses or community centers, these groups of women and men wanted to understand their ordinary day-to-day living in the light of faith. They became what is now known as basic ecclesial communities (BECs) or small Christian communities (SCCs).

Some of the factors that merged to give rise to the BECs were the emerging consciousness of the dependency of Latin American countries on the First World and the need to struggle for justice and liberation; the shortage of priests, resulting in new roles for the laity and religious sisters; Vatican II's recognition of "human development" as part of evangelization; movements and programs that served to raise the literacy level and social consciousness of the people; the insistence of prophetic bishops on the necessary integration of Christian faith and social action; and the example of Protestant sects' knowledge of the Bible and the vitality of their religious gatherings.

BECs proliferated rapidly among the poor in Latin American countries. The BECs are significant to the church both as an instrument of evangelization and as a force for social justice. It is, in fact, from the life and struggles of the poor, particularly of the Christian communities, that liberation theology emerged in Latin America.

The BECs became a "new way of being church"—participative, biblical, and prophetic. Members try to integrate faith and life by using the Bible as the source of strength to engage in transforming society. Besides faith sharing and common prayer and worship, commitment and action are integral to BECs.

Church documents have referred to BECs as "the source of hope for the universal church." However, though they are established worldwide, BECs remain largely a Catholic phenomenon.

Ana María Tepedino
(Trans. Phillip Berryman)

See also: ECCLESIOLOGIES: LATIN AMERICAN, OPTION FOR THE POOR, POPULAR RELIGION.

12

Bibliography
Leonardo Boff, *Ecclesiogenesis: The Base Communities Reinvent the Church*, trans. Robert R. Barr (Maryknoll, N.Y.: Orbis Books, 1986).
Patrick A. Kalilombe, *From Outstation to Small Christian Community* (Eldoret, Kenya: Gaba Publications, 1981).
Julio X. Labayen, OCD, *To Be the Church of the Poor*, ed. Denis Murphy (Metro Manila: CFA Publications, n.d.).

BIBLE

Introduction

With the emergence of the modern missionary movement the Bible became an important tool in the Third World. It arrived as a handbook of missionary propaganda and was seen as a manual that contained valuable materials for church expansion and apologetics. Now, in a changed context, the same book is being appropriated by the Third World people, not necessarily because of its theological propensities but because of its scenarios that parallel their own existential concerns and interests.

The Bible is used in three ways in the Third World. The first is the *nonreaderly use*, in which it is revered as a sacred object and its benefits are seen as beyond the useful advantages of reading. The physical entity of the book takes precedence over the theological capital that lives in its pages, and the book is treated as an object of veneration. A mere touching or possession of it is seen as salvific. As a numinous book, it represents the nearness of God and God's protecting hand.

The second use is the vigorous *rereading* undertaken from the perspective of blacks, women, indigenous people, the poor, and the victims of society. Latin American liberation hermeneutics has given a new meaning to "reread." This means more than to read again, or reinterpret; rather it means to take a fresh look at the biblical data and to *reperceive* the message. Throughout the Third World the old traditions are constantly being renewed in the light of new situations and new demands.

The third use is related to the *peripheral role* it plays in the lives of the faithful, or its nonuse. In the case of early Indian converts, what was important for them was the direct experience of Christ. Other authorities, such as the Bible, creeds, church, and sacraments, were seen as pointers toward Christ. For example, in the Catholic evangelization of Buganda in Africa, it was not the Bible but Catholic catechism and oral transmission that played crucial roles. Linked to this nonuse of the Bible was the call for an opening up of the Christian canon. The aim was to free the Bible from its internal oppression and to add concerns that were missing, namely, the voices and experience of Third World peoples.

Third World biblical interpretation has been eclectic in its methodology. It has profitably employed various methods, ranging from indigenous modes of reading such as the Indian *dhavani*, to Western semiotics, in order to unravel the text. It has introduced a number of reading practices such as "militant reading," "guerrilla exegesis," "cross-textual reading," "dialogical imagination," "calypso exegesis," and so forth. However, the method that still holds sway is the historical critical method and its various manifestations, and this is at a time when the usefulness and effectiveness of the method are being questioned in the West. Most of the interpretative practices in the Third World are based either on subtle or overt use of the historical critical method.

There is a love-hate relationship among the Third World biblical scholars toward the historical critical method. On the one hand, they are fully aware of its colonial intentions and how it was used to degrade other peoples' texts and stories; on the other hand, they themselves have used that same tool to release the text and empower their own people. The supreme examples are Ahn Mung Bu's reading of Mark's gospel in the light of *minjung* experience, and Hisako Kinukawa's appropriation of the same gospel from a Japanese feminist point of view.

The Third World use of the Bible has certain distinctive marks. The Bible's authority depends on a proper preunderstanding; because the starting point for reading the Bible is not objectivity but commitment to eradicate oppression, neutrality is discouraged. The Bible is read not primarily to solve intellectual queries but to come to grips with the everyday problems people face, such as malnutrition, sexual harassment, and rape. Thus, there is a link between study and life. Along with individual reading there is a communitarian reading that is undertaken in collaboration with professional and ordinary readers. The important thing is not to theorize but to set hemeneutical goals that will have an impact on the lives of the people.

The critical question often addressed is the place and function of the Christian Bible amidst the presence of other sacred texts, such as the Hindu *Bhagavad Gita*, the Buddhist *Dhammapada*, the Confucian *Analects*, and stories of African and Native American cultures. The earlier answer of projecting the New Testament as fulfilling the expectations of these scriptures was based on the missionary hope that the Christian Bible would eventually replace other peoples' sacred stories and writings. At a time when these various texts coexist, coalesce, and interact with one another, what is proper is to undertake a cross-textual or parallel reading that will not undermine or privilege one text over the other. While such a reading celebrates the common liberative thrust, it can also expose the gaps, silences, and omissions in the texts. The Christian Bible's place amidst the other sacred writings depends on the acknowledgment that no scripture conveys the full divine-human experience, and that any scripture can help us to see the traces of that experience, if one approaches the sacred writings with openness and sensitivity.

R. S. Sugirtharajah

Bibliography
Hannah W. Kinoti and John M. Waliggo, eds., *The Bible in African Christianity: Essays in Biblical Theology* (Nairobi: Acton Press, 1997).
Kwok Pui-lan, *Discovering the Bible in the Non-Biblical World* (Maryknoll, N.Y.: Orbis Books, 1995).
R. S. Sugirtharajah, ed., *Voices from the Margin: Interpreting the Bible in the Third World* (Maryknoll, N.Y.: Orbis Books, 1995).
Lief E. Vaage, *Subversive Scriptures: Revolutionary Readings of the Christian Bible in Latin America* (Valley Forge, Pa.: Trinity Press International, 1997).

Africa

Discussing the Bible in Africa is as complex as discussing the Bible itself. Covering more than two thousand years of history, the Bible has its roots in Africa. The Exodus event, which gave birth to the Israelite nation through God's Sinaitic covenant with them and forms the fountainhead of biblical history, originated in Africa. The Bible embraces both the Old and New Testaments. Jesus' life and accomplished salvific mission gives birth to the New Testament, hence, for Christians, to the Bible proper. Africa served as God's chosen place for nurturing the Hebrews into "a great nation" (Deut. 26:5) through the leadership of Moses. It also served as God's chosen refuge place for Jesus and his mother against the onslaught of Herod (Matt. 2:13-15).

In the early church, the African patristic scholars Origen, Cyril of Alexandria, and Augustine of Hippo, among others, kept the Bible alive by their commentaries, textual studies, and translations. The Septuagint, the Greek Bible that had its birth in Africa, played a key role in the early Christian proclamation of the gospel of Jesus Christ and served as a literary resource for some of the New Testament authors.

Africa's contribution to the Bible is not limited to the past. Today Africa is the home of a faith-based reading of the Bible among scholars and ordinary readers. Africans see the Bible as God's liberative, life-giving word, rooted in Christ, "the savior of the world" (John 4:42; cf. Acts 4:12). Accordingly, their liberative reading of the Bible takes a number of forms in their search for the fullness of life promised by Jesus (John 10:10).

The ordinary African reader sees the Bible essentially as God's word. As such, it has power and authority to ward off attacks by evil spirits, protect from the enemy's charms, and assist in disclosing a culprit within the community. The Bible gives meaning and direction in life, helps to interpret one's world, and assures us of God's ability to provide for our daily needs (e.g., Pss. 23:1; 27:1; 119:105). The plethora of captions from the Bible placed on vehicles, in homes, and in places of work testifies to this belief. The reading also affirms and celebrates the lordship of Jesus in creation (Phil. 2:11) and readers' convictions that as God's children, nothing can hurt them (cf. Rom. 8:31-38). This faith reading is located mainly, though not exclusively, among Pentecostal, charismatic, and Spirit-centered churches. The reading tends to be "fundamentalistic"; it takes the Bible literally and has little faith in historical-critical, literary, or ideological readings by modern scholars.

Scholarly reading is more critically liberative, without ceasing to be anchored in the faith. One approach explores Africa's presence and role in the Bible itself, "when Israel was in Egypt." Another reviews the damage that selective, imperialistic, and racist readings have caused black Africans. The evils of slavery and apartheid both used the Bible as their alleged divine authorization, citing the so-called curse of Ham (Gen. 9:18-27). Today African scholars reread these texts and disclose that their racist and ideological readings were not only damaging to Africans but also an abuse of Scripture itself. Their reading seeks to highlight and help to eliminate the harmful fruits that such readings bore and continue to nourish in human hearts, even among Africans themselves.

Another reading goes further and sees the Bible itself as an essentially ideological and racist book, with its election theology, its view of Gentiles as "unclean" and its use of God as an excuse to exterminate other nations and forcefully acquire their lands. Originating understandably from apartheid South Africa, this reading asks that the Bible not be simply interpreted in a liberational manner, but that it be completely rewritten and rid of its racist and electionist or exclusionist character.

Other African scholars recognize the human factor in the Bible. As God's word in human language and culture, it embodies the unredeemed realities of limited and historically conditioned human beings in their perception of God, and God's will for humanity as a whole. Though the Bible reflects the life situations of its authors and their audiences, these authors are not the only or even determinative voice in the Bible. The constitutive voice is that of God. Yet this voice has often been drowned or distorted by sinful human voices within the Bible itself and in certain age-old readings and translations. Any oppressive use of the Bible is sinful and cannot be attributed to the biblical God who cherishes all of creation (Ps. 24:1; Wis. 11:24-26). This awareness calls for an attentive reading of the Bible to discern God's own life-giving voice from the culturally conditioned and historically limited human voices. This liberative reading, by far the most dominant, includes inculturation hermeneutics and African women's readings. Its agenda also calls for the liberation of the Bible itself.

These different readings cross border lines, and enrich and challenge one another. Their common ground is the belief that the Bible is God's life-giving and empowering word for all peoples, irrespective of sex, race, and social or geographical location; it invites all readers to become in turn God's life-giving agents for one another.

Teresa Okure, SHCJ

See also: BIBLE: AFRICAN AMERICAN, FUNDAMENTALISM, RACISM, THIRD WORLD WOMEN'S THEOLOGIES: AFRICAN.

Bibliography
L. Cox, I. Mukonyoro, and F. J. Verstraelen, eds., *Rewriting the Bible: The Real Issues* (Gweru, Zimbabwe: Mambo Press, 1993).
Itumeleng J. Mosala, *Biblical Hermeneutics and Black Theology in South Africa* (Grand Rapids, Mich.: Eerdmans, 1989).
Teresa Okure, "Feminist Interpretations in Africa," in *Searching the Scriptures. Vol. 1: A Feminist Introduction*, ed. Elisabeth Schüssler Fiorenza (New York: Crossroad, 1993), 76-85.
Gerald West and Musa W. Dube, eds., "'Reading With': An Exploration of the Interface between Critical and Ordinary Readings of the Bible, African Overtures," *Semeia* 73 (1996).

African American

The African American experience throws into sharp relief one of the major problems faced by all peoples-made-Christians as a result of their experiences of enslavement and colonialization—that of the cultural co-optation (viz. Europeanization) of the Bible and of interpretive approaches to it. Among the several questions raised by conjoining African American experience and the Bible, none is more important than the question of time—whether the study of the Bible ought to begin with a focus on the past, an ancient setting or an ancient text, or on the present, namely, the modern if not the contemporary worlds of those defining what "Bible" is or means. Given the beginnings of the interactions between peoples of color and the Bible in the context of modern slavery and colonialization, and given the European co-optation and over-determination of the Bible, to begin the engagement of the Bible with the focus upon the past is actually to begin on terms that are for formerly enslaved and colonized peoples self-alienating. Only by beginning in their own time, in the modern world that is defined by their physical, sociocultural, and ideological captivity—in which the Bible has played controversial roles—can such peoples begin to position themselves as independent and authoritative readers of sacred texts and thereby read themselves in such texts for the sake of both affirmation and challenge.

African Americans' engagement with the Bible begins with their enslavement in the New World; it continues to this day with diverse and complex engagements. Proposed below is an interpretive schema, a history of "readings," which is also a history of the development of African American identity formation (primarily focused upon the United States).

First reading: wariness of book religion. The Africans who were made slaves in the "New World" were forced for the sake of survival to learn to engage the world controlled by the European slavers. Reports from missionaries of the sixteenth through the nineteenth centuries indicate that the Africans before and during enslavement reacted initially with wariness in response to efforts to convert and catechize them. A major part of the initial difficulty in converting Africans had to do with explaining the belief, so much taken for granted in heavily christianized Europe, that divine power was found in a book. This notion the Africans found at first to be strange, prompting fear and awe and some psychic distance.

Second reading: social critique and social accommodation. Beginning in the late eighteenth century and extending through most of the nineteenth century, and corresponding to the growth of nonestablishment churches and revival movements, African slaves and freedpersons began to encounter the Bible in direct ways and on more independent terms. As there was for the sake of survival an accommodation of sorts to the world of the slavers, so the Bible of the slavers was in this period heard and read. But it was heard and read in opposition to the status quo biblical hermeneutics of the white slavers. It was understood to be a manifesto calling for freedom and a critique of the slaveholding world.

This reading is associated with the largest segments of African Americans over a period of time, stretching from the founding of the independent churches to the modern civil rights movements of the 1960s. The religious-ideological foundation for its prophetic accommodationism is reflected in the popularity of two biblical passages—Galatians 3:26-28 and Acts 10:34-36. These passages express the ironic ideology of the hope of universality of salvation and the kinship and equality of all human beings.

Third reading: radical critique from the margins. In the early decades of the twentieth century, in the wake of the migrations from the agrarian South to the large urban centers of the North, another reading was cultivated. This reading reflected the sentiment of many of those who felt alienated in the new situation. Cultivated mainly in storefront "Christian" churches and in many new formations—the Garvey movement, Father Divine and the Peace Mission Movement, the spiritual churches, the Nation of Islam, the black Jews, to name a few of the most prominent ones—this reading of the Bible and of other sacred texts emphasized the need to reject more sharply both the accommodationist African American churches and white churches and society. What the groups shared was the sentiment that attempts at accommodation and integration into American society were futile. The way of salvation was thought to be the way of radical rejection of the world. The creation of esoteric (extracanonical) sacred texts and esoteric interpretive principles and presuppositions reflected the radical ethos of rejection of the world.

Fourth reading: transcending race. In the late twentieth century another reading of the Bible as a reading of the world became evident. A reaction to both the accommodationist-integrationist and separatist readings and orientations discussed above, this late reading is associated with new evangelical and fundamentalist groups. But such groups are quite different from the evangelical groups that have historically defined "mainline" African American Christianity. These new groups have their origins in early-twentieth-century white fundamentalist camps. Their engagement of the Bible in terms of doctrinal issues and strict literalism has ironically had the force of separating these new groups from mainstream African American groups and enclosing them within a somewhat racially and ethnically diverse religious world in which racial and ethnic issues are relativized or not addressed at all.

Women's readings. Throughout the history of African Americans' engagement of the Bible there is evidence of the special emphases of women's readings. From Phillis Wheatley and many other unnamed, unlettered women to modern womanist scholars, women have been a significant part of each cultural reading identified above. Notwithstanding differences in social statuses, locations, and historical settings, there is also evidence of the special emphases that women have added. What stands out above all is the consistent challenge women have placed upon African American churches to respect within their own communities the prophetic challenge regarding equality of treatment and inclusion.

Vincent L. Wimbush

See also: THIRD WORLD THEOLOGIES IN THE FIRST WORLD: BLACK THEOLOGY IN THE UNITED STATES, THIRD WORLD WOMEN'S THEOLOGIES: AFRICAN AMERICAN.

Bibliography
Cain H. Felder, ed., *Stony the Road We Trod: African American Biblical Interpretation* (Minneapolis, Minn.: Fortress, 1990).
Stephen B. Reid, *Experience and Tradition: A Primer in Black Biblical Hermeneutics* (Nashville, Tenn.: Abingdon, 1990).

Renita Weems, *Just a Sister Away: A Womanist's Vision of Women's Relationships in the Bible* (San Diego, Calif.: LuraMedia, 1988).

V. L. Wimbush, "The Bible and African American Culture," in *Encyclopedia of African American Culture and History*, Vol. 1, ed. J. Salzman et al. (New York: Simon & Schuster Macmillan, 1996), 315-16.

Asia

The reception and appropriation of the Bible in Asia fall into three stages: precolonial, colonial, and postcolonial. In the precolonial days before the advent of modern European colonialism, the Bible was introduced to Asia by those who belonged to the church of the East, popularly known as the Nestorians. The Bible they brought with them was not the Western canon, but the Eastern Bible with the Syriac version known as the Phestto (clear text edition). In India, the Bible remained untranslated into local languages, was rarely read, and often revered as a sacred object by St. Thomas Christians in Kerala. In China, no full translation was undertaken; nevertheless, there were attempts to incorporate biblical materials in Chinese writings. For example, *Jesus Messiah Sutra* follows Matthew's Gospel, and the *Lord of the Universe's Discourse on Almsgiving* contains references to passages in Genesis 1-3, Isaiah 53, Acts 1-2, and Matthew 5-7. These writings creatively infused Mahayana terminologies with Christian concepts. There are two aspects of the precolonial phase: first, the Bible was marginal in the lives of the faithful. It was the sacraments that came to be regarded as the prime media of God's revelation. Second, the Bible found its place among many sacred oracles, both written and oral, and did not threaten to subsume or surpass them.

The second juncture was modern Western colonialism, and with it emerged the modern missionary enterprise. In this phase, the Bible became an important cultural armory to be used against heathenish texts. The British and Foreign Bible Society played an important role in biblicizing the "heathens" by financing the translations and establishing a network of distribution. A collection of narratives that originated in West Asia was now turned into a cultural artifact of the English in the form of the King James Version, and made to act as the umpire of all texts. The colonial use of the Bible was based on the Protestant principle of the self-sufficiency of the Bible. The other legacy was the privileging of the written word over the oral, thereby overlooking the fact that in some cultures hearing, memorizing, and performing are seen as sufficient.

The postcolonial appropriation has two phases. First is the decolonizing hermeneutical practices that took place during the colonial occupation, and are still being continued even after the exit of the invaders. The second is the recent appropriation of current postcolonial theoretical practices for biblical hermeneutics. Hong Xiuquan's altering of biblical texts during the Taiping revolution in order to proclaim himself as God's chosen, K. N. Banerjea's attempt at an intertextual reading of biblical narratives in conjunction with Vedic texts, Matsumura Kaiseki's editing out of canonical material and production of his own version known as the Dokkai Bible, and Panditha Ramabai's own rendition of the Bible into Marathi as a way of redressing the Bible Society's over-Sanskritized version are some examples of an anticolonial mode of interpretation.

The same resistant reading is practiced, after independence, by Indian *dalits*, Japanese *burakumin*, Asian women theologians, and the tribals, whose history has so often and for so long been one of pain and neglect. This time it was not against the missionaries or colonizers, but against their own interpreters whose hermeneutical output was seen as pollution-based and hierarchically and patriarchically influenced. In the Philippines, a predominantly Christian country, an attempt is being made to read the Bible using an important but often neglected tool, namely the eyes of the conscientized poor, to recover the sense of the texts. This exegetical practice has come to be known as taking a "third look" at the biblical narratives.

Though these readings indicate that Asians were not simply the recipients but also dispensers of biblical knowledge, the paradigm that shaped them was the Enlightenment, which among other things privileged the Christian texts and was based on binary thinking: East/West, Hindu/Christian, us/them. Where the current postcolonial biblical interpretation differs is that it concedes the complexities of the contact between the Orient and the Occident and lays a greater emphasis on critical exchanges between, and the mutual transformation of, both. It addresses the colonizing tendencies in both biblical texts and interpretations and the way they collude or subvert the process, and offers rereadings from postcolonial circumstances such as diaspora and hybridity. More important, it turns to the Bible not so much for finding answers but for narratives that remind us about the diversity of human beliefs and experience. Archie Lee, Philip Chia, Kwok Pui-lan, and R. S. Sugirtharajah are the prominent promoters of this mode of interpretation.

In a continent that brims with sacred texts, both written and oral, what postcolonialism tries to do is to enable the Christian Bible to shed its Western pretensions, to rediscover its West Asian roots, and to find a respectable place among them. At a time when religious texts may not be the only place to look for insights into Asia's problems, such a repositioning may not be a bad idea.

R. S. Sugirtharajah

See also: BIBLE TRANSLATION, CHRISTOLOGIES: ASIAN, LIBERATION THEOLO-
GIES: ASIAN, POSTCOLONIALISM, THIRD WORLD WOMEN'S THEOLOGIES: ASIAN.

Bibliography
Carlos H. Abesamis, *A Third Look at Jesus: A Guidebook along a Road Least Trav-
elled*, 3rd rev. ed. (Quezon City, Philippines: Claretian Publications, 1999).
Hisako Kinukawa, *Women and Jesus in Mark: A Japanese Feminist Perspective*
(Maryknoll, N.Y.: Orbis Books, 1994).
Stanley Samartha, *The Search for the New Hermeneutics in Asian Christian
Theology* (Madras: The Christian Literature Society, 1987).
R. S. Sugirtharajah, *Asian Biblical Hermeneutics and Postcolonialism: Contest-
ing the Interpretations* (Maryknoll, N.Y.: Orbis Books, 1998; Sheffield, Eng-
land: Sheffield Academic Press, 1999).
R. S. Sugirtharajah, *Voices from the Margin: Interpreting the Bible in the Third
World*, rev. ed. (Maryknoll, N.Y.: Orbis Books; London: SPCK, 1995).

Caribbean

In the colonial era in the Caribbean, the Bible functioned primarily
as a source for maintaining the Eurocentric status quo. It was an ideological tool to validate the cultural values of the colonial powers. Since
the 1970s, Caribbean biblical scholars have begun to develop a decol-
onized method of biblical interpretation. They have moved away from
methodologies (mainly the Western philosophical analysis) that are detached from the Caribbean situation as a primary means of interpretation. Dreams, visions, spirit, ecstatic dances and healings, which Western biblical scholars, raised in the Enlightenment, regard as irrational or
superstitious, are seen by Caribbean scholars as suitable resources for
Caribbean hermeneutics. Recently, George Mulrain has suggested calypso, a powerful medium in the Caribbean, as a way of engaging with
historical texts.

Pedrito Maynard-Reid

See also: CARIBBEAN EMANCIPATORY THEOLOGY, DECOLONIZING THEOLOGY.

Bibliography
George Mulrain, "Is There a Calypso Exegesis?" in *Voices from the Margins:
Interpreting the Bible in the Third World*, ed. R. S. Sugirtharajah (Maryknoll,
N.Y.: Orbis Books; London: SPCK, 1995).

Hispanic

Biblical interpretation on the part of U.S. Hispanic Americans (or
Latinos/as) from their standpoint as an ethnic minority group within the

United States parallels the rise of Hispanic American theology on the U.S. theological scene toward the end of the 1980s and the beginning of the 1990s. With the rise of theological reflection on the historical experience and cultural reality of U.S. Hispanic Americans, therefore, comes a corresponding interest in biblical interpretation, from the perspective of and with regard to such experience and reality.

Two different and sequential developments can be readily outlined within this newly constituted reading tradition of the Bible. To begin with, the turn to the Bible was profoundly theological in character. The early voices had received their primary training in theological studies, broadly conceived, and turned to the biblical texts for reflection, inspiration, and argumentation in the pursuit of their respective theological constructions. In this first phase, the hermeneutical element remained subordinate to the primary theological aims of the discussion. Subsequently, the use of the Bible became much more of a self-conscious critical activity and thus profoundly hermeneutical in character. Later voices had their primary training in biblical studies and turned to the biblical texts in the light of both contemporary biblical criticism and the aims of the movement as a whole. In this second phase, the theological element remained secondary to the dominant hermeneutical aims of the discussion.

Such concern with biblical interpretation among U.S. Hispanic American theologians and critics in the late 1980s and early 1990s constitutes a clear cultural sign of the times. Its origins can be readily explained in terms of a variety of interrelated developments. In *society*, in the 1960s and 1970s, minority groups turned their attention to their own historical track, present social conditions, and future prospects; in the *academy*, through the 1970s and 1980s, partly as a result of such inquiries, the conception of knowledge changed: across the entire disciplinary spectrum the object of study was now perceived as local and multidimensional and its analysis as contextual and perspectival; in *theological studies*, in the course of the 1970s and 1980s, theological construction began to be avidly pursued in all corners of the non-Western world as well as among non-Western minority groups within the West; in *biblical studies*, from the mid-1970s on, the discipline witnessed enormous methodological and theoretical diversity, with more and more attention focused on the role of reading and readers in interpretation. In the wake of such social, intellectual, religious, and disciplinary transformations, a turn to biblical interpretation among U.S. Hispanic American theologians and critics was simply a matter of time, with the outbreak coming in the years around 1990.

Since then, while the two approaches to the Bible have continued through the 1990s, one, the hermeneutical angle, has emerged as far more vigorous than the other. This approach has shown throughout a strong commitment to the traditional tenets of liberation hermeneutics, whether formulated from the socioeconomic or feminist perspective. This approach has also been concerned throughout with the central discussions on questions of method and theory in contemporary biblical studies. This discussion has become, by way of contrast, ever more populated, varied, and sophisticated.

The tenor of these two approaches may be summarized in terms of five fundamental issues of interpretation. First, with respect to perceived affinity with the text, the theological consensus on correspondence between the people of God and U.S. Hispanic Americans gives way to a much more guarded conception of the Bible as a distant and strange text, whose accessibility to U.S. Hispanic Americans becomes problematic on various grounds. Second, regarding the proposed locus of liberation within the text, the theological consensus that the Bible is a liberating text endures, but the message of liberation is now perceived as far more ambiguous, with the Bible seen, in various ways, as a source of both liberation and oppression. Third, with respect to point of entry into the text, the theological consensus that marginalization and oppression as key to the liberating message of the Bible is preserved, but the process of identification with the people of God on the part of U.S. Hispanic Americans emerges as much more difficult in different ways. Fourth, regarding the question of validity in interpretation, the theological consensus on a reading of resistance persists, but such a reading is portrayed, from different perspectives, as far more complex. Finally, in terms of the perceived agenda of liberation, the theological consensus regarding a highly utopian and subversive vision prevails, but such a vision becomes, from a variety of different angles, much more subtle.

As more and more voices join its ranks, participate in its discussions, and shape its discourse, such sophistication and diversity are bound to grow at an even more rapid pace, making U.S. Hispanic American biblical interpretation an ever more vibrant, complex, and powerful reading tradition of the Bible.

Fernando F. Segovia

See also: THIRD WORLD THEOLOGIES IN THE FIRST WORLD: HISPANIC.

Bibliography
Justo L. González, *Mañana: Christian Theology from a Hispanic Perspective* (Nashville, Tenn.: Abingdon Press, 1990).
Ada María Isasi-Díaz, "La Palabra de Dios en nosotras—Word of God in Us," in *Searching the Scriptures. Vol. 1: A Feminist Introduction*, ed. Elisabeth Schüssler Fiorenza (New York: Crossroad, 1993), 86-100.

Fernando F. Segovia, "Hispanic American Theology and the Bible: Effective Weapon and Faithful Ally," in *We Are a People! Initiative in Hispanic American Theology*, ed. Roberto S. Goizueta (Minneapolis, Minn.: Fortress Press, 1992), 21-50.

Fernando F. Segovia, "Toward a Hermeneutics of the Diaspora: A Hermeneutics of Otherness and Engagement," in *Reading from This Place. Vol. 1: Social Location and Biblical Interpretation in the United States*, ed. F. F. Segovia and M. A. Tolbert (Minneapolis, Minn.: Fortress Press, 1995), 57-74.

Latin America

The use of the Bible in Latin America within the overall setting of a liberating practice of faith is significant and remarkable. It serves as the basis for reflection on religious experience and on reality as a whole. Christian base communities; groups of Christians who engage in a "people's reading of the Bible"; those who are committed to the oppressed, the outcast, and the poor; liberation theologians; and even trained exegetes who work with sophisticated hermeneutical tools—all read it in a manner that is fresh, creative, ecclesial, and committed.

These readings have several distinctive marks.

First, there stands the reality of the poor and oppressed over against those who dominate, the rich and powerful. In Latin America, the Bible, which used to be monopolized by those who wield power, is being regained by a new actor in history, namely, the poor, the outcast, those who mourn. It is precisely in the Bible that their experience of God, their ability to recognize God's presence in their lives, finds a means of communication. It is not only God's word but theirs.

The experience of such a reading—always a rereading—of the Bible is that it is necessary for interpreting the overall situation and gives rise to a profound liberating spirituality.

This reading is driven by a hermeneutical posture: one "enters" into the text from everyday reality with all its conflicts and problems. One then goes deeper into the text to understand its message, and finally one returns to the situation, bringing the contribution of the Word. It is important to emphasize that this "hermeneutical circularity" begins not in books but in life, and therefore it represents a break from traditional readings.

When the Bible is tuned into new situations, it delivers its "reserve of meaning," making it possible to "see" what otherwise remains unseen. It is thus necessary to analyze the biblical text sociologically, and that entails understanding how it reflects the social formation and modes of production in the context in which it was written. Such a socioanalytical reading (from "all four sides": political, economic, social, ideological) is characteristic of Latin America.

Very often the coupling of the hermeneutic and socioanalytical approaches (in addition to the normal and ongoing use of historical-critical methods) makes it possible to enter with some affinity into the reality that gave rise to the biblical text because the earlier "rhetorical situation" was usually also one of conflict, oppression, rejection, injustice, or imperialist invasion with its plunder and destruction.

The hermeneutical interpretation of the Bible, which is a key tool for liberation theology, highlights those textual areas and those events that are more relevant within the vast range of biblical literature, namely, the Exodus (oppression and liberation), the prophetic books (critique of anti-values in society and worship), the historic Jesus (his liberating practices), and the apocalyptic literature (message of hope of the oppressed and the outcast).

This emphasis may seem to be a "canon within the canon" (and so it has been criticized). In point of fact, such an operation is characteristic of any religious tradition with an extensive canon; moreover, it is a legitimate action when the Bible is read as relevant text out of, and for, the situation. Finally, both liberation theology and Latin American exegesis also use the other books and texts in the Bible. But the emphasis on the areas mentioned is significant and praiseworthy.

Another feature of the use of the Bible in Latin America is the fact that it is placed alongside the traditions and sacred texts of the native peoples and in dialogue with them. Various new "hermeneutics" are now emerging—indigenous, black, gender, and so forth—that seek to draw the native cultural and religious values from the ashes of the previous evangelization so that they can take their place in the Christian expression of the faith in a deeply real way (as opposed to the marginal way this was always done). The most significant results are yet to come.

Popular reading of the Bible in Latin America spread explosively in Christian base communities. Something very unusual took place; namely, people were needing and demanding a deeper knowledge of the Bible. As a result of this demand, many Bible scholars threw themselves into the cause of "liberating exegesis" in their research or by working with poor people at the grass roots or at intermediate levels. That led to important initiatives or projects: (a) the institutionalization of annual meetings of Latin American biblical scholars; (b) the creation of a journal with high academic standards but aimed at those leading the people's reading of the Bible, namely, *RIBLA* (*Revista de Interpretación Bíblica Latinoamericana*), published in both Portuguese and Spanish; (c) an Ecumenical Bible Commentary that draws on specifically Latin American exegetical work; (d) many Bible courses, the most outstanding of which is the CIB (*Curso Intensivo de Biblia*—Intensive Bible Course), held every year; and (e) a very useful bibliographical tool titled the Latin American Biblical Bibliography.

Finally, it must be stressed that the greatest manifestation of Bible reading in Latin America is in the community, and that Latin American exegesis, which is at the service of that reading, far from being abstract, is deeply concrete and is at the service of a liberating spirituality.

J. Severino Croatto
(Trans. Phillip Berryman)

See also: BASIC ECCLESIAL COMMUNITIES, HERMENEUTICAL CIRCLE, LIBERATION THEOLOGIES: LATIN AMERICAN, SOCIAL LOCATION.

Bibliography

J. Severino Croatto, *Biblical Hermeneutics: Toward a Theory of Reading as the Production of Meaning*, trans. Robert R. Barr (Maryknoll, N.Y.: Orbis Books, 1985).

Carlos Mesters, *Defenseless Flower: A New Reading of the Bible*, trans. Francis McDonagh (Maryknoll, N.Y.: Orbis Books, 1989).

Pablo Richard, "Indigenous Biblical Hermeneutics: God's Revelation in Native Religions and the Bible," in *Text and Experience: Towards a Cultural Exegesis of the Bible*, ed. David Smith-Christopher (Sheffield, England: Sheffield Academic Press, 1995).

Leif E. Vaage, *Subversive Scriptures: Revolutionary Readings of the Christian Bible in Latin America* (Valley Forge, Pa.: Trinity Press International, 1997).

Third World Women

Women in the Third World began to interpret the Bible consciously from feminist perspectives in the late 1970s. The Bible has been used both as a tool of colonial and patriarchal oppression and as a resource for women's liberation and empowerment. Third World women theologians need to reclaim the authority to interpret the Bible for women's struggles. Ecumenical networks, such as the Circle of Concerned African Women Theologians, the Asian Women's Resource Centre for Culture and Theology, and the Women's Commission of the Ecumenical Association of Third World Theologians, provide support for national, continental, and intercontinental dialogues on the Bible and theology.

Several common issues have emerged as Third World women interpret the Bible. The first focuses on a postcolonial reading of the Bible, which challenges the hegemony of Western interpretation, exposing its co-optation by colonial and neocolonial interests. Western male scholars have always dominated biblical studies, and most feminist works on the Bible are done by Western women. Postcolonial feminist criticism looks at the Bible from the vantage point of women who are often multiply oppressed by race, class, and colonialism. It examines how marginalized women in the Bible, such as slave women (e.g., Hagar) and poor women, are rendered invisible, consigned to "otherness," and denied speech. It reconstructs a counter-discourse that challenges the power dynamics inscribed in the text, in its historical transmission, as well as in white feminist interpretation. It lifts up the voices of contemporary marginalized female readers: women among the *dalits*, migrants, indigenous peoples, minorities, and diasporic communities.

Multicultural and multifaith hermeneutics are important because Third World women live in multilayered religio-cultural worlds. While male theologians have looked for similarities between the biblical tradition and their cultures in attempts to inculturate Christianity, women theologians indicate there are oppressive and liberating elements in both the Bible and their own cultures. A critical cultural hermeneutics is needed to demystify the claims of a homogeneous national culture, debunk the romanticizing of a patriarchal past, and expose violence done to women. Also needed are tools and methods to synthesize liberating motifs and elements from both the Bible and indigenous cultural traditions.

Since many Third World women live in oral cultures and many are illiterate, oral interpretation of the Bible is often the dominant mode of study. Using storytelling, drama, poetry, and performance, Christian women construct religious meanings, challenge male hierarchy, and reclaim women's subjectivity. One of the goals of oral interpretation is to make the text relevant to the present.

Feminist perspectives on the Bible from Asia, Africa, and Latin America vary widely. Many Asian Christian women believe in the authority of the Bible, and some lift up as role models women such as Miriam, Deborah, Hannah, Mary Magdalene, and Mary the mother of Jesus. Others bring Asian myths, legends, and cultural resources to interact with biblical stories through the process of dialogical imagination. Since Asian people have recited and chanted their scriptures for millennia, some women employ dramatization, storytelling, and creative performances to reclaim the voices of biblical women.

Hisako Kinukawa of Japan applies cultural anthropology to show that the social structure defined by honor and shame can be found both in the New Testament and in some Asian societies. She demonstrates that women's struggles against impurity, pollution, and alienation in the first centuries are relevant today. Lee Oo Chung and other Korean theologians adopt a sociopolitical reading to interpret the concepts of shalom and jubilee in the quest for the unification of Korea. Kwok Pui-lan from Hong

Kong proposes a postcolonial reading of the Bible that pays attention to the connections among colonialism, sexism, and anti-Judaism and to the multiple subjectivities of women in the Bible.

African women read the Bible in the context of survival, hunger, disease, economic, and religious exploitation. Some utilize a sociocultural approach to compare women's situations in Africa and in the Bible, such as cultural taboos surrounding blood, marriage, polygamy, and sexuality. Others stress women's ministry in the church by pointing to Jesus' liberating attitudes toward women and to their roles in the early church. The Kenyan theologian Musimbi Kanyoro calls for a cultural hermeneutics to unpack the layers of cultural interpretations women have inherited. Mercy Amba Oduyoye of Ghana develops interpretative principles for myths, folktales, and proverbs in African culture. Such hermeneutical insights can be brought to bear to interpret the multilayered and oral traditions of the Bible.

African women biblical scholars are interested in understandings of mission in the Bible. Teresa Okure of Nigeria reclaims the Samaritan woman as a model and analyzes her dialogue with Jesus at the well. She uses the story to illustrate a new concept of mission. Musa Dube of Botswana employs postcolonial theories to reread the stories of the Samaritan woman and the Syrophoenician woman, showing how the stories have been misused by missionaries to further colonial interests.

While Latin American male theologians have spoken of God's preferential option for the poor in the Bible, Latin American women bemoan women's status as the poorest among the poor. They approach the Bible for resources to support their struggle against injustice and multiple oppressions. Some integrate social analysis of the Latin American situation with critical readings of the Bible, while others focus on the prophetic ministry of women in the Bible and the church. Women in Christian base communities have integrated theories and praxis, applying biblical insights to social transformation.

Women theologians in the Catholic tradition stress the importance of Mary in popular religiosity. Ivone Gebara and María Clara Bingemer use new anthropological perspectives to study Mary in the Bible, emphasizing her roles in the historical destiny of her people and in ushering in the kingdom of God. The Protestant theologian Elsa Tamez reinterprets the central concept of justification by faith in Paul, arguing that sin cannot be understood abstractly as individual guilt. Justification by faith is liberation from structural sin, and it brings freedom and new life in Christ.

Kwok Pui-lan

See also: FEMINIST THEOLOGIES IN THE THIRD WORLD.

Bibliography
Hisako Kinukawa, *Women and Jesus in Mark: A Japanese Feminist Perspective* (Maryknoll, N.Y.: Orbis Books, 1994).
Kwok Pui-lan, *Discovering the Bible in the Non-Biblical World* (Maryknoll, N.Y.: Orbis Books, 1995).
Teresa Okure, "Feminist Interpretations in Africa," in *Searching the Scriptures. Vol. 1: A Feminist Introduction*, ed. Elisabeth Schüssler Fiorenza (New York: Crossroad, 1993).
Elsa Tamez, *The Amnesty of Grace: Justification by Faith from a Latin American Perspective*, trans. Sharon H. Ringe (Nashville, Tenn.: Abingdon, 1993).

BIBLE TRANSLATION

The Bible is the most translated book in the world. At the end of 1998, for example, at least one book of the Bible had been translated in 2,212 of the world's estimated 6,000 or so languages.

The first major translation of the Bible, the *Septuaginta*, was translated from Hebrew to Greek between the second and third centuries, B.C.E., in the North African city of Alexandria, a city central to the dissemination of Hellenistic culture and values. This translation thus incorporated Hellenistic thought forms and categories.

The next influential translation is that of the medieval European scholar St. Jerome (331-420), in the era of pax Romana, with Latin as the lingua franca. Commonly known as the *Vulgata*, because of its "vulgar" language, Jerome's translation was not based on the Greek *Septuaginta* but on the original Hebrew source texts. While Jerome's Latinized scriptures could not completely eliminate the Hellenistic layer, the new Latin text was inextricably linked to Caesar and the church, as well as to Roman culture and ideology.

Those who challenged the hegemony of Jerome's translation did so at their peril. John Wycliffe (1330-1384) and William Tyndale (1490-1536) are among those who paid with their lives. The proliferation of new translations during and after the Protestant Reformation reflected a weakening of the Roman empire, the church, and one dominant language, and the emergence of new empires and languages. The influential translation of Martin Luther (1483-1546) in German or the so-called Authorized King James Version in English (1611), among others, were products of this development.

The emergence of new power centers and the colonization of non-Western cultures and peoples created opportunities for their evangelization by the emerging Christian powers. This wave coincided with the modern missionary era. During this period, translation into the languages and cultures of colonized lands was first done by missionary translators who learned the languages of these lands. A second stage was characterized by close collaboration between native translators and missionaries who played the role of exegete or technical adviser. The final stage is characterized by the presence of qualified native speakers as full translators in their own tongues and cultures.

Translation does not happen only between languages (a source and target language) but is, at the same time, always a process of negotiation and exchange between cultures and their respective power relations. The problem of transforming the categories, concepts, and textual practices of one language into those of another is at the heart of the translation process, but there is also the problem of the translators themselves. They are constrained in many ways—for example, by their own ideology and by what the dominant institutions expect of them. In other words, no translation is a neutral, pure reflection of the original text.

Translation is a complex work. For example, how do you translate the God of the Bible in terms of the "god" or "gods" of another culture? How do you change the categories and concepts of biblical religion to terms understood by those of native traditional religions? In general, however, the local god, religious terminology, and categories are usually hijacked and christianized, or infused with new biblical meaning, as happened with the local god Mungu of the Swahili. How does one treat the case of the Iraqw of Tanzania, where "god" is feminine and so reflected in the grammatical system? Clearly, it is impossible to christianize the grammatical categories of any language without creating serious anomalies. Does replacing "Mother Looa," the God of the Cushitic Iraqw, with "Mungu," the God of the Swahili in his Christian garb, solve the problem?

Some of the numerous problems posed by translation across cultures are intractable and not always amenable to simple solutions. Does one "foreignize" or does one domesticate? Contextualization and inculturation, now in vogue, are about domesticating the foreign. Foreignizing is the norm, however, which, in a colonial context, may go hand in hand with alienation.

Translation is never a neutral tool. It is an instrument of ideological and theological formation—within the limits of fidelity and faithfulness to the source text. It operates at the cutting edge of inventing the terms of theological discourse. It can promote liberation or oppression. In this process, translators are active participants in molding the tools for the expression of the faith.

Aloo Osotsi Mojola

See also: BIBLE: INTRODUCTION, COLONIZATION, CONTEXTUALIZATION, INCULTURATION, INDIGENIZATION.

Bibliography
Roman Alvarez and M. Carmen-Africa Vidal, eds. *Translation, Power, Subversion* (Clevedon, England: Multilingual Matters Ltd., 1996).
Eugene A. Nida and Jan de Waard, *From One Language to Another: Functional Equivalence in Translating* (Nashville, Tenn.: Thomas Nelson Publishers, 1986).
Douglas Robinson, *Translation and Empire: Postcolonial Theories Explained.* (Manchester, England: St. Jerome Publishing, 1997).
William A. Smalley, *Translation as Mission: Bible Translation in the Modern Missionary Movement* (Macon, Ga.: Mercer University Press, 1991).

BLACK CONSCIOUSNESS

Black consciousness, in its theological context, arose in the mid- to late 1960s both in the United States and in South Africa. As a movement, it defined how one gained consciousness of being black. In the United States, prior to becoming "black," African Americans had accepted the name of "Negro," even though this rubric suggested that blacks were defined, controlled, and, thereby, oppressed by whites. South African blacks struggled against comparable derogatory descriptions given to them by white Christians. Instead of *kaffir*, "colored," or "Bantu," Africans, like their black American counterparts, accepted "black" as an overarching designation of self-definition. The question "How does one be black and Christian?" challenged both sides of the Atlantic. In response, a black theology of liberation arose, between 1966 and 1969, as the theological arm of larger liberation struggles. The spirit of liberation that permeated the black consciousness efforts in urban areas in the United States and in African townships and some rural lands was the same spirit of liberation of Jesus Christ. Black consciousness within black theology emphasized two trajectories—culture and politics. Being created black by God meant that one had the right to self-identity (i.e., an accent on a cultural theology) and a right to self-determination (i.e., a move toward a political theology).

Dwight N. Hopkins

See also: APARTHEID, KAIROS DOCUMENT, RACISM.

BLACK THEOLOGY

(See **Third World Theologies in the First World: Black Liberation Theology in Britain** and **Black Theology in the United States**)

BURAKUMIN LIBERATION THEOLOGY

In Japan, the *burakumin* minority have been oppressed for more than four hundred years. Discrimination against them remains severe in the areas of marriage, housing, and employment. It clearly illustrates what oppression means in seemingly homogeneous Japanese society today.

It is not easy to establish the historical origin of the *burakumin*. According to some sources, it goes back to the Heian period (794-1185). Its religious roots lie in a combination of two factors: the Shinto idea of pollution, and the Buddhist abhorrence of killing animals, a practice that polluted those involved in disposing of dead people and animals and thus prevented them from participating in religious rites. They were seen as filth (*eta*) and as non-people (*hinin*), and were settled in ghettos (*buraku*). This discrimination was institutionalized during the Tokugawa period (1603-1867) when these groups were seen as inferior castes and were ranked below warriors, farmers, artisans, and merchants. Though the present-day *burakumins* no longer undertake activities such as slaughtering animals, they continue to carry the taint. One of the earliest movements to take up the cause of *burakumin* liberation was the Suiheisha (Levellers Association), founded in 1922, which drew its ideas from Marxism, Buddhism, and Christianity. The Suiheisha's symbol was a cross of thorns. The Christian church missed an early opportunity to join with the *buraku* cause when Kagawa, a Christian leader of that period, had a disagreement with the Suiheisha movement.

In his book, *A Theology of the Crown of Thorns* (1991), Teruo Kuribayashi relates the liberation of the *burakumin* to the biblical theme of liberation. He analyzes the adaptation of the biblical symbol of Jesus' crown of thorns by the *burakumin*, which was chosen, in part, to contrast with the Japanese imperial throne of chrysanthemums. More important, Jesus' crown, now seen in passive, devotional, and contemplative terms, becomes a symbol that points to the pain of the outcastes and also reveals the hope of their final victory. It has become a symbol of liberation for the untouchables of the world.

Teruo Kuribayashi

C

CAPITALISM

Capitalism is an economic system based on private ownership of the means of production and on free market competition. The means of production are capital—such as materials, machines, and money—and labor. Workers sell their labor power to the owners of capital at current market rates.

The capitalist system maintains that this is the best way to distribute profits and losses, as it rewards efficiency and punishes inefficiency among free competitors. However, this assumption makes little sense to the poor, who have never been able to bargain freely with the owners for fair wages. It is even less convincing to Third World workers, whose poverty is a consequence of colonialism and of the deprivations and unrestrained exploitation they have suffered for generations. Karl Marx's critique of working conditions in the nineteenth century is also applicable to working conditions of the Third World poor today: owners of capital retain "surplus value" as they pay in wages less than the value created by the workers, whereas these latter are forced to work in order to barely subsist.

Capitalism, which arose in the wake of medieval mercantilism, has gone through several stages. Elimination of state regulation was the main claim of liberalism. The industrial revolution allowed capitalism to consolidate itself in the nineteenth century, due to high levels of economic growth in Britain, France, and the United States. Characteristic of capitalism are recurring crises, such as the Great Depression of the 1930s, which compel it to undergo adaptive transformations and to allow some extra-economic regulations. After the collapse of the Soviet Union, capitalism apparently won out over socialism. Today, with the help of the cybernetic revolution, it has developed into a system of globalized neoliberalism, where the process of deregulation moves toward the elimination of all remaining state control over economic activities.

Manuel Ossa

See also: DEPENDENCY THEORY, DEVELOPMENT, GLOBALIZATION, MARXISM.

Bibliography
Robert Brenner, "The Economics of World Turbulences: A Special Record of the Economy 1950-1958," *New Left Review* 229 (1998).

C. Colclough and J. Mannor, eds., *States or Markets? Neo-liberalism and the Development Policy Debate* (New York: Oxford University Press, 1995). Hans-Peter Martin and Harold Schumann, *The Global Trap: Globalization and the Assault on Prosperity and Democracy*, trans. Patrick Camiller (London and New York: Zed Books, 1997).

CARIBBEAN EMANCIPATORY THEOLOGY

The Caribbean region remains one of the most complex and enigmatic areas of the world. It is a difficult area to define, since some of its territories are islands and some are located on the continental mainland. There is a multiplicity of languages, customs, and religions, as well as a plethora of industrial, commercial, ideological, and political connections with external centers of power and control. None of this should be entirely surprising, since the Caribbean was originally plundered by European mercantilist greed and resettled as plantations based mainly on the economic potential of African slave labor. In sum, the history of the Caribbean has been a progression of conquest, plunder, exploitation, colonialism, independence, and neocolonialism. Caribbean people today, whether at home in the region, or abroad in the diaspora, are still in search of the true meaning of the "emancipation" that was signed into law as early as 1834. Emancipation for them is still both a sociopolitical struggle as well as a deep religious quest.

Thus Caribbean emancipatory theology takes its departure from the social and historical realities of poverty, dependence, alienation, and fragmentation. It is grounded on the irrevocable conviction that, in the midst of these realities, God is the sovereign free God who wills that all persons should be free. It seeks to reinterpret anew the gospel tradition that all are created in the image of God, and that that *imago Dei* is not a call to submission to the rich and powerful, but rather a summons to concrete and historical communion with the unconditionally divine. Emancipatory theology seeks to renounce all modern forms of slavery and bondage. It seeks to affirm the full worth and dignity of persons in their rich and distinct diversity. It seeks to create new forms of spirituality, and to join in solidarity with those who take their call to freedom as a gift from God rather than as a privilege granted by any human agency. It seeks to *cultivate* the art of Christian freedom, to *celebrate* the gift of divine freedom in song, dance, and praise, and to *communicate* the good news of human freedom in modes of cultural liberation and social praxis.

Kortright Davis

See also: BIBLE: CARIBBEAN, CHRISTOLOGIES: CARIBBEAN.

Bibliography
Kortright Davis, *Emancipation Still Comin': Explorations in Caribbean Emancipatory Theology* (Maryknoll, N.Y.: Orbis Books, 1990).

CHARISMATIC MOVEMENTS

(See **Pentecostalism**)

CHILDREN

There is a growing consensus that "children" refers to persons from birth to eighteen years of age, in accordance with the United Nations Convention on the Rights of the Child. All faiths have been concerned with the well-being of children in the Third World. The formal education of children was introduced and undertaken mainly by Christian churches since colonial times, until progressive, nationalist, or independence movements gave the state more responsibility for educating them. In a similar way, religious groups have created charitable institutions to protect vulnerable children. Today the tendency among progressive Christians is not only to deliver needed services but also to advocate for better public policies for children, based on the new vision that children have rights and that governments must implement and promote them.

The movement for children's rights emerged from practical experiences in caring for children, new sociological and political challenges, and scientific developments. Perhaps the most important influences have been (a) the feminist movement with its questioning of patriarchal institutions; (b) the urbanization process, especially in developing countries, exposing children to exploitative labor, drugs, and risks in the streets; (c) medical science, revealing the importance of the first five years of life and the preventable nature of the most devastating diseases of the past; and (d) the development of modern psychology, especially its discovery of the impact of early experiences on adult psyches, as well as the irreversible damage that can occur in infancy.

The global children's rights movement has had three moments of formal expression. In 1924, the League of Nations proclaimed the Declaration of Geneva. In 1959, the United Nations issued the Declaration of the Rights of the Child. Both of these were simple declarations promoting the rights of children to welfare. In 1989, the United Nations adopted the Convention on the Rights of the Child (CRC), which legally binds the countries that ratify it to introduce its principles and regulations into their national laws. The CRC is a comprehensive treaty that not only consolidates previous international laws on children but also establishes new standards to protect children, the rights of children to information, to freedom of expression, and to advocates who will assist in protecting their rights. The CRC is the sole UN convention that has reached nearly universal ratification; only Somalia and the United States have not ratified it.

The main source of global data on children, available in several languages, is UNICEF, which in recent reports presents a disheartening picture of children. In Africa, children have become the most vulnerable victims of the AIDS epidemic; they have also been enlisted as soldiers and the majority lack the most elementary social services. In Latin America, the numbers of abused children, street children, and exploited working children are growing. In Asia, the use of children in prostitution and bound labor has no limits, and the marginalization of the girl child continues. None of these problems is exclusive to any continent. In all the developing countries, a lack of public resources keeps some 130 million children of primary school age out of school. These realities are rooted in macroeconomic trends related to the debt crisis, a global increase of unemployment, and the liberalization and globalization of the capitalist economy.

The plight of the world's children raises hard questions about the meaning of mission today and about the priorities of religious groups of all faiths. It questions the usefulness of isolated projects and, instead, demands concerted actions. It challenges the absence of any discussion of children's concerns in current theological work. If the subject of liberation theologies is the poor, the marginalized, the exploited, and those victimized by human structures, how is possible that children's needs and concerns have not received specific and serious reflection by theologians? Indeed, how inclusive is theology if, to paraphrase the Gospel of Matthew, it is done "not counting [the needs of] women and children"? While in the past two decades women's theology has flourished, enriching our faith perspectives and our vision of God, children still do not count.

Mercedes Román

See also: OPPRESSION, POVERTY, VIOLENCE.

Bibliography
Maureen Junker-Kenny and Norbert Mette, eds., *Little Children Suffer*, *Concilium*, 1996/2 (Maryknoll, N.Y.: Orbis Books; London: SCM Press, 1996).
Douglas Sturn, "On the Suffering and Rights of Children: Toward a Theology of Childhood Liberation," *CrossCurrents* 42 (Summer 1992): 149-173.
U.N. General Assembly, *The U.N. Convention on the Rights of the Child* (New York: United Nations, November 20, 1989).

UNICEF, *The State of the World's Children* (New York: UNICEF, 1999 [annual publication]).
UNICEF, *The Progress of Nations* (New York: UNICEF, 1999 [annual publication]).

CHINESE THEOLOGIES

Four separate encounters have occurred between Christianity and China in the past fourteen centuries. Indigenous theological thinking, however, did not really begin in China until the twentieth century, when Chinese Christians began to move out of the shadow of Western Christianity. In the 1920s, against the background of political and intellectual hostility toward the Christian religion, the first challenge was to establish a truly Chinese leadership and organization. In 1926, six Chinese Catholic bishops were consecrated by the pope, despite the opposition of the missionaries. In 1927, the Protestant Church of Christ in China was established as a Chinese church based on the principles of self-government, self-propagation, and self-support.

The second challenge was to develop a Chinese apologetic in tune with the social and cultural changes of the time. Chinese theologians began by dissociating themselves from the Western form of Christianity. They sought to show that Christianity was a universal religion not confined to any particular culture and yet at home in all cultures, including China. They also had to demonstrate that Christian values could be part of the spiritual reconstruction of the Chinese nation. Although they succeeded in raising awareness of the church's role in society, they failed to provide a viable alternative to the predominant ideologies of the time—nationalism and communism. Catholic theology was too hampered by a rigid scholastic theology imposed from Rome, and Protestant theology put too much emphasis on individual salvation.

T. C. Chao (Zhao Zichen), the doyen of Protestant theology in this period, believed that the Chinese church must go through a double purification—institutional and doctrinal. The trappings of Western denominationalism and alien liturgies must be rejected. Central cores of the Christian faith must be reinterpreted to conform to rational and scientific worldviews; "unscientific" concepts such as the virgin birth and miracles must be purged from Christian belief. Only then would the person of Jesus and the salvific event of the cross become relevant to humanity's search for meaning and relief from suffering. Chao also believed that Confucianism, the dominant tradition in Chinese culture, should be regarded as part of the revelation of God. Chao's pursuit was cut short by the triumph of the Communist movement. The new faith, "scientific" and atheist, rejected both Confucianism and Christianity as feudal superstitions. Political pressure was put on the churches to adapt to the new regime.

The theological enterprise, as in the 1920s, had to begin again by a series of corrective measures. K. H. Ting (Ding Guangxun), the best-known Christian leader from the 1950s onward, proposed three stages of development: (a) a positive evaluation of atheism, (b) a new understanding of sin and grace, and (c) the rediscovery of the Christ-like God. In the first stage, Christianity must recognize the validity and achievements of Communist ideals and invite them to a fuller and deeper dialogue on the meaning of human struggle by relating their efforts to the ongoing creative, redemptive, and sanctifying actions of God. Second, Christians must realize that saying no to sin is not sufficient. They should see that the majority of God's people are not only sinners but have been sinned against by exploitative structures. Third, a Christian theology must move from the language of doom and damnation to recognize the universal dimension of God's love as expressed in the "cosmic Christ" in Pauline and Johannine scriptures. Ting believed that traditional christologies could not bridge the gap between the Judeo-Christian tradition and Chinese culture, or between the institutional church and the revolutionary movements in history. An understanding of Christ, not bound by history, institution, or culture, would be necessary to free the Chinese church from its theological confinement. The concept of the "cosmic Christ" not only serves as a corrective to traditional theologies, it acts as the omega point of history toward which all humanity, Christian or otherwise, is attracted and it maintains a prophetic scrutiny over the actions of church and society.

At the end of the twentieth century, however, Christianity in China must meet challenges other than communism. In fact, as an ideology, communism has completely collapsed, resulting in a "spiritual void" in a society lacking a coherent system of beliefs and values. Many again turn to the Christian churches for personal salvation and refuge from social and economic turbulence. There is also a new intellectual interest in Christianity, sometimes as a religion and sometimes as a cultural system. Many study the Christian religion and tradition, attracted to the fundamental concept of the individual as a person supported by a transcendent ground of being. Few are "converted" as such, but many actively seek a dialogue between Christianity and Chinese culture and history. This sets a new stage for Christian thinking in China.

Edmond Tang

See also: CHRISTOLOGIES: ASIAN, COSMIC/METACOSMIC RELIGIONS, DECOLONIZING THEOLOGY, MALAYSIAN THEOLOGIES, MYANMAR THEOLOGY, TAIWANESE THEOLOGIES, VIETNAMESE THEOLOGY.

Bibliography
Chen Zemin, "Theological Construction in the Chinese Church," *Chinese Theological Review* (Holland, Mich.: Foundation for Theological Education in Southeast Asia, 1991).
Ralph R. Covell, *Confucius, the Buddha & Christ: A History of the Gospel in Chinese* (Maryknoll, N.Y.: Orbis Books, 1986).
Wang Weifan, "Changes in Theological Thinking in the Church in China," *Chinese Theological Review* (Holland, Mich.: Foundation for Theological Education in Southeast Asia, 1986).
Raymond L. Whitehead, ed., *No Longer Strangers: Selected Writings of K. H. Ting* (Maryknoll, N.Y.: Orbis Books, 1989).

CHIPKO MOVEMENT

In India, women's expressions of resistance against the desecration of creation date back to the 1730s, when the women, children, and men of Khejadali, a Bishnoi village in Rajasthan, led by a woman called Amritha Devi, stopped the maharaja of Jodhpur's men from cutting the sacred *khejri* trees in their village. Willing to sacrifice themselves, they clung to the trees, defying the sword of the maharaja's men. Recognizing the value of the Bishnoi action, the maharaja promulgated a decree that no trees were to be cut in that area.

This event inspired the *Chipko* movement (*chipko* means "to cling"), which began in the early 1970s, in the Gharwal region of the Himalayas and has since spread. The movement aims at saving the hills from commercial exploitation and from the threats of landslides and severe soil erosion. This largely women-centered movement focuses on creating a sustainable, renewable forest system and on supporting and restoring food and water resources. The movement strongly affirms the feminine principle in Indian spirituality of valuing all of creation as sacred and as something to be preserved. These words by a Chipko activist, Chamundeyi, sum up the spirit of the movement:

Sister, it is a fight to protect
Our mountains and forests
They give us life
Embrace the life of the living trees and streams
Clasp them to your hearts. . . .
The fight for life has begun. . . .

Aruna Gnanadason

See also: ECOFEMIST THEOLOGY, ECOLOGY, TRIBAL THEOLOGIES.

Bibliography
Vandana Shiva, *Staying Alive: Women, Ecology and Development* (London: Zed Press, 1989).

CHRISTOLOGIES

African

At both formal and informal levels, African people are formulating christologies that are meaningful and relevant to the varying situations on the continent. As Charles Nyamiti (Kenya) and others have pointed out, African christology is bound to be pluriform. There are denominational differences (for example, between Catholics and Protestants), political and cultural differences (such as tribal and national differences, Anglophone versus Francophone, and differences between East, West, and Southern Africa), and a variety of theological approaches (such as those based on the oral tradition or using the inculturationist or liberationist models). However, throughout Africa unifying elements of emerging christologies include a strong reliance on the Bible and church traditions; an emphasis on African traditional teachings and the use of indigenous African symbolism and imagery; and significant consideration of the sociocultural context, the real situations in which Africans live.

Widely accepted images or understandings of Jesus are Christ as the Greatest Ancestor (John S. Pobee, Ghana), Christ the Proto-Ancestor (Bénézet Bujo, Congo/Zaire), and Christ the Brother-Ancestor (Charles Nyamiti, Tanzania). Jesus is also understood as healer, liberator, chief, or elder brother. Use of these images is often dependent on the historical, cultural, or social context and responds directly to the needs of Christians for relief from hunger, suffering, injustice, or oppression. In Ghana, for example, certain features of the religio-cultural heritage of the people influence the development of both formal and informal christologies. These include the pervasive presence and power of the Spirit and the constant need to equip oneself spiritually for life's contingencies; the tendency to emphasize the spiritual dimension of social experiences and the belief that spiritual powers can intervene in all aspects of human life; and the tendency to view religion as a means for survival and for enhancing all of life.

These resilient features of our cultural heritage have immensely colored and influenced the formulation of christological statements, particularly by the "new" or "popular" churches, otherwise known as charismatic, African instituted, or independent churches. Members of these churches have interpreted the gospel in ways relevant to African realities through popular "gospel" music and other creative forms of expression. In these churches, an all-embracing Being, Jesus, helps people cope with concrete situations, ranging from hunger, barrenness, broken relationships, unemployment, fear of evil spirits and diseases, to death.

African women express their relationship with Jesus in particular christological images. Christ becomes truly friend and companion, liberating women from the burden of disease, and from the ostracism of a society riddled with taboos and patriarchal assumptions about women. Women are honored, accepted, and sanctified, whether single or married, mothers, or without children. A pregnant woman without primary health care available might see Jesus as the great and efficient midwife who helps ease the pain of childbirth. African widows, whose lives are often characterized by misery and poverty, might perceive Jesus as husband.

African Christians affirm a strong belief that Jesus enhances their entire life, which includes prosperity, fertility, virility, good health, and total protection from any evil spirit or source of fear. One might arguably conclude that the main emphasis of African christologies is what Jesus can do to effect positive change in people's lives. This is *not* to say, however, that Africans ignore the Being of Jesus Christ, for one cannot separate the Being from his actions. The pragmatic attitude to religion and the holistic view of life clearly underscore the perception of Jesus Christ as a Being who cannot be limited to a particular model. Jesus Christ is the miraculous, all-embracing, wonderful Being who builds people up, particularly the excluded and those at the fringes of society, and leads them to experience the love of God.

Such varying bases of christologies raise certain issues, such as how African christological models, based on the use of African symbolism and imagery with their multiple interpretations and meanings in specific African contexts, can benefit the universal community of Christians. The image of Christ as ancestor is a good example. Some have argued that because the meaning of the word "ancestor" is culturally specific, Jesus Christ cannot be an ancestor to all Africans and to the entire Christian community or to all humanity. Yet, the concept of Jesus Christ as ancestor can enrich the church's universal understanding of Christ if the ancestor is seen as a symbol of perfection and of relationships that are eternal, that extend beyond death. African ancestors, whose exemplary lives are worthy of emulation, are believed to be very concerned with the well-being of the members of the community. Jesus Christ as ancestor, then, is another way of saying that Jesus continues to live, to influence the lives of people, and to give them abundant life, according to his promises.

Elizabeth Amoah

See also: AFRICAN INDEPENDENT CHURCHES, BIBLE: AFRICA, LIBERATION THEOLOGIES: AFRICAN, THIRD WORLD WOMEN'S THEOLOGIES: AFRICAN.

Bibliography

Elizabeth Amoah and Mercy Amba Oduyoye, "The Christ for African Women," in *With Passion and Compassion: Third World Women Doing Theology*, ed. Virginia Fabella and Mercy Amba Oduyoye (Maryknoll, N.Y.: Orbis Books, 1988), 35-46.

J. N. K. Mugambi and Laurenti Magesa, eds., *Jesus in African Christianity: Experimentation and Diversity in African Christianity* (Nairobi: Initiatives Publishers, 1989).

Robert J. Schreiter, ed., *Faces of Jesus in Africa* (Maryknoll, N.Y.: Orbis Books, 1991).

Thérèse Souga and Louise Tappa, "The Christ-Event from the Viewpoint of African Women," in *With Passion and Compassion: Third World Women Doing Theology*, ed. Virginia Fabella and Mercy Amba Oduyoye (Maryknoll, N.Y.: Orbis Books, 1988), 22-34.

African American

Each generation of Christians must answer the question: "What does it mean for Jesus, a first-century Palestinian Jew, to be Christ (the Messiah, the incarnate one)?" The answer is inevitably shaped by a particular community's social, historical, cultural, and political context. Instead of a singular or universal christological understanding, various christologies emerge from diverse communities of people who attempt to understand fully the significance of God's revelation in Jesus.

Black christology reflects a long tradition of black Christians probing the meaning of Jesus Christ in their struggle for life and freedom in a society that would deny them both because of their blackness. This christology begins with the notion that Jesus brings God down to earth and is God's intimate presence in human history. The central symbol, the black Christ, signifies black people's witness to a Christ who walks with them, talks with them, and understands their tears and pain.

Black christology is not grounded in the Nicaea/Chalcedon tradition but rather in the experience of slavery. While the Nicaea/Chalcedon tradition tends to minimize the significance of Jesus' earthly ministry, enslaved Africans highlighted this ministry in their attempts to reconcile their Christian faith with their enslavement. Relying on the gospels' witness to Jesus as opting for the downtrodden and oppressed, and recognizing the poignant similarities between their condition as chattel and Jesus' crucifixion, enslaved Christians testified in diverse ways that Jesus Christ was black.

Blackness in enslaved Christianity was not a statement about Jesus' ethnicity or skin color but a testimony to his existential commitment to the life and freedom of the black enslaved. Jesus was a trusted friend who understood their agony, grief, and struggles. Grounded in the resurrection, the enslaved also believed that Jesus would deliver them from the tyranny of slavery. A christology emerged that defined Jesus Christ as one who opposed white racism and affirmed black humanity.

Though variously interpreted, the black Christ remains a characteristic feature of contemporary black christology. The pioneering black theologian James Cone argues that Jesus Christ takes on the very condition of blackness in America. He also explains that the blackness of Christ means Christ is an unequivocal liberator of black people from white racism. Cone recognizes the universal symbolic meaning of the black Christ when he says blackness signifies those that are oppressed, meaning people of the Third World.

Another pioneering black theologian, J. Deotis Roberts, argues that because Christ is for everybody, Christ is black, just as Christ can be white or any other color of people. Roberts further explains that the black Christ is at once a reconciler and liberator with the ultimate concern of reconciling white people and black people.

A second generation of black male theologians, including Dwight Hopkins, George Cummings, Josiah Young, and Mark Chapman, is attempting a more comprehensive understanding of the complexity of black oppression by acknowledging the presence of classism and sexism within the black community. Their black christologies are also more intentionally linked to African and other Third World christologies.

The most recent black christology emerges from black female theologians who identify themselves as womanist and explore black christology from the particular struggles of black women. Womanist christology points to the multidimensional character of black oppression and stresses the interactive impact of race, gender, and class oppression on black women's lives. Womanist christology employs a diversity of symbols to clarify the meaning of the black Christ and highlights those persons, especially black women, who have worked to move the black community toward wholeness and freedom.

Jacquelyn Grant, a pioneer in womanist christology, concludes that Christ today is a black woman. She disavows the centrality of Jesus' maleness in determining what it meant for him to be Christ. Similarly, Kelly Brown Douglas says that the black Christ can be a black woman. Douglas stresses, however, that the black Christ is seen in the face of anyone, male or female, who fights for the life, freedom, and wholeness of the black community. Douglas further recognizes that the complexity of black oppression includes heterosexism and homophobia. The Roman Catholic Jamie Phelps emphasizes Christ as one who provides "life-engendering hope" and a "life-engendering way of life" for black men and women as they encounter the numerous dimensions of their complex oppression, be it socioeconomic, psychological, or institutional.

Kelly Brown Douglas

See also: BIBLE: AFRICAN AMERICAN, THIRD WORLD THEOLOGIES IN THE FIRST WORLD: BLACK THEOLOGY IN THE UNITED STATES.

Bibliography
James H. Cone, *A Black Theology of Liberation*, 20th anniversary ed. (Maryknoll, N.Y.: Orbis Books, 1990).
Kelly Brown Douglas, *The Black Christ* (Maryknoll, N.Y.: Orbis Books, 1994).
Jacquelyn Grant, *White Woman's Christ, Black Woman's Jesus* (Atlanta, Ga.: Scholars Press, 1989).
Jamie T. Phelps, OP, "Inculturating Jesus: A Search for Dynamic Images for the Mission of the Church among African Americans," in *Taking Down Our Harps: Black Catholics in the United States*, ed. Diana L. Hayes and Cyprian Davis, OSB (Maryknoll, N.Y.: Orbis, 1998), 68-101.

American Indian

Although very little has actually been written on this subject, over the generations since the missionization of American Indians began, Indian people and especially Indian clergy, as peoples of oral cultures, have spoken about it. The story of Jesus was by no means strange to Indians on their first hearing, since every Indian community, representing a variety of distinct cultures and languages, had stories that prepared them to make sense of Jesus. Indeed, many Indian clergy have come to speak of those old stories and religious traditions as the appropriate Old Testament for Indian Christians. Deeply religious, traditional Indian people have a long history of relating to the Sacred Other in stories and ceremonial acts.

Countless figures from traditional stories could be fruitfully understood as christological figures: from Corn Mother and Rabbit Boy to White Buffalo Calf Woman and even Coyote. No, these stories are not the same as the Christian gospels, but they function in similar, salvific ways for the people, always pointing to the need for divine assistance in living a successful life. They involve human manifestations of the Sacred Other and can include miraculous births. The immediacy of the divine, radically experienced in tension with their clear notion of divine transcendence, means that traditional Indians live with a constant awareness of the Sacred Other as present and functioning in the life of the community.

On the other hand, a certain overlay of cultural language imposed upon the gospel makes Christian affirmation difficult for Indian people, even as many accede to it. For instance, the Christian claim for the absoluteness of the Christ event will be screened out by most Indian Christians who are not yet ready to consign their ancestors, some from the immediately past generation, or their present relatives, to the eternal damnation that supposedly awaits nonbelievers.

Other language usages can be equally alienating or co-optive of Indian people. The use of the word "lord" in reference to Jesus is a prime example. Indian cultures were far more egalitarian than hierarchical European cultures. Since Indian communities in North America lacked any cultural concept of lordship, the concept had to be learned before any affirmation of Jesus' lordship could be made. The only notion of lordship that functioned or functions experientially in Indian communities derives from the lordship of European and Amer-European colonial domination. Hence, the simple affirmation of the lordship of Jesus is culturally tortuous for Indian people. It necessarily involves a prior affirmation of lordship, which is in itself a violation of traditional Indian culture. Moreover, the affirmation of lordship functions inherently as a subtle religious legitimization of European and Amer-European hegemony as the colonial rulers of American Indian lands and peoples.

Thus, a truly liberating christology for American Indian people must find different metaphors to talk about the salvific presence of the Christ in the world. Instead of the hierarchical notion of lordship, Indian preachers will sometime invoke the more egalitarian notion of Jesus as brother, a radically different but equally biblical metaphor (Gal. 3:26). Likewise, the Pauline notion of freedom (Gal. 5:1) becomes important for many Indian clergy, since it would seem to allow continued participation in Indian culture and cultural activities, including the ancient traditional ceremonies of our peoples (so also an Indian reading of Romans 14). The question Indian people will press with their mainline denominations, then, are these: How free are we? Does Christ set us free to pray and participate in traditional tribal ceremonies? Or does Christ bind us to a new law of Christ and Christ alone?

The word "Christ" is itself a metaphor rooted in the Jewish culture and language of Hellenistic Palestine. Christ, messiah, and *messhiach* all translate into English as "anointed one," playing metaphorically on the Israelite notions of kingship, first of all, and of prophet and priest. How can we begin to unpack this metaphor in any American Indian language or culture? Must we necessarily become intellectually versed in Hellenistic Jewish culture and in the traditions of the Hebrew Bible before we can affirm Jesus and gain spiritual unity with Christendom? Or must we merely come to an intellectual affirmation of the most current Amer-European interpretation of these things (in their latest Lutheran, Presbyterian, Catholic, Episcopal, or Methodist guises)?

Once we begin to claim the freedom to interpret the metaphor of Christ from within our own cultures, then a broad range of metaphors becomes available to Indian people. These will necessarily include the possibility that the Christ had long come to Indian people in the form of the ancient manifestations of the divine that have always functioned and still function as salvific presence in our traditional ceremonial life.

(George) Tink Tinker

See also: ABORIGINAL THEOLOGY, COLONIZATION, DECOLONIZING THEOLOGY, INDIGENOUS THEOLOGIES, THIRD WORLD THEOLOGIES IN THE FIRST WORLD: NATIVE AMERICAN, THIRD WORLD WOMEN'S THEOLOGIES: NATIVE AMERICAN.

Bibliography
George E. Tinker, "Jesus, Corn Mother and Conquest: Christology and Colonialism," in *Native American Religious Identity: Unforgotten Gods*, ed. Jace Weaver (Maryknoll, N.Y.: Orbis Books, 1998).
George E. Tinker, "American Indians and Jesus: Towards an EATWOT Christology," *Voices from the Third World* (December 1995).
Achille Peelman, *Christ Is a Native American* (Maryknoll, N.Y.: Orbis Books; Ottawa, Canada: Novalis-Saint Paul University, 1995).

Asian

Jesus, the man of Nazareth, is the Christ, the one in and through whom we have the saving knowledge of God. Asian theologians have brought out in a challenging manner the meaning of this confession in formulations made in the context of different social, political, cultural, and philosophical backgrounds.

Inculturation christologies. Indian Hindus who focused on the nature of the person of Jesus Christ did many of the early christological reflections in Asia. While their articulations reveal a genuine fondness and awe for Jesus, their attempts disclose loyalty to the traditions to which they belonged since they drew only upon images from the Hindu philosophical systems that they hoped would bridge the gap between the two faiths. The result was a mystical and metaphysical interpretation of the person and work of Christ. Their christological affirmations provide a variety of images: Jesus as the great teacher, guide, and messenger delegated with power from God to set an example (Raja Ram Mohan Roy); Jesus as the divine man, who through his self-emptying becomes filled with God (Keshab Chandar Sen); Jesus, the son of Man who seeks the last, the lost, and the least (Rabindranath Tagore); Jesus the supreme *satyagrahi* (Mahatma Gandhi); Jesus as Jivanmuktha, the one who has attained liberation while alive (Swami Vivekananda); Jesus as Advaitin, the one who has realized destiny with Brahman (Swami Akilananda); the mystic Christ (Radhakrishnan).

The efforts of these pioneers inspired several Indian Christians to develop christological articulations rooted in the Indian culture. Hence Jesus has been identified as *logos* or *cit*, or consciousness, but fully human and fully divine (Brahmobandhav Upadhyaya); as *prajapati* or Lord of the created world (K. M. Banerjee); as incarnation or *avatara* (Sadhu Sundar Singh and V. Chakkarai); as the *antaryamin* or the immanent Christ (A. J. Appasamy); as Adi Purusha or the historic figure permanently human (P. Chenchiah); and as the eternal *Om* or *logos* (S. Jesudasan). A later development in Asian Christian theology, particularly in India, saw an emphasis on humanization and liberation of people in the social and political realm. Much of this was done within the context of rising nationalism and the need for dialogue between religions. Jesus Christ was therefore referred to as the Hidden One (J. N. Farquhar); the Crown of Hinduism (R. Panikkar); the Acknowledged Christ (M. M. Thomas); and so on. It is well known that the roots of Indian Christian theology are found in the experiences of theologians who are mainly from the upper caste/class communities. An authentic contextual theology to them meant an adaptation or adjustment to the dominant ethos in India, which therefore included the acceptance and continuance of the caste structure. Influenced by the Hindu philosophical systems and other Hindu literature such as the Vedas and the Upanishads, their theology differed from that of the Christian masses who were poor and illiterate and belonged to the Scheduled caste groups. Their articulations of Christ did not challenge but protected the interest of the dominant castes. Christological thinking has also been informed by the distinct Indian concept of "guru" or teacher, which enables one to perceive Jesus as the revelation or presence of God in a freer manner while at the same time transforming the understanding of the term itself when Jesus' teachings and works are considered (M. Thomas Thangaraj).

Popular christologies. Outside the mainline theological circles are the many popular christologies, which range from the traditional to the radical: Jesus as one who bestows prosperity, the magician, the miracle man, the stiff and the stern judge, the spiritual being and world-negating God, the eschatological Christ, to name a few. The work of Jesus is understood to be that of one who has been sent to call the people to repentance and a life of adoration of God. This focus on the spiritual dimension of salvation places Jesus over the cultural conflicts of caste, religion, gender, language, and class and therefore outside the debate, so to speak. The infant Jesus is also worshipped as a symbol of protection in times of danger and hardship and as the bestower of wishes. Many Asian Christians identify with the Christ of the cross and pay little attention to resurrection. Their vision does not go beyond the satisfaction of their immediate personal needs and hence lacks a social dimension. Yet there are others for whom Christ is a model to be emulated in the struggle for liberation. "To have faith in the incarnate, crucified and resurrected Christ means to be part of his revolutionary task to liberate man" (Salvador Martinez).

Christologies and religious pluralism. Challenged by religious pluralism, Asian christological thinking over the past decade has, with the realization that religious pluralism is something to be valued and not merely tolerated, embarked on the project of bringing the "person of Jesus in conjunction with other religious figures, into a revitalizing and enriching encounter with them and with Christian faith itself" (Sugirtharajah). Explorations have been made into the similarities between Jesus and other religious figures, resulting in connections being made between Jesus and Krishna and the salvation they both offer (Ovey N. Mohammed); Jesus and the Buddha as two enlightened individuals (Seiichi Yagi), both involved in the act of human liberation (Aloysius Pieris). In the light of the Chinese concept of *yin* and *yang*, Jesus has been conceived as the way of change and progress and has provided new insights into the understanding of humanity/divinity, death/resurrection, and creation/redemption (Jung Young Lee). Within the Islamic context, it has been suggested that christological affirmations need to be divested of ideas, images, and language that are offensive to the Islamic community and focused instead on the "greatness of God," as exemplified in Jesus (Alexander Malik). Other have proposed a God-centered christology that is also mystery (Stanley Samartha); or Jesus as one among the many manifestations of the Universal Word (Michael Amaladoss).

Liberation christologies. At present, christological reflections stand at a new crossroad. Asian theologians are attempting to articulate christologies that take into consideration the massive and acute suffering of the Asian people, the widespread poverty, injustice, ethnic, caste, racial, and religious differences, and the increasing violence that characterize Asian communities. Against this backdrop, Asian theologians have articulated christologies within a theological paradigm with a liberation stance. Hence, we have Jesus identified as "pain-love"—who embodies the pain of the Asian people through the passion of his own pain on the cross (C. S. Song); Jesus as the center moving toward those at the periphery (Kosuke Koyama); Jesus as the prophet, a subversive-creative individual (Sebastian Kappen); Jesus as the hope and the way to liberation (Michael Rodrigo); and the *minjung* Christ as one who is not the Christ of the kerygma but the historical Jesus who associates and lives with the *minjung*. For the *dalits* in India, Christ embraces them in their suffering, rejection, and shame. Jesus, by virtue of his humanity, his roots, his solidarity with the outcastes, his total identification with the poor, his being the servant God and the suffering servant, and most of all because of his dying on the cross and exemplifying brokenness, for allowing himself to be crushed, split, and torn, by virtue of his experience of Godforsakenness is the prototype of a *dalit*. Jesus is therefore a *dalit* in the fullest sense of the term, one who belongs to the realm of the outside, the region of carcasses and defilement.

Asian women have generally found the traditional images of Jesus as suffering servant, Lord, Emmanuel, Messiah, or the representative human being to be most meaningful. But attempts are also being made to reinterpret some of these images, particularly those affirmations that seem to glorify suffering so much that suffering becomes a value in itself, and thereby a trap for women which ensnares them. In their struggle to overcome their oppression and experience liberation, women are using religio-political symbols and motifs to understand Jesus and see him as the liberator, the revolutionary, and the political martyr (Philippines); the mother, woman, shaman, and worker (Hong Kong and Korea); the bread of life that keeps women alive; the Tree of Life (Lucy D'Souza); and the cross (Judith Sequeira). More recently, Asian women are looking into the goddess traditions and making linkages between them, the biblical wisdom tradition, and Jesus. This allows for connections between Christian feminists and other goddess-centered feminists, and between historical and mythological worldviews, and provides Asian Christian women with wholly feminine symbols and images as possible alternatives for understanding Jesus Christ.

Monica J. Melanchthon

See also: BIBLE: ASIA, ECCLESIOLOGIES: ASIAN, INCULTURATION, INTERRELIGIOUS DIALOGUE, THIRD WORLD WOMEN'S THEOLOGIES: ASIAN.

Bibliography
"Any Room for Christ in Asia," Leonardo Boff and Virgil Elizondo, eds., in *Concilium* 2 (1993).
Virginia Fabella, "A Common Methodology for Diverse Christologies?" in *With Passion and Compassion: Third World Women Doing Theology*, ed. Virginia Fabella, MM, and Mercy Amba Oduyoye (Maryknoll, N.Y.: Orbis Books, 1988).
R. S. Sugirtharajah, ed., *Asian Faces of Jesus* (Maryknoll, N.Y.: Orbis Books; London: SCM, 1993).
Peter Phan, "The Christ of Asia" in *Studia Missionalia* 45 (1996).

Asian American

Compared with African American and Hispanic American theologies, Asian American theology is a much younger sibling. Asian American history began in 1848, when the Chinese, first among Asians, went to the United States looking for work. Between 1850 and 1882, over three hundred thousand Chinese, mostly male, came as "sojourners" to acquire quick fortunes and return to their homeland but ended by staying on as immigrants. California, with its newly discovered gold and with railroad and agricultural industries in need of cheap labor, was the state of choice for Chinese immigrants. They were joined in 1860 by the Japanese immigration, which reached its peak around the turn of the century, and by the Koreans on a large scale in 1903. The Protestant churches were active among the early Asian immigrants, but with the coming of the Filipinos and the Vietnamese, the presence of the Roman Catholic Church became noticeable. Besides these nationalities, there are other groups, including Indians, Pakistanis, Malaysians, Cambodians, Laotians, Hmong, and Thai. Clearly, "Asian American" denotes an ethnically, racially, linguistically, culturally, and religiously very diverse group.

Most Asian American theologians, that is, those who are of Asian origin but work mainly in the United States, have been trained in the West and are well acquainted with Western theologies. While benefiting from American, European, and South American theologies, Asian American theologians attempt to construct their own distinctive theologies, and especially christologies. On the one hand, they make use of the Asian resources, such as Asian peoples' stories, Asian religious traditions and rituals, Asian philosophies and literature. On the other hand, they theologize from their experiences of marginalization as immigrants in the United States.

Among Asian American theologians who have developed a distinctive christology is Jung Young Lee, a Korean United Methodist. Understanding reality as essentially marked by change, he paints Jesus as the "perfect realization of change." Furthermore, viewing the immigrant as one who lives "in-between" and "in-beyond" two worlds, he presents Jesus as the marginal person par excellence. Choan-Seng Song, a Taiwanese Presbyterian, wrote a christological trilogy in which Jesus is described as the "crucified people" who is presently working in Asia in the power of the Spirit to liberate Asians from all types of oppression. From his Confucian heritage, Peter C. Phan, a Vietnamese Roman Catholic, portrays Jesus as the "Elder Brother" and the "Ancestor" in addition to being a liberator. Anselm Kyongsuk Min, a Korean Roman Catholic, develops a theology in which Jesus is seen as being not only in solidarity *with* others but receiving solidarity *of* others. David Ng, a Chinese Presbyterian, paints Jesus as primarily a person gathering others into a community (*koinonia*). Andrew Sung Park, a Korean United Methodist, views Christ as healing not only sin but also *han* (the deep sense of anger and pain caused by prolonged oppression) and racial conflicts.

Women Asian American theologians have also been engaged in constructing a christology from a feminist and antipatriarchal perspective. Rita Nakashima Brock, for one, rejects the notion of Jesus as the savior and the Christ. For her, Jesus is but one of the participants in the embodiment of the redemptive "Christa/Community" in which the erotic power of "heart" flows in mutual relation and brings about the healing of brokenheartedness. Other theologians strongly criticize the androcentric and patriarchal christology of the West that takes the maleness of Jesus as normative.

These and many other portraits of Jesus by Asian American theologians have no doubt enriched Chalcedonian christology with resources and insights derived from their varied cultures. As people rooted in two cultures, they are in a position to bring together the theologies of both East and West in a new theological synthesis.

Peter C. Phan

See also: THIRD WORLD THEOLOGIES IN THE FIRST WORLD: ASIAN AMERICAN, THIRD WORLD WOMEN'S THEOLOGIES: ASIAN AMERICAN.

Bibliography
Rita Nakashima Brock, *Journeys by Heart: A Christology of Erotic Power* (New York: Crossroad, 1992).
Kwok Pui Lan, "On Color-Coding Jesus: An Interview with Kwok Pui Lan," in *Postcolonial Bible*, ed. R. S. Sugirtharajah (Sheffield, England: Sheffield Academic Press, 1998), 177-88.
Peter C. Phan and Jung Young Lee, eds., *Journeys at the Margin: Toward an Asian-American Autobiographical Theology* (Collegeville, Minn.: Liturgical Press, 1999).

Caribbean

Theologians in the Caribbean have always insisted on the need for Christ in the Caribbean to reflect its peoples and spaces. But what is authentically Caribbean and relevant to discourse on christology in the Caribbean? In theological reflection in the Caribbean three main positions attempt to bear this responsibility.

The first position uses cultural and literary sources in the Caribbean as the bases for theological reflection as well as for analyses of racial and social stratification as a means of understanding the complex cultural patterns of the region. This position is a break from the old christology, which saw the region as mission territory needing to hear the words of Christ.

The second position sees the struggle for justice in its social, political, and economic forms as central to the message of Christ and Christians. These two positions are by no means mutually exclusive, and theologians in the region have always freely incorporated both into their reflections. Regardless of the theological position, it is clear that theology in the region is a reaction to and is formed by the experience of colonization and its contemporary mercantilistic expression of globalization.

In response to this, a third position uses historical method as the basis for theological reflection. Rather than viewing the historical importance of the Caribbean as a theater of personalities or absentee landlords, the region is understood as a geographic space that is shaped by its material relations and must be looked at over a long time span following distinct yet intermeshing cycles of human agency, culture, and economics. This reading exposes the forced character of Caribbean reality and the forced context of theological reflection in that reality. The task of christology in the Caribbean is thus that of giving the faces of Jesus in the Caribbean an anchored presence in the history of the region.

Gerald M. Boodoo

See also: BIBLE: CARIBBEAN, CARIBBEAN EMANCIPATORY THEOLOGY, DECOLONIZING THEOLOGY.

Bibliography
Patrick Anthony, ed., *Theology in the Caribbean Today 1: Perspectives* (St. Lucia: Archdiocesan Pastoral Centre, 1994).
Jason Gordan, "Clash of Paradigms: Report from the Caribbean," in *Liberation Theologies on Shifting Grounds*, ed. Georges DeSchrijver (Leuven, Belgium: Leuven University Press, 1998), 365-379.
Howard Gregory, ed., *Caribbean Theology: Preparing for the Challenges Ahead* (Jamaica: Canoe Press, University of the West Indies, 1995).

Hispanic

Every christology is a reflection on the power and the meaning of the Jesus story. As such, all christologies are written from a particular context and with a particular audience in mind. Hispanic christologies take as their point of departure the marginalization that Hispanics have experienced within the United States because of their *mestizo* identity— never fully mainline U.S., never fully Latin American.

From within the experience of marginalization, the Galilean identity of Jesus is a fundamental point of Hispanic christology. Pure-minded Jews of Judea marginalized Galileans while, at the same time, the Greeks and Romans of Galilee marginalized them as Jews. The Galileans, like U.S. Hispanics, were thus twice marginalized. It is from within this experience of exclusion that Jesus proclaims the reign of God wherein all will be welcomed. The reign of God refuses to accept marginalization, exclusion, and rejection. Jesus is the rejected cornerstone that becomes the cornerstone of the new creation. It is society's reject who now rejects all rejection and does so precisely in the name of God, who is Abba, *Papacito*, to all.

It is in this Galilean Jesus that U.S. Hispanics find the true meaning and mission of their experience of rejection and marginalization. What the world sees as rejection is for God election, not for privilege but for mission. Their christology, based on the Galilean Jesus and the reign of God, defines the true identify and mission of the Hispanics in the U.S.

Virgilio P. Elizondo

See also: BIBLE: HISPANIC, *MESTIZAJE* CONSCIOUSNESS, THIRD WORLD WOMEN'S THEOLOGIES: HISPANIC.

Bibliography
Virgilio P. Elizondo, *Galilean Journey: The Mexican-American Promise*, rev. ed. (Maryknoll, N.Y.: Orbis Books, 2000).
Roberto S. Goizueta, *Caminémos con Jesus: A Theology of Accompaniment* (Maryknoll, N.Y.: Orbis Books, 1995).

Latin American

The understanding of Jesus Christ of a given church, time, or people cannot be limited to their theological (dogmatic) definitions, but is also seen in the place that Christ plays in their faith, their religious attitudes, their piety, their iconography, their celebrations, and even their folklore. In this sense, there have been and are very different "faces of Christ" in Latin America.

The French theologian Georges Casalis characterized the christology of the Iberian conquest and colonization with two images frequently present in Latin American iconography: first, the "heavenly monarch," the exalted Christ who has total and discretionary power; and, second, the "crucified victim," the powerless and wounded Christ with whom suffering indigenous people can identify. Both images have found expression through the conquest, as in the defense of the right of conquest in the work of a Spanish theologian like Sepúlveda, or in the identification of Christ with the suffering and "crucified" native people, so forcefully portrayed by Fray Bartolomé de Las Casas.

This latter, dominant motif has concrete expression in popular piety and in the different miraculous "Christs" venerated throughout Latin America, to whom people address their petitions and from whom they expect help. Thus, the merciful Christ is also the powerful healer, the hand stretched to help. This "christology" could be extended to include the motif present in the "maternal face of God" (the Virgin) and the saints. There is also a "prophetic christology" present in popular charismatic leaders that is acknowledged in popular lore and images. Included are popular outlaws, "black Christs," and even political figures.

The dominant christology in Protestantism stresses Christ the Savior who atones for sin, liberates human beings from a miserable and "lost" life, creates a new community of love, and ensures eternal life. In Protestant piety, the image of the Savior is also that of the "friend" to whom one can entrust all one's problems and worries and from whom one receives help and comfort. In Pentecostal piety, in particular, Christ is the source of power, health, and abundance. Here, christology and pneumatology are almost totally identified.

In recent Latin American theology (frequently called "liberation theology"), some of these christological motifs—although in different forms in popular Catholic and Protestant piety—have been taken up, recast, corrected, and articulated in biblical and theological reflection. Well-known theologians, such as Gustavo Gutiérrez, Leonardo Boff, Jon Sobrino, Juan Luis Segundo, Victorio Araya, Jaci Maraschin, and many others, have produced significant theological works. Although there are differing articulations of these theological christologies, it is possible to discern some themes common to both Catholic and Protestant theologians.

First, Christ is the place to meet God. God has made Godself visible and available in a human life; the Christian is a person who believes that God is as Jesus Christ has said and shown. Second, we meet and know God in Jesus' words and actions. Latin American theology has privileged the "historical Jesus," not in a literalistic understanding of the gospels but in the total picture they give us of Jesus' "program" revealed in his actions and words. The content of this program is the kingdom or reign of God—the reign of life, justice, and mercy. The response to this call means repentance, conversion, and "following" the Christ. Third, the identification with the poor—in its broad sense of the excluded, the weak, the discriminated against, the materially impoverished—is central to Jesus' program. Discipleship means taking on the cause of the poor. Fourth, the death of Jesus is understood as his absolute and total faithfulness to his mission and, at the same time, the way in which God unmasks sin, corruption, and injustice through God's own self-giving. In this sense, as the fourth gospel says, his death is his triumph. This is God's vindication of Jesus' life and program.

Feminist christology in Latin America begins with the experiences of the oppression of women and a corresponding rereading of the Bible. It places special emphasis on retrieving the person of Jesus, his humanity, his suffering, and his relationships with oppressed women in which health and integrity are restored through words and deeds. The close relationship between Jesus and oppressed women, the healing of their bodies, the recognition of the role of women in the Jesus movement, and the critique of patriarchal institutions are important in the liberative hermeneutics of Latin American women. They are being rediscovered as fundamental to the gospel. The Jesus movement is retrieved and understood as a resurrection movement of women and men, who, in a discipleship of equals, perform resurrection actions to restore life. Jesus is seen as a symbol of transformation, capable of encompassing human yearnings for relationships of fullness, justice, compassion, and tenderness. He is a symbol open to new perspectives such as ecological salvation. The attitudes, behavior, and respect shown by Jesus for the life of each being open up the possibility of new relationships with the land and our planet.

José Míguez Bonino

See also: LIBERATION THEOLOGIES: LATIN AMERICAN, OPTION FOR THE POOR.

Bibliography
Leonardo Boff, *Jesus Christ Liberator* (Maryknoll, N.Y.: Orbis Books, 1978).
José Míguez Bonino, ed., *Faces of Jesus in Latin America* (Maryknoll, N.Y.: Orbis Books, 1985).
Juan Luis Segundo, *Jesus of Nazareth, Yesterday and Today* (Maryknoll, N.Y.: Orbis Books, 1987-88).
Jon Sobrino, *Jesus the Liberator: A Historical Theological View* (Maryknoll, N.Y.: Orbis Books, 1993).

COLONIZATION

Colonization is a method of physical and symbolic control characterized by the act of settling a community into a region or country of a different cultural, religious, and political ethos. The word "colony" was coined during the Roman Empire and literally means to cultivate and inhabit a foreign region. Processes of colonization require the active control and dominion of cultures by the incoming power, which by means of superior military and political force can effectively excercise substantial power over others. As a political system, colonization can be found as early as the second century, when the Roman Empire extended from Armenia to the Atlantic Ocean.

Colonization processes, however, cannot be reduced to foreign expansions such as the British Empire's colonization of India, Africa, and the Americas, and Spanish and Portuguese expansions in the Americas, Africa, and Southeast Asia. For instance, in Latin America, civilizations such as the Aztec and the Inca grew by annexing and controlling other nations and groups. In India, during the fifteen century, the southern region was colonized by the Vijaynagara Empire. Colonization processes are complex enterprises that require more than military superiority. They also demand cultural, religious, and political erasure by acts of banning the language used in the region as well as religions, dress, and social organizations.

The role of theology has always been important in these processes, as the symbolic spiritual configurations of a nation have proved to be a site for national identity and resistance. Christian theology was key to British colonization processes in India and Africa, which were implemented by missionary enterprises. In Latin America, the Spanish and Portuguese empires found in Roman Catholicism a most powerful ally in reconfiguring nations, which then became subjects of those empires. Christianity also contributed to the development of colonial wealth by exploiting the people and pillaging natural resources.

From a Christian perspective, the effects of colonization may be seen in two main areas. First, new power alliances were produced between the colonizers and the colonized, such as, for instance, gender alliances. Women frequently found themselves in positions of less power after the colonizing process because patriarchal alliances established traditions of women's cultural oppression based on the European religious norm of excluding women. Privileging one group to allow it to oppress another is a tactic that has been used to divide colonial societies. It has also brought cultures of corruption to colonized nations. Second, national struggles for political and cultural identity have sometimes been hindered by the newly acquired religious identity of the colonized nation. In Latin America, for instance, Christianity needed to be subverted in order to start the wars of independence. It was renegotiated by the colonial subjects, giving birth to forms of liberation theologies. Latin American liberation theology was one of the first attempts to work with a theological praxis that decentered (desacralized) neocolonial interests. Similarly, the Scriptures were reread and reinterpreted using a postcolonial perspective in order to sanction the people's right to insurrection.

Colonization processes differ according to context and they have been superceded at the end of the twentieth century by neocolonialism. Globalization, with its emphasis on the integration of markets, has initiated a new era in colonial practice. Exclusion from international markets has become a new category to describe the marginalized in poor countries and provides a new challenge for postcolonial theologies.

Marcella Althaus-Reid

See also: Decolonizing Theology, Globalization, Liberation, Post-colonialism.

Bibliography
David Batstone, Eduardo Mendieta et al., *Liberation Theology, Postmodernity, and the Americas* (London: Routledge, 1997).
Marc Ferro, *Colonization: A Global History* (London: Routledge, 1997). Ania Loomba, *Colonialism/Postcolonialism* (London: Routledge, 1998).

CONTEXTUALIZATION

The term "contextualization" was introduced to the theological world in 1972 by the Theological Education Fund (TEF) of the World Council of Churches, which was then headed by Shoki Coe of Taiwan. Before then, such terms as adaptation, accommodation, inculturation, and indigenization were more commonly used to designate ways of expressing theology in a non-Western context, utilizing the native culture and thought expressions as the basis of theological formulation. According to TEF, contextualization does not ignore traditional culture but goes beyond it in a dynamic way, taking into account contemporary phenomena, such as the struggles for justice and the changes wrought by technology, which are part of Third World reality. Moreover, while contextualization stresses local and situational concerns, "it draws its basic power from the Gospel which is for all people."

It has been claimed that all theologies, because they are born out of social conditions and needs of a particular context, are in a sense "contextual." In the past, however, there was no conscious effort to understand the context. Philosophical abstractions, church doctrines, and biblical texts—rather than concrete situations and experience—were used as the starting point of theology. This was true of Western theology, which was taught as "universal theology," applicable to all times and contexts.

Contextualization is now understood in different ways; in general, however, it connotes taking a critical look at the local context (with its historical, socioeconomic, political, cultural, ethnic, racial, and religious dimensions) as well as the impact of outside forces (such as the imposition of a global market and a homogenized culture) on the people.

Contextual theology takes on various forms, the most widely known being Third World liberation theologies; these involve not only a serious analysis of the context and the people's situation but they also seek the transformation of unjust and oppressive structures and practices therein. Liberation theology in Latin America, black theology in South Africa, *minjung* theology in Korea, *dalit* theology in India, and the theology of struggle in the Philippines are examples of contextual theologies.

Women's theologies in the Third World, insofar as they are liberational, are also contextual. The Institute of Contextual Theology in South Africa is an instance of an institutional effort to develop and promote this type of theological expression.

Although contextualization has played an important role in the formation of Third World theologies, it has its critics. Some Third World theologians claim that in light of the global nature of contemporary challenges to life, contextual theologies, no matter how well developed and essential for the context, are inadequate to inspire liberative action that must also be global.

Virginia Fabella, MM

See also: *DALIT* THEOLOGY, DECOLONIZING THEOLOGY, INCULTURATION, INDIGENIZATION, LIBERATION THEOLOGIES, THIRD WORLD THEOLOGIES IN THE FIRST WORLD, THIRD WORLD WOMEN'S THEOLOGIES.

Bibliography
Bulletin for Contextual Theology in Southern Africa and Africa (Scotville, South Africa: School of Theology).
Theology in Context: Information on the Theological Contributions from Africa, Asia, Oceania, and Latin America (Aachen, Germany: Missio, Institute of Missiology [semi-annual publication]).

COSMIC/METACOSMIC RELIGIONS

Theologians have employed the term "cosmic" in three different ways. First, there used to be a tendency among Western theologians to use the term "cosmic" to describe nonbiblical religions such as Hinduism, Jainism, and Buddhism, which postulate that existence is eternally cyclical and that salvation is an escape from that endless recurrence of births. These were contrasted with the biblical religions (Judaism, Islam, and Christianity), which were termed "noncosmic" because they give a unilinear historical character to the cosmos and its redemption. This usage is not very common today.

Other theologians, such as Pierre Teilhard de Chardin, who interpreted the evolutionary view of the cosmos (the whole creation) within the framework of Pauline *enkephaliosis* (recapitulation of all in Christ), described the process of redemption as the gradual "Christification of the cosmos." This image of Christ, who thus permeates the whole universe with his resurrectional activity (radial energy), came to be called the "Cosmic Christ." Many theologians in both the East and the West sometimes explain salvation within the plurality of religions by appealing to the concept of the Cosmic Christ.

A third meaning of the term "cosmic" emerged within the Ecumenical Association of Third World Theologians (EATWOT) in 1979 when the primal religions (also called tribal, clannic, or "animistic"), together with the *popular* forms of the major religions (such as folk Buddhism and popular Hinduism), began to be called by that name. The focus of this type of religiosity is *this world*, including the world of the departed, insofar as this world is a *sacred* locus of religious experience. The word "cosmic," connoting sacred third-worldliness, was coined to differentiate it from the Western concept of the "secular," which is identified with the nonsacred or the a-religious. Thus, "polytheism" is rejected in this scheme as a misnomer for reverence toward "cosmic forces," meaning natural or preternatural powers (*devas* in South Asia; *nats* in Burma; *phis* in Thailand, Laos, and Cambodia; *kamis* in Shinto Japan; *bons* in Tibet; and ancestors in Confucianism).

By contrast, a transcendental, meaning a "metacosmic," reality or a horizon, is the ultimate salvific goal in the major world religions, both in the gnostic religions (*Brahman-Athman* of the Upanisadic seers, *Nirvana* of the Buddha or Mahavira, *Dao* of Daoism) and in agapeic religions (*Yahweh* of Moses, *Abba* of Jesus, and *Allah* of Muhammed). These metacosmic religions usually spread by sending their roots into the cosmic religiosity of a given culture, which explains the cosmic or popular base of all metacosmic religions.

Aloysius Pieris, SJ

See also: POPULAR RELIGION.

Bibliography
Raimon Panikkar, *The Cosmotheandric Experience: Emerging Religious Consciousness* (Maryknoll, N.Y.: Orbis Books, 1993).
Aloysius Pieris, SJ, "Towards an Asian Theology of Liberation: Some Religio-Cultural Guidelines," in *Asia's Struggle for Full Humanity*, ed. Virginia Fabella (Maryknoll, N.Y.: Orbis Books, 1980).
Aloysius Pieris, SJ, *An Asian Theology of Liberation* (Maryknoll, N.Y.: Orbis Books, 1988).

CROSS-TEXTUAL HERMENEUTICS

The notion of cross-textual hermeneutics comes from reflection on the problems of Christian identity in the particular multiscriptural context of Asia. Cross-textual hermeneutics deems questionable the traditional Christian denunciation of the truth claims and values of other religious traditions and cultures. It holds that Asian Christians should venture to read their own classical texts and the biblical text together, and let one text shed light on or challenge the other, so that creative dialogue and integration can take place. Only then can a fuller identification with the two textual traditions, which we can claim as our own, be achieved.

Long before Christian scriptures arrived, the people of Asia had already been nurtured for centuries by their own classics and scriptures. More important, these Asian scriptural traditions are still living, developing, and thus have tremendous vitality today. They continue to shape the lives of Asian people even if they have become Christian. It should be added that "scriptural" culture in the literary sense may not be universal in all Asian countries, as classical and religious teachings are also found in oral traditions handed down from generation to generation. In either case, Asian culture is characterized by the multiplicity and diversity of its religious traditions and spirituality.

However, this Asian situation has not been respected by many theologians who persist in upholding certain presuppositions for doing theology and for interpreting scripture that are dependent on their social location. Some see the church and its historical traditions as the guiding principle for hermeneutics; others underline the unique revelation of biblical truth; some include the universality and the absolute claim of the Christian faith. Many others champion christological positions, and liberation and feminist theologians advocate the experience of the suffering and oppressed. All these positions, except perhaps that of the feminists, tend to create judgmental attitudes toward non-Christian texts and the cultural context from which they originate. The danger of not seriously taking into account culture means that cultural texts may easily be subsumed in the gospel or subordinated in the hermeneutical process.

Cross-textual reading takes seriously Asian religiosity and the cultural values in Asian classics and scriptures; it strives to integrate divine activities in Asian history with those witnessed in the Bible. It values the common human religious quest as a necessary guiding principle, and takes the search for the sacred in the mundane as a significant presupposition. Both the Christian text and the cultural text are affirmed as equally significant and valid for the religious quest they pose and for the similar human religious dimension of life they address, although differences do exist because of their varied historically and culturally bound conditions.

Cross-textual hermeneutics suggests that there may be multiple "crossings" between an Asian text and a biblical text. Both texts must be read in the context of the reader, and the social location of the community must be seriously considered. No one text should hold absolute sway over the other. Surely there are liberating as well as enslaving elements in both texts, and the negative or enslaving elements must be challenged and judged. Each provides the necessary contour against which the other can be seen in a proper light. It is the existence of "the other" that strengthens the understanding of our own identity.

The cross-textual approach also takes "crossings" between the text and the reader into consideration. On the one hand, the reading process is shaped and governed by the social location and power dynamics of the reader. In fact, readers are neither passive nor autonomous. When taking an active role in reading the biblical text, they bring a perspective to the text and critique it from their cultural or social text. On the other hand, the reader's life has to be examined, critiqued, and claimed by the text. Interpretations, however, must be tested in dialogue in a community of interpreters or a "community of inquiry."

In reading the Bible through Asian eyes, we are encouraged to grasp the meaning of the text in the light of the people's suffering and struggle for social justice. Perhaps these "crossings," if they are genuinely executed, help us to go beyond cultural boundaries and to focus on the human quest that is common in both texts. Cross-textual hermeneutics may be a painful endeavor, but it is, nonetheless, necessary for the enrichment of both the gospel and culture.

Archie C. C. Lee

See also: BIBLE: ASIA, CHRISTOLOGIES: ASIAN, INCULTURATION, INDIGENIZATION, INTERRELIGIOUS DIALOGUE, POSTCOLONIALISM, SOCIAL LOCATION.

Bibliography
Kwok Pui-lan, *Discovering the Bible in the Non-Biblical World* (Maryknoll, N.Y.: Orbis Books, 1995).
Archie C. C. Lee, "Cross-Textual Hermeneneutics on Gospel and Culture" in *Asia Journal of Theology* 10 (1) 1996.
R. S. Sugirtharajah, *Asian Biblical Hermeneutics and Postcolonialism: Contesting the Interpretations* (Maryknoll, N.Y.: Orbis Books, 1998).

CULTURE

A particular people (nation, tribe, ethnic group) has its own culture, its distinct way of living, loving, eating, playing, and worshiping. "Culture" may refer to the musical and visual arts, modern influences on life, an acquired tradition, or to regulations that bind the life of a community. Culture can be a double-edged sword: it can form community identity and it can also be used to set apart or oppress those whom culture defines as "other." Participation in culture is so natural and ubiquitous that most people take culture for granted.

Dialogue on matters of culture is still largely undeveloped. On one hand, "It is my culture" implies that others do not have the right to question a practice. On the other hand, people fear to question acts considered part of the culture of another group because such questions might imply that the other culture is inferior. In the past, cultural judgments have often been based on false colonial distinctions that maintained a belief in the superiority of Northern cultures over Southern cultures. Current debates on culture generally promote intercultural understanding and depart from a frame of reference that defines culture from a position of power.

Rethinking culture in theological terms requires affirming realities within every culture and in using appropriate terminology, because the communication of the gospel occurs only through the use of culture. All cultural beliefs and practices should be tested and affirmed for their life-giving potential or condemned for their alienating and death-causing factors.

Though missionaries treated cultures of the Third World people as demonic and superstitious, nonetheless, they used that same pagan culture to wean the people from their erring ways. The earlier generation of Third World theologians, as a way of celebrating their self-identity, used the local culture as a medium to convey the gospel. Recently, however, theologians have been using insights from their culture critically to articulate the message of God. There is also an increasing awareness of the flowing out of Third World cultures into the West, and the rapid penetration of Western cultures into the Third World.

Musimbi R. A. Kanyoro

See also: INCULTURATION.

D

DALIT THEOLOGY

Dalit theology, a contextual reflection of the liberation movements in India, arises from the "pain-pathos" of *dalit* Christian communities. It manifests itself in two complementary ways: the resistance of *dalits* to counter the reach of dominant theologies, and creative construction to circulate themes of *dalits'* experience of the Divine One.

Indian society comprises four castes: priests, rulers, traders, and laborers. Yet, a significant 16 percent of Indian society lives outside these castes. These outcaste collectives have taken on the name *dalit*, which means "broken" and yet striving people. *Dalits* were considered too polluted to participate in the social interactions of the Indian community: they were untouchable and even unseeable. Statistics acknowledged by the Indian government show that every hour an average of five *dalits* are raped; every day five *dalits* are killed; every day fifteen *dalit* houses are burned.

Christianity became an avenue for pursuing *dalit* emancipation. Between two-thirds and three-quarters of the Indian Christian community are *dalits*. In the 1980s, Christian theology set about to reclaim the significance of this historical fact for its own enrichment. The *resistive current* of *dalit* theology is a countertheology that empowers *dalit* Christians to say no to the dominant theologies of the Christian West and the Brahminic East. This dissent must be interpreted within the hegemonizing design of the colonizing West and the homogenizing propensity of Brahminic Hinduism.

The *constructive strand* of *dalit* theology asserts the epistemological judgment that "pain-pathos" is the birthing place of theological knowledge; it taps into the symbolic representations of this experience that are available in *dalit* culture and religion. Substantive themes of *dalit* theology are thus imaginatively worked out by correlating the knowledge of suffering *dalit* communities of the faithful presence of the Divine One (the God-with-us) with the knowledge of striving Christian *dalit* communities of the unfailing presence of Jesus Christ (the God-for-us). *Dalit* theology thus is a contextual rendition of Indian liberation theology.

Sathianathan Clarke

See also: BIBLE: ASIA, CHRISTOLOGIES: ASIAN, LIBERATION, LIBERATION THEOLOGIES: ASIAN.

Bibliography
Sathianathan Clarke, *Dalits and Christianity: Subaltern Religion and Liberation Theology in India* (New Delhi: Oxford University Press, 1998).
V. Devasagayam, ed., *Frontiers of Dalit Theology* (Madras: ISPCK/Gurukul, 1997).
James Massey, *Dalits in India: Religion as a Source of Bondage or Liberation with Special Reference to Christians* (New Delhi: Mahohar, 1995).
Arvind P. Nirmal, ed., *A Reader in Dalit Theology* (Madras: Gurukul, 1991).
M. E. Prabhakar, *Towards a Dalit Theology* (Madras: Gurukul, 1989).
John C. B. Webster, *The Dalit Christians: A History*, 2nd ed. (New Delhi: ISPCK, 1994).

DECOLONIZING THEOLOGY

The decolonization of theology presupposes an understanding of what it means "to decolonize," as defined by former colonies. Unlike the definition usually found in Western dictionaries, which speaks of the "withdrawal" of settlers from a territory, leaving it independent, former colonies see it as "ridding" their country of the settlers, who more often than not, were invaders or illegal immigrants. These "settlers" acquired and maintained their colonies with a view to their exploitation, especially economic, precipitating swift erosion of the freedom, dignity, life, and culture of their original inhabitants. On the whole, colonists withdrew only when forcibly thrown out.

Like a colonized territory, theology in the Third World needs decolonizing, its theological landscape having been invaded, disturbed, and destroyed by theologies from the outside. Our situation as former colonies is that either the theological soil of our Christian existence has been used to grow foreign crops that we do not need or use, or it has been left fallow while theologies raised abroad were imported, but neither assimilated as nourishment nor welcomed as a force for social change. Decolonizing would therefore imply and demand rejection of theological imports or imitations; reappropriation of our theological soil and its possibilities; sowing of this soil with our own needs, hopes, and struggles; and careful gathering of our theological harvest with which to foster human life and humanizing visions.

The project of decolonizing theology is not new, but was intensified during the second half of the twentieth century. For example, in 1976, the Ecumenical Association of Third World Theologians (EATWOT) announced a radical decolonization of theology through a Copernican revolution in theology's method, as well as in its concept, content, and goal. The primacy of praxis over theory was affirmed, along with the primacy of social analysis and involvement over detached philosophical speculation. In various parts of the Third World in the late 1960s and beyond, theologies began to emerge that were based on the struggles for justice and freedom and that took Third World cultures and contexts seriously.

A negative but necessary aspect of our starting point is a critique of Western theology, which has comfortably cohabited with imperialism, the slave trade, genocide, plunder, and mammon worship. Since theology is a critical reflection on life in the light of faith, the first step in decolonizing theology is to reexamine the colonially imposed definition of theology and to redescribe it. Theology will then no longer be an attempt to explain away suffering, including that caused by colonialism, nor to promote resignation to oppression.

Decolonizing theology and building authentic Third World theologies thus means helping theology spring from the underside, letting faith articulations arise from the search of the marginalized for relevance; being faithful to the theological method of the primacy of praxis over theory; taking seriously women's contributions to faith and life and community, so that theology ceases to be colonized by patriarchy; addressing indigenous, tribal, *burakumin*, and *dalit* concerns; stepping with Jesus into the people's religion and culture and identifying with the righteous poor of the land; engaging in a deep, cutting critique of the feudal-capitalistic system, without which no effective decolonization is possible; listening to God's word spoken outside the Judeo-Christian tradition; and celebrating theological pluralism.

Theology, in its beginnings, processes, and conclusions, must be open to challenges. Thus theology is always on the way. In brief, Third World theology aims not at being a perfect system but at being nourishment for life and a plan of action for people who seek meaning in life and freedom.

Samuel Rayan, SJ

See also: CONTEXTUALIZATION, EATWOT, INCULTURATION, INDIGENIZATION.

Bibliography
Jean-Marc Éla, *African Cry*, trans. Robert Barr (Maryknoll, N.Y.: Orbis Books, 1986).
Gustavo Gutiérrez, *A Theology of Liberation*, trans. and ed. Sister Caridad Inda and John Eagleson, 15th anniversary ed. (Maryknoll, N.Y.: Orbis Books, 1988).
Aloysius Pieris, SJ, *An Asian Theology of Liberation* (Maryknoll, N.Y.: Orbis Books, 1988).

DECONSTRUCTION

Deconstruction is both a philosophical and a literary movement in contemporary Western thought. Philosophically, it is associated with

Jacques Derrida and a series of works beginning in the late 1960s. The central tenet is that language is endlessly unstable and indeterminate (*différence*), frustrating all attempts to establish grounds of certainty and truth. Literarily, it is associated with a number of American critics (Yale School) in the 1970s and 1980s. The main goal is to show how texts collapse by foregrounding the internal contradictions that undermine all claims to coherence. The process of deconstruction is going on in Third World theologies without using the term; indeed, decolonizing theology is a form of deconstructionism. All theological construction, Western or Third World, would represent attempts to repress *différence*.

Fernando F. Segovia

See also: DECOLONIZING THEOLOGY, EPISTEMOLOGICAL BREAK, MODERNITY/ POSTMODERNITY, PARADIGM SHIFT.

DEPENDENCY THEORY

"Structural dependency" was proposed in the 1960s and 1970s as an explanation for the Third World's unequal, perverse development. A key notion for liberation theology, it maintains that "peripheral" economies in the Southern Hemisphere have been integrated with industrial "centers" into an international marketplace, which enforces subordination because it does not allow equitable competition. Terms of trade tend to deteriorate steadily as Third World countries' exports of raw materials do not compensate for the ever increasing costs of imported industrial goods. Economic growth becomes impossible, despite profit for a few. Thus, the North's welfare is inextricably linked with the South's debt and poverty.

Once a useful tool employed by liberation theologians, dependency theory is now seldom used as it fails to take sufficient account of the inner dynamics of the individual countries or the vast dimensions of the world of the poor.

Manuel Ossa

See also: DEVELOPMENT, GLOBALIZATION, SOCIAL ANALYSIS.

Bibliography
Fernando Enrique Cardoso and Enzo Faletto, *Dependency and Development in Latin America*, trans. M.-M. Urquidi (Berkeley: University of California Press, 1979).

DEVELOPMENT

The concept of development became prominent after the end of World War II with the emergence of a large number of newly independent countries in the Third World. Development was equated with Western industrial capitalism and was seen as the way these newly independent countries (the "underdeveloped" or "developing" countries) would catch up with the West (the "developed" countries). Associated with pure economic growth, the term was criticized as failing to express the idea of promoting true human well-being through societal transformation. In the 1980s, terms such as "human development" and "sustainable development" became more common, but in the 1980s, in the context of globalization, development was again equated with economic growth at the cost of justice.

Although the development approach was given theoretical elaboration by Western scholars and became the basis of Western policies, the inherent contradiction of this model was evident. The Third World itself is the product of the European capitalist system, so genuine development for the Third World requires the elimination of the structures of dependency imposed on it by this Western-dominated system. With the advent of globalization, these structures were reinforced rather than eliminated.

After the precipitation of a debilitating debt crisis in Third World countries, stringent conditions were imposed on their governments through structural adjustment programs and trade liberalization policies. These impositions simply increased the economic vulnerability of the Third World and diminished the prospects for long-term growth and genuine development; furthermore, they prevented governments from adopting national economic policies oriented to justice or social policies geared toward promoting distributional equity and providing basic standards of living.

In the beginning, ecumenical thinking on development gave equal importance to growth and justice. However, it also challenged the order and predictability that development claimed, and affirmed that development could be destabilizing. As development gradually became identified with the status quo, ecumenical thinking began to reject development and speak instead of liberation.

Two key concepts became central to ecumenical thinking about development and liberation. One is the crucial role of participation. Justice demands that it be participatory and not merely distributive. The other key idea is that of people. Participation is not by people in general, but by the marginalized and oppressed who form the majority in the Third World and who had too often been ignored.

A new development paradigm is needed that puts people at the center of development, regards economic growth as a means not an end, protects the life opportunities of future generations, and respects the natural system on which all life depends.

Ninan Koshy

See also: CAPITALISM, DEPENDENCY THEORY, GLOBALIZATION, THIRD WORLD DEBT.

Bibliography
C. Furtado, *Development and Underdevelopment* (Berkeley: University of California Press, 1975).

Manfred Bienefeld, *Rescuing the Dream of Development in the Nineties* (Institute of Development Studies, paper 10: University of Sussex, England, 1992).

David A. Smith and Josef Borocz, eds., *A New World Order? Global Transformation in the Late Twentieth Century* (Westport, Conn.: Praeger, 1995).

E

EATWOT

The Ecumenical Association of Third World Theologians (EATWOT) was founded in 1976 to promote "the continuing development of Third World Christian theologies which will serve the church's mission in the world and witness to the new humanity in Christ expressed in the struggle for a just society" (Article 2, EATWOT Constitution). The association is committed to fostering "new models of theology which would interpret the gospel in a more meaningful way to the peoples of the Third World and promote their struggle for liberation." Among these new models are Latin American theology of liberation, black theology of liberation, *minjung* theology in Korea, *dalit* theology in India, and the theology of struggle in the Philippines.

The years before EATWOT's foundation were a period of awakening for Africa, Asia, and Latin America. People were becoming aware that the dire conditions in their countries were due not to lack of human or natural resources but to long years, even centuries, of economic, political, and cultural domination and exploitation by powerful nations of the West in collaboration with local elites. At the same time, Christians were becoming conscious that the "universal" theology they had received from the West was not relevant to their continents and needed reformulation to make it meaningful to peoples aspiring for a more just world order.

Against this backdrop twenty-one theologians from Africa, Asia, and Latin America, and one black theologian from the United States, met in Dar es Salaam in August 1976 for an "ecumenical dialogue of Third World theologians." Their purpose was to share an analysis of their reality, an evaluation of the church's presence, and a survey of alternative theological approaches. Despite differences in racial and cultural backgrounds, religious affiliations (Catholic, Protestant, Orthodox), and theological orientations, the participants unanimously rejected the dominant theology of the West as irrelevant to their contexts. Despite disputes and tensions, they found the exchange so worthwhile that they agreed to form an association for future dialogue. Thus EATWOT was born.

For the founding members, "Third World" was not a strictly geographical designation but a quality of life and social condition characterized by poverty and different forms of oppression and marginalization. Thus EATWOT members are those who not only live and work in Third World situations but who do theology from the vantage point of the poor and oppressed. While the term "Third World" has come into question, especially with the demise of the "Second World," EATWOT maintains it as constitutive of its theological identity.

EATWOT has become an important forum of mutual challenge and enrichment for Third World theologians who previously worked in isolation, allowing them to speak with a concerted voice. Besides conferences on national, continental, and intercontinental levels, exchanges among members are made possible through official publications (books and a semiannual journal, *Voices from the Third World*) and individual writings, as well as through the work of EATWOT's three commissions: the Working Commission on Church History in the Third World (established in 1981), the Commission on Theology from Third World Women's Perspective (1983), and the Intercontinental Theological Commission (1986).

Moreover, EATWOT has contributed to breaking theology from its exclusively Western moorings. Besides reformulating theology from a Third World perspective, the primacy of liberation praxis, the move from a philosophical/metaphysical approach, the departure from traditional epistemology, and the use of critical and comprehensive analysis of reality as integral to theology are elements that indicate a paradigm shift in theological thinking and methodology and a reversal of the conventional academic model of Western-based theology.

EATWOT also faces a number of long-standing challenges. Foremost among these are the incorporation of Third World women's perspectives and the emancipating theological insights of racial and ethnic groups, indigenous communities, *dalits*, and other marginalized peoples; a reinterpretation of scripture that takes into account gender, racial, cultural, and religious differences; the inclusion of the ecological and cosmic dimensions in liberation theology and spirituality; and, very important, the recognition of the theologians' own sexist and racist biases in reformulating theology. Newer challenges come from the destructive consequences of economic and cultural globalization on Third World peoples, resources, and environments, as well as the impact of high technology and emerging ethical and moral issues. No Third World theology can be done in a serious way without taking into consideration these new challenges. At the same time, Third World theology must be accompanied by an alternate political vision that can be translated into action to bring about a just world. One perennial challenge persists: to assist the church in redefining its mission in the light of Third World reality and experience, so that the fullness of the gospel will truly be available to all.

EATWOT has a constitution and an executive committee, and holds a general assembly every five years; however, it has no permanent secretariat. To facilitate its work, EATWOT has divided itself into four regions: Africa, Asia, Latin America, and a region for "minority groups" (called the "diaspora" in the original constitution) in other parts of the world. While membership is limited to those who belong to those four regions, it is not restricted to professional theologians, but is open to any Christian woman or man in related fields who wishes to actively promote Third World theology as an alternative voice.

Virginia Fabella, MM

See also: LIBERATION THEOLOGIES, THIRD WORLD, THIRD WORLD THEOLOGIES IN THE FIRST WORLD, THIRD WORLD WOMEN'S THEOLOGIES.

Bibliography
Leonardo Boff and Virgil Elizondo, eds., *Theologies of the Third World: Convergences and Differences, Concilium* 199 (Edinburgh: T & T Clark, 1988).
Virginia Fabella, MM, *Beyond Bonding: A Third World Women's Theological Journey* (Manila: EATWOT and the Institute of Women's Studies, 1993).

ECCLESIOLOGIES

African

In Africa the central task for ecclesiology is how to construct a church that is truly African and truly Christian. African ecclesiologists and theologians in general have proposed various approaches to achieve this goal during the past three decades. The main thrust in all of these approaches, however, is on building the church as a community through participation and sharing by the members.

In the 1970s, the Roman Catholic bishops of Eastern Africa, and subsequently of the whole continent, proclaimed small Christian communities (SCCs; also known as basic ecclesial communities or BECs) to be the best model for the church in Africa. According to this model, the government and structure of the church follow the principles of locality and subsidiarity. But in the majority of cases, SCCs have not been enabled to function in that manner, due mainly to the clerical character of the church.

In 1994 the African synod of Catholic bishops, held in Rome, proposed the family as another model, describing the church as the "family of God." The synod was, in fact, summarizing and adopting the insight of African Catholic theologians whose depiction of the African church included such symbols and analogies as "clan," "kinship," "lineage," "relationship" or "solidarity," and "communion." The Holy

Trinity, which is understood as a life of communion and community, seems analogous to the life of communion and community that exists in traditional Africa among the living, the recently dead, and the ancestors. For African Catholic ecclesiologists this understanding of the Trinity is paradigmatic for understanding the nature of the church. The participation in life by the living, the recently dead, the ancestors, and the yet-to-be-born thus becomes a fundamental element in African Catholic ecclesiology.

Feminist theology in Africa has, in principle, little difficulty with the model of church as family, but with one important proviso: the understanding of family in Africa must be purified of its traditional patriarchal and hierarchical theoretical and structural overtones if it is to serve as an adequate symbol of a just, nonsexist church. Feminist theologians insist that the concept of family in Africa must recognize and integrate within itself the human rights and dignity of African women and children.

Protestant ecclesiology in Africa emphasizes the paradigm of community for the church as well, and uses the idioms of "fellowship," "mutuality," and "celebration" to describe it. All of these descriptions depict the communal activities of participation and sharing central to African traditional living. The Pentecostal churches, capturing the African person's desire for fullness of life in this world, build their ecclesiology, which is often practical rather than dogmatic, around communal prayer and healing. For them, the church is an instrument of Christ, meant to heal the body by miraculously curing disease and the soul by driving away evil spirits. It is an ecclesiology with wide appeal among all sectors of the African population because it responds to Africa's moral philosophy, which sees suffering as an act of evil powers.

The churches that have captured this appeal most radically are the African-initiated churches (or AICs). Their ecclesiology and church structure often revolve around one or several charismatic personalities who often have powers of healing and exorcism. Sometimes these churches collapse, or survive but greatly weakened, after the death of their charismatic leader, unless they have established firm structures of shared leadership. Yet even in the AICs, with their apparent emphasis on the charismatic leader, the church is still viewed as a communion of members and community, and ecclesially perhaps even more so than in the mission churches. This is expressed there through flamboyant liturgies of song and dance.

The relationship between and among the churches, known as interreligious dialogue and ecumenism, has been a preoccupation of most major mission churches in Africa only during the past thirty years. But, although there is now the Organization of African Instituted Churches, similar to the Protestant All Africa Conference of Churches, both with headquarters in Nairobi, Kenya, ecumenism has not been high on the agenda of AICs. In fact, a few reject it altogether as heresy.

Laurenti Magesa

See also: AFRICAN INDEPENDENT CHURCHES, BASIC ECCLESIAL COMMUNITIES, BIBLE: AFRICA, CHRISTOLOGIES: AFRICAN, INCULTURATION, INDIGENIZATION, LIBERATION THEOLOGIES: AFRICAN; THIRD WORLD WOMEN'S THEOLOGIES: AFRICAN.

Bibliography
J. N. K. Mugambi and Laurenti Magesa, eds., *The Church in African Christianity: Innovative Essays in Ecclesiology* (Nairobi: Initiatives, Ltd., 1990).
Charles Nyamiti, *Christ as Our Ancestor* (Gweru, Zimbabwe: Mambo Press, n.d.).
Mercy Amba Oduyoye, *Hearing and Knowing: Theological Reflections on Christianity in Africa* (Maryknoll, N.Y.: Orbis Books, 1986).

Asian

Ecclesiology assumes various modes in Asia. The complex and diverse traditions, histories, and situations of the churches partly explain the absence of a uniform ecclesiology. Two significant issues for Asian Christians are how to live as a Christian community amidst other religious communities, and how to supplant the Western institutional practices of the different denominations. Although Asian mainline Protestant denominations have maintained, in general, the ecclesiologies of their parent churches, there is a growing group of Asian Christians who have come up with different forms of being church, for example, communities centering around individual Christian gurus such as Subha Rao in India, and Christians exercising their faith in secret as do members of *Sivakasi* in South India. Some of the most promising developments in forming new ecclesiologies are originating with Asian Catholics. In spite of factors inevitably working in favor of a pluriformity of ecclesiologies in Asia, common orientations are discernible.

Emphasis on the local church. The ecclesiologies arising from Asia emphasize the local church, the body of Christ "real-ized" in a particular people, their traditions, cultures, and life situations. The mystery of the incarnation of the Word of God is the paradigm for the church's "taking on flesh" in the lives of peoples. Thus the world inhabited by Asian peoples is not simply the external setting in which the life of the church unfolds but is constitutive of the church's identity and mission. The church "happens" in the meeting of the gospel and the Spirit with the peoples of Asia and their "worlds."

The mission of evangelization and the church. The mission of the church is evangelization, the proclamation of the good news of salvation. Asian ecclesiologies stress that evangelization must be related historically, culturally, and contextually to the realities of Asia. From this perspective, mission builds up a truly local church, in the "intersection" of the gospel with a people. In turn, the whole local church evangelizes. Mission is not merely a consequence of the local church's identity and constitution; rather, it is constitutive of its very being. In Asia, mission as the heart of the church's being is motivated by faith in Jesus, deepened and nurtured by a life of contemplation, held in high esteem by the cultures and traditions of Asia.

Dialogue. The mode of mission for the local churches in Asia is dialogue. In the early 1970s, ecclesiologists identified three areas of life in Asia with which the church was called to dialogue: the poor, the cultures, and the religions of Asia. Liberation, inculturation, and interreligious dialogue are thus the three concrete forms of mission. This triple dialogue remains basically valid today. Dialogue is a way of existence for the church in Asia and not just a way of mission. Thus it is asked to proclaim and share its experience of the living Christ in a dialogue of life, in solidarity, and in witness. An attitude of deep respect for openness, listening, and attentiveness to the partners in dialogue must pervade the missionary approaches and the very style of life of the church in Asia.

The church as discipleship of Jesus in the service of life in Asia. There is a growing awareness that the peoples of Asia search for a fuller life. The church must serve as the sign of Jesus' service of life. Christian discipleship must afford to Asian peoples, especially those of other faiths, an experience of the kingdom of life inaugurated in the ministry, death, and rising of Jesus. In this context, the disciples of Jesus arc called to be truly the *church of the poor*, serving, nurturing, enhancing, and protecting life, especially of the teeming millions of Asia's poor.

Communion of communities. With the retrieval of the Trinitarian communion as the origin, model, and goal of the church, ecclesiologies in Asia stress the aspect of communion in the being and mission of the church; the new way of being church in Asia is by being a communion of communities. Communion resonates with the value of harmony, prized by most Asians. The basic ecclesial and human communities in Asia are often presented as the model of communion.

Special issues. A number of special issues have challenged ecclesiologists in Asia. The first is the unique but difficult situation of the church in China. With a Catholic episcopate selected by the local church rather than appointed by Rome, the "independent" status of the church in China has opened new discussions on the meaning of communion in the universal church, on the episcopate, and on the role of the successor of Peter in the church.

A second interesting model of ecclesiology is found in the *Iglesia Filipina Independiente* (IFI), which originated in the Philippines in the late nineteenth century during the revolution against Spanish colonial rule. The ecclesiology of the IFI follows many of the biblical, pastoral, and missionary orientations of the Roman Catholic Church, especially after Vatican II. Its unique quality, however, springs from its fidelity to its historical roots, its break from Rome, and its particular discipline.

Apart from the ecumenical perspectives arising from dialogue between mainline Christian groups, there is not much "ecumenical ecclesiology" in Asia. However, a third innovative ecclesial model that is ecumenical in nature originated in the early 1980s when Asian churchwomen began searching for egalitarian, nondiscriminatory ways of being church. The Women Church in Korea is a concrete living out of an alternative ecclesiology that affirms the creation of women and men in the image of God and ensures equality in church structures, membership, and ministry. The term "women" is used as a symbol of the least and oppressed whom Jesus chose to serve. Women Church is committed to fostering just relationships among human beings and with the rest of creation. It is inclusive in its membership and language, participatory, and multiform in its worship and ministry.

Luis Anthony G.Tagle

See also: CHINESE THEOLOGIES, INCULTURATION, INTERRELIGIOUS DIALOGUE, LIBERATION, MISSION.

Bibliography
Franz Josef Eilers, ed., *For All the Peoples of Asia: Federation of Asian Bishops' Conferences Documents from 1992 to 1996* (Quezon City, Philippines: Claretian Publications, 1997).
John Gnanapiragasam and Felix Wilfred, eds., *Being Church in Asia, Volume I, Theological Advisory Commission Documents (1986-92)* (Quezon City, Philippines: Claretian Publications, 1994).
Aloysius Pieris, SJ, *Fire and Water: Basic Issues in Asian Buddhism and Christianity* (Maryknoll, N.Y.: Orbis Books, 1996).
Gaudencio Rosales and Catalino Arévalo, eds., *For All Peoples of Asia: Federation of Asian Bishops' Conferences Documents from 1970 to 1991* (Maryknoll, N.Y.: Orbis Books, 1992).
Edmond Tang and Jean-Paul Wiest, *The Catholic Church in Modern China: Perspectives* (Maryknoll, N.Y.: Orbis Books, 1993).

Latin American

Latin American ecclesiology defines itself as liberation ecclesiology, and, in taking shape as a theological discipline, it uses the same methodology as liberation theology. Its starting point is the praxis of Christians called together by the Spirit to build the church in the historic and social context of the continent. This ecclesiology is ecumenical even though it has been developed primarily by Catholic theologians.

Ecclesiology draws on two sources in Latin America. The first is the bishops' conferences at Medellín (1968) and Puebla (1979), and the assemblies of the Protestant CLAI (Latin American Council of Churches) in Lima (1982), São Paulo (1988), and Concepción (1995). The second source is the accumulated experience of the churches over the past thirty years, characterized by the experience of communion, increasing charisms, the following of Jesus even to martyrdom if needed, the option for the poor, a commitment to human rights, and the experience of an ecumenism that is more experiential than doctrinal.

The resulting church has certain characteristics.

The church of the poor. Christians from different confessions have come to see more clearly the unjust reality of poverty and have found themselves to be indispensable "to the poor." The poor are present in the church and are a privileged space from which God addresses us (Matt. 25). This is what Puebla called "the evangelizing potential of the poor." The church of the poor, which excludes no one, has a universal mission. In Catholic ecclesiology and in liberal Protestantism, this concern finds expression in making an "option" for the poor.

Church of the poor as people of God. When Vatican II defined the church biblically as the people of God, it set in motion a "Copernican shift," thereby overcoming the notion of the church as authoritarian and centralized. Latin American ecclesiology advanced and specified this universality and democratization: "people of God" became "poor people of God." This is the church of the beatitudes (Matt. 5:1-12; Luke 6:20-23).

Church at the service of the reign of God. Jesus proclaims the reign of God and understands it as a new order, the establishment of the right of the poor. The historic liberation that Jesus embodied when he multiplied bread (Mark 6:30-44) and healed the sick (Luke 5:17-26) is a sign that proclaims the eschatological reality of the reign. Evangelization is a liberating proclamation of the spread of the reign. The church of the poor is a sign that is at the service of the reign of God. Feminist ecclesiology points out that there were both male and female disciples in the Jesus community and that the eschatological reign, where there will be no difference, must be anticipated now in a community of equals.

Church as sacrament of historic liberation. Vatican II presents the mission of the church as salvation, and the ecclesiology of Latin America does so as liberation. This is integral liberation "from all slaveries" (Medellín) and "from personal and social sin" (Puebla). Salvation *within* history becomes an integral part of the evangelizing mission. This entails demythologizing the metaphysical aspect of discourse about salvation, which can no longer be disconnected from actual history. However, renewed Protestant ecclesiology points out that liberation also means symbolizing or sacramentalizing God's saving action in history. For feminist theology, it is crucial that faith and evangelization come out of the full experience of men and women.

Church and Christian base communities. Christian base communities are an original contribution by Latin America. These small communities are led by lay people, stirred up by the Spirit, who meet periodically to review their lives in the light of God's word and to plan their participation in building church and society. They attest to a church that is not clericalized or centralized. The base communities are composed primarily of poor people who believe that poverty does not result from chance but is caused by systems of injustice and oppression. They constitute an ecclesiological experience that is a new model of church.

A surprising development that has emerged from both Protestant Pentecostals and the Catholic charismatic movement is a *rediscovery of the Holy Spirit*, who has often been absent from both Catholic and Protestant traditions. In reaction to the Christomonism of traditional ecclesiology, a charismatic vision of the community of faith is emerging that includes a diversity of gifts at the service of the community.

Latin American ecclesiology reveals the great vitality of the grassroots church; nonetheless, it still encounters difficulties. First, women believe that it has not articulated adequately their massive presence and contributions. Second, its spontaneity and creativity tend to be repressed by Roman centralism. Third, the spread of charismatic groups is lessening its social commitment. Even so, theological reflection strives to respond to these challenges and continually finds responses, both new and old.

Sergio Torres González
(Trans. Phillip Berryman)

See also: Basic Ecclesial Communities, Bible: Latin America, Christologies: Latin American, Option for the Poor, Third World Theologies: Latin American.

Bibliography
Leonardo Boff, *Church: Charism and Power*, trans. John Dirkmeier (New York: Crossroad, 1985).
Julio De Santa Ana, *Towards a Church of the Poor* (Geneva: World Council of Churches, 1979).

ECOFEMINIST THEOLOGY

In the Third World, ecofeminist theology emphasizes that the survival and sustainability of nature are inextricably linked with the survival of all human life, particularly of women, who bear the greatest consequences of the degradation of the earth. It lifts up the idea that all creation is one sacred body that integrates all forms of life.

Born of women's daily struggles for life, ecofeminist theology affirms the value of women's work, women's sexuality (including their demand for control over their productive and reproductive capacities), women's relationships to the earth, women's spirituality, and women's yearnings to reconstruct all unjust relationships in society. Sex role divisions of work in the Third World usually ensure that women do the most strenuous kinds of work and in close proximity to the resources of the earth— food and fuel gathering and collecting of water from distant places. Therefore it is women who have a vested interest in conserving the resources of the earth and women who have been most concerned with maintaining the bond with creation.

Ecofeminist theology is also built on critiques of the dominant models of development and of patterns of life that are based on growth and profit, rather than on sustainability. In many cases, these models of development continue the subjugation and exploitation of colonization. Ecofeminism questions the assumption that Western-style industrial development is possible in all countries today, even those that are essentially agricultural. Ecofeminists note that the violence of development and the violence inflicted on creation are linked closely with violence against women. Both women and creation are too often appropriated, used, abused, and then discarded when considered "worthless." Thus, Third World ecofeminists often challenge traditional understandings and analyses of society.

Ecofeminist theology also challenges patriarchal understandings of scripture, the hierarchical dualisms that undergird most Western theologies, and the excessive anthropocentrism of such theologies. In many cases, the rediscovery of earth-centered and often female-centered powers of cosmic religiosity has inspired ecofeminist theologians to articulate an alternative vision that is more in keeping with the traditional spirituality of the people of the earth. Such a vision centers on the restoration of the soil and its nourishment for the production of food; it also emphasizes humanity's responsibility for the earth and the sacredness associated with land and with rituals surrounding the planting of crops and the harvesting of grains.

Ecofeminist theology also claims that our modern world has lost the power of the feminine in much of our spirituality. Asian ecofeminist theology, for instance, recognizes the concept of motherhood as a possible theological construct to redefine our inextricable bond with creation and to understand our relationship to the world, to ourselves, and to each other. In Third World cultures, mother goddesses are most often represented as virgin, mother, or fertility symbol; they represent, therefore, the power to create, regenerate, and sustain life. The mother goddess, wherever she is found, is an image that inspires and focuses the perception of the universe as an organic whole. It has been said that the Divine Mother is not the ruler of the world but the world itself.

Third World ecofeminist theology has made women conscious of their responsibility to all of creation and has given rise to a new spiritual energy that leads them to find God. Ecofeminists offer these insights as a resource to theology.

Aruna Gnanadason

See also: CHIPKO MOVEMENT, ECOLOGY, FEMINIST THEOLOGIES IN THE THIRD WORLD.

Bibliography
Ivone Gebara, *Longing for Running Water: Ecofeminism and Liberation*, trans. David Molineaux (Minneapolis, Minn.: Fortress Press, 1999).
Rosemary Radford Ruether, *Women Healing Earth: Third World Women on Ecology, Feminism, and Religion* (Maryknoll, N.Y.: Orbis Books, 1996).
Vandana Shiva, *Staying Alive: Women, Ecology and Development* (London: Zed Press, 1989).

ECOLOGY

Once a minor topic in biology, ecology is now a universal political discourse and a significant theological category that can mobilize many people. Ecology exists on four different levels: environmental ecology, social ecology, mental ecology, and holistic ecology.

The concern of *environmental ecology* is that the environment not be excessively disfigured. It seeks to preserve the quality of life and to keep species from becoming extinct. It pursues technologies that are less contaminating, and it emphasizes technical solutions. It seeks to correct the voracious excess of existing worldwide industrialization, whose plundering always entails high ecological costs. If we do not care for the planet as a whole, we may destroy parts of the biosphere and ultimately render our own life impossible. Use of nuclear weapons, the assault on nature, or a worsening of social injustice between North and South would suffice for that to come about.

Social ecology considers not only the natural environment, but also human beings and society located within nature. Social ecology studies the type of relationships, whether benign or aggressive, that societies develop toward nature. It advocates sustainable development, meaning the kind of development that provides for the basic needs of human beings today without sacrificing the earth's natural capital or ignoring the needs of future generations.

The kind of society built up in recent centuries can prevent sustainable development from taking place. Its model of development systematically plunders the earth's resources and exploits the labor force, creating millions of victims. A theology of ecological liberation hears the cry of the poor and the cry of that great poor figure, the earth itself. Both must be liberated.

Mental ecology, also called deep ecology, holds that the causes of the earth's deterioration are not found simply in the kind of society and development we have at present, but also are rooted in our mind-set today, whose roots extend from earlier periods into modern history. We bear within ourselves violent instincts, the will to dominate, and shadowy archetypes that pull us away from kindness toward life and nature. Their expression is called anthropocentrism, which views other beings only in relationship to human beings: everything else is there for our pleasure. This claim forgets that all beings are interdependent and important.

It is crucial that a new alliance be established with the earth, with feelings and attitudes able to change people's awareness, such as kindness, compassion, the sense of respect toward all beings, and veneration of the magnificence of nature. This can be attained only if the dimension of the feminine is first retrieved within men and women. By means of the feminine, human beings are opened to care and sensitized to the mysterious depth of life; they recover their sense of wonder and awe, which helps respect the earth.

Finally, the fourth type of ecology, *holistic* or *integral ecology*, takes as its starting point a new vision of earth. It began in the 1960s when the first spaceships with humans aboard were launched. For the first time, human beings viewed earth from beyond the earth. From that standpoint, the earth and human beings are seen not in juxtaposition to each other but as a single entity. The human being is the earth at its stage of feeling, thinking, consciousness, and love. The earth is part of the universe. All forces are connected and calibrated in such a way as to make possible the existence of the earth and our here and now.

Holistic ecology seeks to familiarize human beings with this total, all-embracing view. It awakens in human beings the awareness of where they fit into this vast whole. Human beings are spiritual beings who can listen to the message of all things; who can rejoice with them; who can praise and thank that Intelligence that orders all and that Love that moves all; and who sense that they are ethical beings responsible for the portion of the universe in which they live, namely, the earth, which outstanding scientists view as a living superorganism that has been called "Gaia."

This cosmic vision requires a new civilization and a new kind of religion, one able to reconnect (*re-ligar*) God and world, world and human being, human being and spirituality of the cosmos. God is in all, and all is in God (panentheism). The incarnation of the Son means taking on matter and becoming part of the cosmic process (the cosmic Christ of St. Paul and Pierre Teilhard de Chardin). The manifestation of the Holy Spirit is revealed as energy inspiring the entire creation. The Blessed Trinity is a play of inter(retro)relationships among the divine Persons. The universe is created in its image and likeness; it is a most intricate fabric of relationships where everything has to do with all at all times and in all places. As planetary consciousness grows, so does the conviction that ecology is becoming the context for all human problems. Caring for the earth and its vast riches means caring for ourselves and assuring our common future.

Leonardo Boff
(Trans. Phillip Berryman)

See also: CHIPKO MOVEMENT, COSMIC/METACOSMIC RELIGIONS, ECOFEMINIST THEOLOGY.

Bibliography
Thomas Berry, *The Dream of Earth* (San Francisco: Sierra Club Books, 1990).
Leonardo Boff, *Cry of the Earth, Cry of the Poor*, trans. Phillip Berryman (Maryknoll, N.Y.: Orbis Books, 1997).
Rosemary Ruether, *Gaia and God: An Ecofeminist Theology of Earth Healing* (San Francisco: Harper, 1992).

ECUMENISM

"Ecumenism" derives from the Greek word *oikos*, which means household. While *oikoumene* refers to the whole inhabited earth, ecumenism, in its current and popular usage, refers to cooperation among and between Christian churches. Ecumenism is marked by the churches' search for unity in doctrinal and ecclesiological matters. Attempts to discuss and come to common understanding and, if possible, mutual recognition of practices such as baptism, Eucharist, and forms of ministry have enabled denominations to merge or share resources. To date, ecumenical dialogues have been most prevalent between and among the so-called historical Christian churches, including Roman Catholics, Orthodox, Anglicans, Lutherans, and so on, although today ecumenism also includes dialogue with other religious traditions of the world. This latter form of ecumenical dialogue often brings with it a certain tension as to how to reconcile Christian mission and evangelism with respect for the traditions of people of other faiths. It is worth noting that in most international ecumenical dialogues, women, peoples of the Third World, and lay people are still underrepresented.

Though often ecumenical activities are seen as Western-propelled, we should not overlook the impetus provided at the embryonic stages by Asians such as Samuel Azariah (India) and C. T. Chao (China). Nor should we overlook the colonial context that compelled ecumenical cooperation in the Third World and challenged the uselessness of imported denominational divisions.

After World War II many ecumenical organizations sprang up to gather Christian witness to respond to the aftermath of the war. Among them was the World Council of Churches (WCC), which currently has a membership of Protestant, Orthodox, and Coptic churches as well as a limited number of Pentecostal, evangelical, and African-initiated churches. The denominational membership of the WCC is a strength as well as an impediment, particularly when differences in doctrinal and cultural stances become bargaining tools for power within the ecumenical movement.

Ecumenism has also been marked by Christians attempting to find common ground in confronting political and social challenges, such as apartheid and political dictatorships, and by acting together on humanitarian issues such as disaster relief, development work, and refugee assistance. More recently, economic, environmental, cultural, and gender issues have also joined its agenda. Current issues of contention include the presence and leadership of women and homosexuals in the church, especially in the ordained ministry; the position of dominant churches regarding the political stance of national governments (such as in Rwanda and the former Yugoslavia); the challenge of evangelicals to the historical churches; and questions of proselytism.

Today ecumenism is expressed locally and internationally through many organizations, including older ones such as the Young Women's Christian Association (YWCA) and newer ones such as Bread for the World. Third World ecumenism is realized through national and regional councils of churches, theological bodies such as the Ecumenical Association of Third World Theologians (EATWOT), the Circle of Concerned African Women Theologians, or the Ecumenical Bishops' Forum in the Philippines. Major ecumenical achievements in the South include the formation of national churches such as the United Church of Zambia or the Church of South India.

Musimbi R. A. Kanyoro

See also: MISSION.

EPISTEMOLOGICAL BREAK

Epistemology is the branch of learning that studies the nature and limits of knowledge. It explores the ways by which one arrives at knowledge and also the structure, origin, and criteria of knowledge. Epistemology is closely linked with a hermeneutics, which is context oriented. Traditionally there have been *deductive* and *inductive* epistemologies. Deductive epistemology implies that one begins with certain presuppositions and applies them to the present situation, seeking to understand it and arrive at knowledge. Inductive epistemology looks at data, analyzes it, and lets the results of the analysis lead to knowledge. Deductive and inductive epistemologies need not necessarily be mutually exclusive.

Theologies followed in the Third World were mostly imported from the West and followed the deductive approach. This had to be abandoned and theologies had to be developed that would be relevant and meaningful, relating faith to the life situations of the people. At the first ecumenical meeting of Third World theologians held at Dar es Salaam in 1976 they affirmed, "We reject as irrelevant an academic type of theology that is divorced from action. We are prepared for a radical break in epistemology which makes commitment the first act of theology and engages in critical reflection on the praxis of the reality of the Third World."

J. Russell Chandran

See also: DECOLONIZING THEOLOGY, DECONSTRUCTION, EATWOT, PARADIGM SHIFT.

Bibliography
Tissa Balasuriya, ed., *A Rainbow in an Unjust World. Voices from the Third World* XV/2, (Colombo, Sri Lanka: EATWOT, 1992).

ESCHATOLOGY

Eschatology designates last things, the final judgment and afterlife, the end of the world and its accompanying events. From a Christian perspective, the major issues that comprise eschatology include the imperfections of the present situation; the imminence, unexpectedness, and urgency of the eschatological event; the need for preparation, which calls for positive moral action and repentance; judgment, meaning rewards and punishment; and the establishment and inauguration of newness and perfection.

A major concern of Third World theologians is the relationship between the present situation and eschatology as a future event. For example, Western missionaries and the church in general have tended to encourage Christians in the Third World to overlook present injustices culminating from other factors, such as colonialism, neocolonialism, and globalization, and to look forward to future heavenly bliss. The unacceptability of this stance is manifest in the numerous movements of social transformation, political change, justice, and liberty that are a reality to be reckoned with in many countries and even within churches in the Third World. The call and desire are for action and change toward eschatological experience here and now. Merely waiting for the coming of the Lord is viewed as an expression of weakness, poverty, helplessness, and downtroddenness.

In the African context, there has been controversy over John S. Mbiti's view that in Africa the future is virtually absent because events of the future have not yet taken place; because they have not been realized, they cannot constitute time. Mbiti also maintains that time does not "run" anywhere and is an uneasy concept for Africans. The rejoinder that should be promoted for Africa, the Third World, and elsewhere is that time is not mathematical but human.

Mary Getui

See also: REIGN OF GOD, SALVATION.

Bibliography
K. C. Abraham and Bernadette Mbuy-Beya, eds., *Third World Theologies: Commonalities and Divergences* (Maryknoll, N.Y.: Orbis Books, 1990).
Pablo Richard, *Apocalypse: A People's Commentary on the Book of Revelation* (Maryknoll, N.Y.: Orbis Books, 1995).

ETHICS

(See **Moral Theology/Ethics**)

F

FAITH AND SCIENCE

The conflict between faith and science started with Galileo, although Charles Darwin, with his theory of evolution as opposed to creation, is perhaps better known in Christian circles. The conflict was often a dialogue, or the lack of it, between experts. It is said today that the advance of science is one cause of secularization, although secularization itself may be more an opposition to the church as an institution and to its control of the secular world, including science, than a denial of God. Third World people are generally too religious to be secularized so easily, apart from the fact that contemporary science itself is often mediated through the educational and medical institutions of Western mission efforts. In general, Third World people have not lived the relation between faith and science as a conflict. Through contemporary cosmologies, for example, a whole new way of looking at the world is emerging, which speaks directly to an awareness of God and of ultimate reality.

The Asian religions, too, react differently to science. They are not as fundamentalistic as those sections of Christianity or Islam that are bound to a literal interpretation of the Bible or the Qur'an. Both Hinduism and Buddhism believe in two spheres of reality and truth, which can be roughly characterized as "this-worldly" and "transcendent." Science has to do only with this-worldly reality; it cannot affect faith/religion, which deals with the transcendent (or Absolute). To the Westerner this division might seem like living in two worlds, but Asians are quite comfortable with such an approach.

Today, some New Age movements seem to find an easy concord between science and faith. For example, some practice astrology "scientifically." Some modern cosmologies may resonate with the cosmologies of Asian religions as phrases like the "Tao of physics" indicate, and contemporary ecological reflection seems to find inspiration in the more holistic Asian traditions. On the other hand, science has often been accused of being hegemonic and exploitative in its relation to nature; however, some would suggest that such a hegemonic attitude to nature can be traced back to the biblical theory of creation.

Sarojini Henry

See also: COSMIC/METACOSMIC RELIGIONS, THEOLOGICAL METHODOLOGIES.

86

Bibliography
Ian G. Barbour, *Religion in an Age of Science* (London: SCM Press, 1990).
Paul Davies, *God and the New Physics* (London: J. M. Dent, 1983).
Arthur Peacocke, *Theology for a Scientific Age*, 2nd ed. (London: SCM Press, 1993).
Fraser Watts, ed., *Science Meets Faith* (London: SPCK, 1998).
Gyan Prakash, *Another Reason: Science and the Imagination of Modern India* (Princeton: Princeton University Press, 1999).

FEMINISM

As an ideological category, feminism reached the Third World at the end of the 1970s. It has no single form. Based on an analysis of women's oppression, its main strands have been classified as liberal, radical, or socialist, although there is some overlap, and the terms "cultural" and "Marxist" are also used. In the 1980s, the "sameness/difference divide" was introduced, the former minimizing the difference between women and men and the latter maximizing the difference in favor of women. The emergence of ecofeminism and the voices of Third World women in the 1990s have exposed the limitations of feminisms: the former, for their anthropocentric thrusts, and the latter, for their Western orientation.

Some Third World women clearly call themselves feminists. Others, however, prefer such designations as "women's liberation movements." Still others identify feminism only with white Western women's experience. As a result, they criticize the disregard for Third World women's historical experience of colonialism and imperialism, other oppressions due to color, caste, or creed, and the destruction of the land and environment for the sake of Western economic expansion. Third World women who consider the experience of colonization and imperialism as crucial to their analysis define their feminist ideology as postcolonial.

Women theologians in the Third World who do liberation theology generally accept the type of feminism (without necessarily using the term) that underscores the intersection of sex, race, and class in its analysis and affirms the need for a new society that promotes respect and right relationships not only among women and men but with the rest of creation.

Arche Ligo

See also: FEMINIST THEOLOGIES IN THE THIRD WORLD, THIRD WORLD WOMEN'S THEOLOGIES.

Bibliography
Chilla Bulbeck, *Re-Orienting Western Feminisms: Women's Diversity in a Postcolonial World* (Cambridge: Cambridge University Press, 1998).

Virginia Fabella, MM, and Mercy Amba Oduyoye, eds., *With Passion and Compassion: Third World Women Doing Theology* (Maryknoll, N.Y.: Orbis Books, 1988).

FEMINIST THEOLOGIES IN THE THIRD WORLD

This all-encompassing term refers to the religious vision articulated by Third World women and men to describe a new model of society and civilization that is free of systemic injustice and violence due to patriarchal domination. It seeks to affirm new paradigms of social relationships that can fully sustain human dignity and the integrity of creation, as well as eliminate the current patriarchal system of unequal power relationships that subjugate and exploit the poor, especially women and children around the world. This vision emerges from the struggles of diverse socio-ecclesial movements for justice, for liberation, and for self-determination. It establishes a deliberate conversation with critical feminist theory and feminist movements and shares the end purpose and commitment of all liberation theologies. It provides inspiration to transform all unjust realities so that the world truly reflects God's glory and salvation.

Third World feminist theology adopts a twofold point of departure: women's experiences of resistance, survival, and struggle against patriarchal systems of domination and dehumanization, and women's shared experiences of hope, of a life-giving spirituality, and of a common effort to eliminate all forms of social and domestic violence. This point of departure does not mean that feminist theology is done "for" or "by" women alone; rather, it shows a shift in the ways of doing theology from the dominant androcentric worldview to a holistic way of articulating the human religious experience. Third World feminist theology takes into account the diversity of experiences, cultures, and realities, but it also recognizes that the faith experience can occur within a complex and conflictive capitalist societal model that continues to exert its colonial and neocolonial dominance over the entire Third World. Through its globalizing processes, the current world model has increased awareness of human interdependency; however, it has also multiplied the impoverishment and exclusion of entire peoples due to its tendency to absorb and concentrate social power and resources. This model reproduces patriarchal oppression by promoting militarism, sexism, racism, homophobia, and ecological degradation. In this context, feminist theology asserts that religion, the churches, theology, and spirituality cannot contribute to the maintenance of forms of societal, ecclesiastical, and cultural patriarchy.

In its plural form, the term "Third World feminist theologies" designates the distinct theological discourses rooted in the particular realities of the Third World, each with varied levels of conversation with Third World feminist theory and native feminist movements. Taking into account the diversity of critical feminist analyses, all Third World feminist theologies share the following principles of theological construction: (a) women and men possess a God-given inviolable dignity that must be protected; sexism and racism are considered to be sins against God and humanity; (b) the common good of humanity entails honoring and promoting women's rights as human rights; (c) the integrity of the earth requires a relationship of respect, care, and harmony because the human being and the cosmos constitute an interconnected historical reality; (d) the fullness of life for all, especially a better quality of life for women and children who are poor, is the universal and absolute principle for a new way of living; (e) justice is a constitutive dimension of the gospel and an essential dimension of Christianity; therefore, all forms of violence against women are regarded as sin against God and humanity; (f) full participation of women in church and society is a basic principle for attaining a just and peaceful world; (g) structural exclusion of the poor and of women is an evil and an injustice that must be eradicated by establishing new social relationships based on solidarity, mutuality, and equalization of power.

In sum, Third World feminist theology is a shared perspective that raises a socio-theological critique of all forms of domination rooted in patriarchal society, church, and religion. As a critical reflection on the people's experience of God within our struggles for justice and liberation, this theology accompanies critically all struggles for life with its liberating religious vision of a just world order and a reconciled humanity.

María Pilar Aquino

See also: FEMINISM, THIRD WORLD WOMEN'S THEOLOGIES.

Bibliography
María Pilar Aquino, *Our Cry for Life: Feminist Theology from Latin America* (Maryknoll, N.Y.: Orbis Books, 1993).
Virginia Fabella, MM, and Mercy Amba Oduyoye, eds., *With Passion and Compassion: Third World Women Doing Theology* (Maryknoll, N.Y.: Orbis Books, 1988).
Virginia Fabella, MM, and Sun Ai Lee Park, eds., *We Dare To Dream: Doing Theology as Asian Women* (Hong Kong: Asian Women's Resource Centre, 1989; Maryknoll, N.Y.: Orbis Books, 1990).
Mercy Amba Oduyoye and Musimbi R.A. Kanyoro, eds., *The Will to Arise: Women, Tradition, and the Church in Africa* (Maryknoll, N.Y.: Orbis Books, 1992).

FOLKTALE/MYTH

(See **Myth/Folktale**)

FUNDAMENTALISM

Today we live in a world of crisis—in authority, identity, and religion. The crisis of religious identity leads to a crisis of moral identity and that in turn affects the very basis of personal and social life. This is a dominant reality in the Third World. In such a context, religious fundamentalism is appealing and popular.

Religion is the home and the nurturing ground of fundamentalism, which claims, generally, that its authority stems from the pure word of God. Fundamentalism abstracts a set of strict rules from scripture in order to elaborate a narrow and exclusive religious system. As a religious-political movement, fundamentalism often uses religion to rally people in order to capture or influence political power and awaken nationalism.

Religious fundamentalism is sweeping across the Third World. It is appealing to people because it explains the crisis in society in simple religious terms and argues that the situation in society cannot be changed unless society recaptures its religious roots. The God of the fundamentalist is most often hierarchical, patriarchal, intolerant, and unforgiving. Religious fundamentalism tends to be exclusivist, militant, self-righteous, puritanical, and aggressive.

Rienzie Perera

Bibliography
John Augustine, ed., *Religious Fundamentalism: An Asian Perspective* (Bangalore: South Asia Theological Research Institute, 1993).

G

GLOBALIZATION

Globalization can be understood as uniting the world for the common good of all. In this sense it is desirable and can lead to the greater happiness and fuller humanity of all peoples. But globalization as commonly known in the Third World refers to a new development model of a globally integrated market economy. It has different strands, impacting one another toward exponential growth of global interdependence, but their overall effect is to incorporate all peoples into a single world unit for production, consumption, trade and investment, information flow, and culture. This global system imposes itself as the only viable alternative available to economic and social life. While the system benefits the rich and powerful, it has adverse consequences on the majority poor of the Third World.

Globalization may be defined as the transnationalization of capital and the standardization and homogenization of consumer tastes. As a global extension of the principles and practices of capitalism, it is also called capitalistic or economic globalization. Its process and policies are determined by the affluent nations, mostly those of the West, headed by the United States, and powerful financial institutions, such as the World Bank, International Monetary Fund (IMF), and World Trade Organization (WTO). These financial agencies have created policies called the Structural Adjustment Programs and imposed them on poor (and often debtor) countries. These include trade liberalization, foreign investments, privatization of public-sector enterprises, and promotion of export crops and industries. These policies are supposedly intended to bring about rapid industrialization, a transfer of technology, and the availability of credit and foreign aid in the form of loans, grants, or investments that enable debt repayment. On the whole, however, they have not improved the lot of the poor nations.

The real movers and beneficiaries of the process are in fact the global transnational corporations (TNCs) that control the greater share of the production, trade, finance, transportation, insurance, and communications media in the world. In dire need of foreign investments, the local governments of debtor countries are constrained to offer incentives to the TNCs, which may include guarantees for foreign capital, cheap labor, adequate infrastructures, and flexible labor and environmental laws, often at great social cost to the debtor country. In many Third World countries, national planning has been replaced by corporate strategic planning under the aegis of the TNCs, aided by the Washington-based World Bank and IMF.

The argument for globalization is that the productivity of the world increases; marvelous technological advances that include long-distance instantaneous communication are available to all; the world's resources are used more efficiently; and thus humankind's needs are more readily satisfied. But poorer peoples face many drawbacks from such globalization. For example, cheaper food imports discourage local agriculture and make the poor countries dependent on the advanced countries for food; local industries are forced to close down or be integrated within the dominant TNCs; unemployment escalates when TNCs decide to relocate to another country where labor is cheaper. Poor countries thus compete with other poor countries, while competition between TNCs is reduced by mergers, takeovers, monopolies, and oligopolies.

A particular and essential characteristic of present-day globalization is the power and mobility of global capital. This recent development provides avenues for immense financial profit-making without entering the productive process. The sudden outflow of large amounts of speculative currency was one of the main causes of the financial, economic, and social crises of the Southeast and East Asian countries that broke out in July 1997.

Globalization has had gravely harmful effects on the poorer sections of most societies in the Third World. The system produces what can be sold to the rich but not the necessities of the many poor. Globalization commercializes most aspects of life: education and health services, transportation and water supplies, even leisure and sports. Harassed by the burden of debt service payment, governments are forced to reduce public expenditures for social services. Worsening social conditions lead to increasing social discontent, crime, violence, and civil conflicts.

Unemployment has increased in most Third World countries, which has led to both internal and external migration of labor and populations—as migrant workers, settlers, refugees. Women are pressured to go abroad (many as domestics or entertainers) due to the inadequacy of the family income. This disrupts family life, distorts family values and relationships, and leads to the neglect of children, and, in many cases, the harassment and degradation of women and increased violence against them.

A further ill effect of globalization on the Third World is the homogenization of culture. The mass media promote a global Western-style monoculture in food, dress, leisure, music, and sports. It dictates not only what people must eat, drink, and wear but what they must feel, desire, and think. This diminishment of local culture has affected Third

World peoples unfavorably. It is important to note that the destruction of a culture is often the first step in eliminating a people.

The process of globalization has also been responsible for ecological devastation and environmental pollution in the Third World. The air, water, sunlight, soil, forests, and various life forms have been affected adversely by the modern industrial, commercial culture, which fails to establish a sustainable relationship with the natural world. With the wasteful lifestyle of the rich the world over, resource depletion and environmental pollution have become life-threatening to both present and future generations.

Former colonies in the Third World see globalization as a form of re-colonization that does not require military intervention. The governments of developing countries have to maintain the system, with the support of the local elite, to survive in power.

Committed groups and movements in the Third World, however, do not see globalization as inevitable or irreversible; nonetheless, they realize that a sustained struggle is required against the globally organized power of the TNCs, the rich countries, the World Bank/IMF/WTO alliance, and the collaborating local elite. Experience and critical analysis of the system and its negative effects have led committed citizens to opt, instead, for genuine development and liberation of the people, especially the poor, the marginalized, the excluded. They see that any strategies they pursue must include alternative goals and means of realizing the vision of a new world order that can give hope and happiness to all. This requires consciousness-raising programs and demands people-empowering activities, networking, national coalitions, and transnational alliances that can lead to an alternative economy and society. A counter-culture that truly respects humans and nature alike needs to be fostered by grassroots movements and alternative mass media.

Religious groups of all persuasions have also become aware of the negative values of capitalistic globalization, which are diametrically opposed to the precepts of world religions. The religions stress the sisterhood and brotherhood of all peoples, which would require a change in the present relationships and societal structures to accept all persons as equal in dignity and rights.

Third World theologians and socially concerned Christians see the motivation and practice of capitalistic globalization as basically contrary to the core teachings of Jesus Christ. Whereas Jesus teaches love and service of neighbor, the motivation of globalization is primarily to maximize profit. Jesus teaches the beatitudes: blessed are the poor in spirit, those who seek justice, whereas globalization blesses and benefits the rich and excludes the poor. Jesus' mission is to liberate the oppressed; globalization worsens the oppression of the poor and oppressed. Due to this fundamental contradiction, Christians are enjoined to be a counter-movement for right relationships among all humans as well as with the rest of creation.

As contextual theology, all Third World theology must seriously study and critically analyze globalization, which affects every people and every context. To meet the challenges of this global system, doing Christian theology in the Third World must begin with the experience of the poor and powerless, the principal victims of globalization—peasants, laborers, indigenous and tribal peoples, fisherfolk, and urban slum dwellers, particularly the women among them.

The struggle against the system of globalization requires a spirituality that entails a firm commitment to the values of the reign of righteousness, that is, an option for the liberation of the oppressed. This option includes a vision of justice for all humanity and nature that presents alternative values, relationships, and structures.

Tissa Balasuriya, OMI

See also: CAPITALISM, LIBERATION THEOLOGIES, THIRD WORLD, THIRD WORLD DEBT.

Bibliography
David C. Korten, *When Corporations Rule the World* (West Hartford, Conn.: Kumarian Press and San Francisco, Calif.: Berrett Koehler Publishers, 1995).
Felix Wilfred, ed., *Globalization or Peripheralization? Jeevadhara: A Journal of Christian Interpretation* (Kerala, India), 25/145 (January 1995).

GOD

The God of Jesus Christ is God crucified in Christ and in the poor and the excluded of the earth and God liberator, who raised Jesus from the dead and who establishes righteousness and justice. More than provident, God takes the side of the poor and liberates them from slavery and oppression. Thus God is the God of the poor. God is seen and understood from the poor and has become incredibly small with those little ones. God shows a preferential love for the poor, because God is poor, because God suffered injustice and death. This preferential love is expressed in the announcement to the poor of God's reign. God's reign is at hand, and the poor appear as the privileged receivers. God is the one who comes in the reign as good news to the poor.

God of history, present in history, acts within it and identifies with the poor of history; God's face and action are hidden in them. Even though history is the place where God manifests God's self, no historic act is capable of containing or setting limits to the divine presence and action. God's presence will always remain utopic. God is transcendent. God enables life in plenitude beyond the limits of oppression, overcoming death, assuring life. The transcendence of God manifested itself in the historic life of Jesus, who constantly looked to God so as to be obedient to God's sovereign will, allowing God to be God in his own life. God's hidden presence in history with those at the margins of history means that God is to be sought there.

God of the people makes covenant with the people in their organization and struggle for liberation. God of the Exodus walks before the people when confronting the powers of domination.

God is love, in loving solidarity. Love between humans is the privileged mediation of the encounter with God. God is suffering love. God is not indifferent to the suffering of victims nor of the suffering caused by history. Through love and solidarity God became poor, was condemned, crucified, and died.

God is the God of life. Life and death are everyday experiences in the Third World. In the small Christian communities, God is experienced in their own lives and in the fulfillment of abundant life, including the material means that make life possible. God is a living God, present in the creation and the permanent re-creation of life by the strength of the Spirit. The God of life, who gives life, has assumed human life with its beauty and richness.

God is joy and hope that invade the heart, hope in liberation, joy and hope that give strength for the struggle. More than that, God is joy in knowing that one is recognized by God with dignity, subversive joy that nourishes and encourages the pilgrim.

Silvia Regina de Lima Silva

See also: OPTION FOR THE POOR, REIGN OF GOD, TRINITY.

Bibliography

K. C. Abraham and Bernadette Mbuy-Beya, eds., *Spirituality of the Third World* (Maryknoll, N.Y.: Orbis Books, 1994).

Gustavo Gutiérrez, *The God of Life*, trans. Matthew J. O'Connell (Maryknoll, N.Y.: Orbis Books, 1991).

Pablo Richard et al., *The Idols of Death and the God of Life: A Theology*, trans. Barbara E. Campbell and Bonnie Shepard (Maryknoll, N.Y.: Orbis Books, 1983).

H_____

HAN/HAN-PURI

Han is the accumulated feeling of resentment, anger, sadness, and resignation experienced by the Korean people that arises from injustices suffered, from the sinful interconnection of classism, racism, sexism, colonialism, neocolonialism, and cultural imperialism that are part of the Korean people's daily lives. It has been called the people's "root experience" or "collective unconsciousness." Like a cancer in the soul, *han* debilitates and oppresses. The most *han*-ridden people are the *minjung*, those Koreans who are dominated, exploited, marginalized, and repressed politically, economically, socially, and culturally. In Korea, women are often the "*minjung* of the *minjung*," suffering the greatest *han*.

Han-puri, a term originating from the Korean shamanistic tradition, is a releasing or untangling of *han*. Although shamans have special rituals for this, *han-puri* can take other forms, from dancing and other artistic performances, to "rumor mongering" (as indirect vindication), to peasant uprisings and student demonstrations against the government. Thus, *han-puri* not only liberates but can also stimulate creativity or lead to social change.

Han and *han-puri* are the core of *minjung* theology as well as of Korean women's theology. It was a growing consciousness of *han* in the 1970s that led to the birth of *minjung* theology. Similarly, as Korean women became aware of their gender-specific oppression, in addition to the suffering they shared with men, they launched a theological movement. Both theological movements are Korean expressions of liberation theology; they are thus *han-puri*, releasing women and men from the bondage of *han*. By identifying the roots of *han* and working together to overcome them, Korean people can experience the peace and healing of true liberation.

Chung Hyun Kyung

See also: MINJUNG THEOLOGY, SHAMANISM.

Bibliography
Chung Hyun Kyung, *Struggle to Be the Sun Again: Introducing Asian Women's Theology* (Maryknoll, N.Y.: Orbis Books, 1990).
Andrew Sung Park, *The Wounded Heart of God: The Asian Concept of Han and the Christian Doctrine of Sin* (Nashville, Tenn.: Abingdon Press, 1993).

96

Jae Hoon Lee, *The Exploration of the Inner Wounds: Han* (Atlanta, Ga.: Scholars Press, 1994).

HERMENEUTICAL CIRCLE

The hermeneutical circle attempts to relate the critical reading of historical reality (with its political, economic, cultural, gender, ethnic, and other oppressions) to a reinterpretation of sacred texts to discern the liberating message of a religious tradition. This hermeneutical task entails relating the "world of the text" (the text as witness to a story, a vision, a faith) to the "world of the reader" (with the life circumstances in which the text is received). The reinterpretation of texts takes place in the search for new understanding and organizing of life and in response to daily struggles for greater freedom and justice. This endeavor leads to a new interpretation and formulation of attitudes and the contents of faith. The hermeneutical circle is completed only with the community's action to transform reality and with its celebration of life.

The hermeneutical circle, which links action and reflection, has been used by many liberation theologians and feminist theologians in the Third World. The most articulate proponent of this interpretative method was Uruguayan theologian Juan Luis Segundo, who identified four stages in this open-ended and evolving hermeneutical circle. First, one becomes aware of reality, leading to an analysis and a suspicion of the operating ideologies. Second, this awareness leads to a critique of the ideological superstructure and theology in particular. Third, this critique in turn leads to a mistrust of how the Bible and theology have been interpreted. Fourth, this exegetical suspicion leads to an appropriation of the Bible in a liberative way. In Latin American theology this process is called "see, judge, act, and celebrate." Some theologians have spoken of a "hermeneutical dance" because these steps are not always sequential and the task itself is subject to continual reexamination. The noun "circle" is used because the task must ever begin again in order to be critical of new realities. The process appeals to the "reserve of meaning" in the texts, making them valid in various historic, social, and cultural circumstances.

Néstor Oscar Míguez
(Trans. Phillip Berryman)

See also: BIBLE.

Bibliography
J. Severino Croatto, *Biblical Hermeneutics: Toward a Theory of Reading as the Production of Meaning* (Maryknoll, N.Y.: Orbis Books, 1985).
Juan Luis Segundo, *The Liberation of Theology* (Maryknoll, N.Y.: Orbis Books, 1976).

HIERARCHY

(See **Patriarchy/Hierarchy**)

HOLY SPIRIT

Jesus spoke often of God as his Father and our Father. He also referred to the Spirit whom the Father and he were gifting to us for our rebirth. Thus, God is Trinity, a communion of three persons, distinct, inseparable, equal, eternal. Within the Trinitarian mystery the Spirit is the relatedness and mutuality of the Father and the Son; in the divine family the Spirit is dynamism, love, and joy. The three live in and for each other, and act together. Christian reflection and debate, lasting some four centuries, and mediated by the experience of a community life of radical sharing, blossomed into the beautiful insight that the absolute and ultimate Source/Goal/Reality is community, not solitude. We must move beyond the days or centuries of Christomonism and pre-Trinitarian monotheism, and insist that the Ultimate is Trinity, communion, a fellowship of total sharing among equals who thus provide the model on which to pattern a new world order.

"Father" and "Son" are names adopted from family relationships and are suggestive of personhood; "Spirit" is neither. The Spirit is described as the promise of the Father, the paraclete or advocate, and the Spirit of truth. Also used as symbols of the Spirit are realities noted for their dynamism, strength and power, freshness, innocence, mystery and beauty. Among such symbols are breath, wind, storm, flame, water, stream, dove, and cloud. But the finest symbol of sacrament of the Spirit is Jesus himself with his radicalism and tenderness, his tears and his laughter, his parables and endless journeys, his subversive interpretation of customs and laws of society and religion, his special fondness for, and table fellowship with, the lowly and the outcast, his placing of mercy above sacrifice and compassion above recital of creeds. Today the Spirit's best everyday sacrament would be any mother anywhere.

God transcends gender, yet "Father" and "Son" denote the masculine. What of the Spirit? In the first four centuries C.E., Syrian and Jewish Christianity spoke of the Spirit as feminine, as Mother, even as Eve, complementing the comparison of Christ to Adam. The Spirit's motherhood, like Eve's and unlike the church's, embraced the whole of humanity. Eventually, this usage waned and disappeared. Theology today again holds that a valid case can be made for depicting the Spirit as Mother, for the activities of the Spirit present striking similarities with the role of a mother. The role of the Spirit is found in activities commonly associated with mothers: comforting, nourishing, inspiring, supporting, enveloping, giving birth, teaching us to pray.

The Spirit's motherly role has consequences for the church. First, those who have the ministry of ruling in the church must remember that Christ is Lord in the power of the Spirit who is maternal and gentle. The only power in the church is the charity of the Spirit. Second, Christ and the Spirit are two principles that together constitute the church. A theology of the Spirit and devotion to her must help correct the excessive masculinity and imbalance in a church based on legal power. Third, they should also lead to some reevaluation of high goddess cults found in various ancient traditions.

The presence and action of the Word and the Spirit mark the beginning, the unfolding, and the crowning of all the creative and redemptive projects of the Father in the beginning of creation when the *ruah* hovered over the waters; of the new creation that is Jesus, when the Spirit overshadowed Mary; and of the church, when the Spirit filled a whole gathering of the women and men who were Jesus' disciples. Today, the Spirit accompanies and guides the evolutionary pilgrimage of the cosmos and keeps renewing the face of the earth; she takes charge of the New World. She abides in the church, interpreting Jesus to her from age to age and enabling her with diverse charisms to carry on her mission. The Spirit is working toward a final liberation of creation from all travail and frustration and its definitive assumption into the freedom of God's children.

The Spirit pervades the universe. The astounding variety and multiplicity of things living and nonliving, of movements, colors, sounds, and spontaneities are the Spirit's work. In the Spirit, creation comes alive as God's self-disclosure, as God's Word nodding to us and beckoning us to dialogue and praise. Everything becomes a symbol, a parable, of the Divine.

The Spirit is present also in the ebb and flow of history. Her action is not restricted to any one person, institution, epoch, culture, or religion. All human quest for truth, beauty, and community, and all humanizing and liberating discoveries and inventions, originate in the promptings of the Spirit abiding deep within. The varieties of talents, tastes, strivings, and symbol systems are the Spirit's gifts. They are interdependent and are meant to complete and enrich one another. The Spirit asks us to cooperate in weaving them into a web of life and a community of love in which the "other" is discerned as a value to be respected and upheld.

All the same, the Spirit-Mother is partial to the poor. It is through the poor that the Spirit acts to take history forward to finer humanity. Jesus, anointed by the Spirit, opts to be poor, to work among the poor and address his gospel to them. He introduces himself as one anointed with the Spirit and sent as liberator of the downtrodden. It is right, then, to discern the Spirit's stirrings and her summons to action in all liberation struggles throughout history. In the Third World, this means the struggles of slaves, colonized peoples, *dalits*, apartheid victims, marginalized women, victims of fanaticism, racism, and imperialist wars. The Spirit calls for radical freedom and radical communion. She comes to transform all hierarchies into God's family and the Body of Christ.

The Spirit grieves when we hurt one another and violate God's image that forms us as women and men. Jesus, too, grieved over the hunger, harassment, and dejection of the crowds, and over the soulless laws and customs of society and religion. At the tomb of Lazarus he broke down and wept; at the sight of Jerusalem, which had refused his ingathering mother-love, he shed tears. As Jesus is a sacrament of the Spirit, his grief is an expression of her grief. The Spirit grieves over our lies and treacheries; over our greed and worship of mammon; over our system of accumulating wealth in a few hands and leaving the masses of the people to starve or sell themselves in order to stay alive; over suffering and humiliation caused by discrimination based on gender, race, caste. She grieves over the endless conflicts in Kashmir, Sri Lanka, Algeria, Sierra Leone, Sudan, Rwanda and Burundi, Mexico, Kosovo, East Timor, and over the two major wars and the many minor wars and internal conflicts; over the holocausts and the genocides; over the conquest of the Americas and the slave system; over colonial destruction of peoples, histories, and cultures; over dictators who have tortured, killed, and "disappeared" thousands and stolen people's moneys; over the support given those dictators by the superpowers; over the continuing production of nuclear weapons and all the threat, waste, and insanity they represent. The list is endless. Endless are the griefs of the Spirit and the pain of God and the crucifixion of the people.

But the Spirit grieves ultimately to wipe away our tears and heal our wounds and make us whole. For the Spirit is *ananda*, joy. To believe is to live in the tension of her grief and her joy, and to love is to resolve the tension, release the joy, and let the dove take to her wings and bear us with her.

Samuel Rayan, sj

See also: GOD, TRINITY.

Bibliography
José Comblin, *The Holy Spirit and Liberation* (Maryknoll, N.Y.: Orbis Books, 1989).
John Crescy, "Woman and the Holy Spirit: From an Indian Perspective," in *We Dare to Dream: Doing Theology as Asian Women*, ed. Virginia Fabella, MM and Sun Ai Lee Park (Maryknoll, N.Y.: Orbis Books; Hong Kong: Asian Women's Resource Centre, 1989).
Samuel Rayan, *The Holy Spirit: Heart of the Gospel and Christian Hope* (Maryknoll, N.Y.: Orbis Books, 1978).

HOMELAND THEOLOGY

(See **Taiwanese Theologies**)

HUMAN RIGHTS

On December 10, 1948, the United Nations approved the Universal Declaration of Human Rights. That document, along with the International Covenant on Economic, Social, and Cultural Rights and the International Covenant on Civil and Political Rights, form what has come to be known as the International Bill of Human Rights. Since then several other protocols and agreements have been approved to prevent various abuses, including racism, apartheid, discrimination against women, torture and inhuman treatment or punishment, and violation of the rights of children.

In the Third World the topic of human rights has broken upon the scene with a deep sense of urgency and also suspicion. Many countries have experienced military governments and so-called democracies that are still far from being truly participatory. It is true that the situation of political and civil rights has improved and that a much greater consciousness exists of the need to respect and protect such rights. In some countries this consciousness has been translated into new legislation. Nevertheless, serious violations still occur, particularly when authoritarian structures seek to maintain power. One of the open wounds is the impunity with which security forces and political leaders operate. Other areas that cry out for justice are abusive judiciary systems, conditions in jails and prisons, the continuing use of torture, and the abuse of power by government or military authorities.

The growing influence of neoliberalism means that economic and cultural rights are continually more restricted. Growing poverty in the Third World violates basic human rights because it limits the possibilities for development and for living in dignity for the majority of the population. The right to peace and to a healthy environment and respect for indigenous peoples are also urgent topics.

Throughout the Third World, churches have played significant roles in human rights, in both their enhancement and their suppression of cultural and theological perspectives. In Latin America, churches have played an important role in the defense of life, focusing on the dignity of the human person, the great masses who are oppressed by poverty, and the defense of those who have taken on the cause of human rights, areas in which the most ecumenical church action occurs.

Laura Vargas
(Trans. Phillip Berryman)

See also: JUSTICE.

Bibliography

Aloysius Pieris, "Human Rights Language and Liberation Theology," in *The Future of Liberation Theology: Essays in Honor of Gustavo Gutiérrez*, ed. Marc H. Ellis and Otto Maduro (Maryknoll, N.Y.: Orbis Books, 1988).

J. Milburn Thompson, *Justice and Peace: A Christian Primer* (Maryknoll, N.Y.: Orbis Books, 1997).

United Nations Development Program, *Human Development Report, 1998* (New York: Oxford University Press, 1998).

I

IDEOLOGY

Ideology is a system of ideas (a way of thinking, a system of logic) and a system of social representations (images, myths, utopias) with which human beings identify themselves, think, and represent themselves within the world in which they live. Ideology transcends the individual and is proper to a group or social movement. The word "ideology" can be understood in both a positive and a negative sense.

Third World theological traditions have used the term "ideology" both negatively and positively. Negatively, ideology is regarded as a discourse that plays a social role in concealing reality and legitimizing domination. In a situation of conflict, we can either enter into the conflict to resolve it or we can deny the conflict exists with a discourse that is false and self-interested and that legitimizes domination. Third World theologies are usually historically engaged theologies that reject any ideological vision of reality. Such theologies take on conflicts within history and identify with the oppressed in their struggles.

Third World theologians use the term "ideology" in a positive sense by urging people to identify themselves and to express themselves out of their own reality—to become historic "agents" who are capable of resistance within the system and who propose and design alternatives. They are generally the poor and others excluded by the power systems, but especially indigenous people, blacks, young people, and women. Theology tries to express their way of feeling, thinking, and believing. It seeks to represent their hopes, utopias, myths, and symbols, and especially seeks to do theology out of their specific culture, ethics, and spirituality.

Pablo Richard
(Trans. Phillip Berryman)

See also: CAPITALISM, FEMINISM, FUNDAMENTALISM, MARXISM, SOCIALISM.

Bibliography
Pablo Richard, *Idols of Death and the God of Life: A Theology* (Maryknoll, N.Y.: Orbis Books, 1983).

IDOLATRY

There are two kinds of idolatry: *perversion*, in which God is manipulated, and *replacement*, in which other gods replace God. The first type

103

tends to be dominant in the churches, while the second is more common in society. In the latter case, consumer goods, technology, or even freedom are transformed into divine subjects, and sometimes human beings are transformed into objects. The perversion of all idolatry lies in the deification of a subject, in whose name domination can be carried out with a clear conscience and without limits. Idolatry is the transcendent root of social sin. In the Third World idolatry is more dangerous than atheism. The problem is not God's *existence* but God's *identity* and *presence*. The question is which God I believe in and where I discover God.

Pablo Richard
(Trans. Phillip Berryman)

See also: GLOBALIZATION.

Bibliography
Pablo Richard, *Idols of Death and the God of Life: A Theology* (Maryknoll, N.Y.: Orbis Books, 1983).

INCARNATION

(See **Christologies**)

INCULTURATION

Inculturation has been described variously, but basically it is the mutual interaction between the gospel and a people with its particular culture whereby both are enriched.

Inculturation was first used as a missiological term in the 1960s, but it gained universal currency in theology only after it was introduced at the Synod of Bishops in 1977. It soon became widely used, largely by Catholics, not only in reference to the church's evangelizing mission, but also in other theological disciplines and aspects of Christian life such as liturgy and catechesis.

While the term is recent, the practice is not. Efforts to adapt the Good News to local cultures stem back to the early days of Christianity. When Christianity became successful in the West, it took on varying accents (Iberian, Anglo-Saxon, Celtic, etc.). It was this Westernized Christianity that prevailed and became normative for all Christians. It was what missionaries brought to the Third World.

During the twentieth century, it became more and more evident that adjustments had to be made for a more effective proclamation of the Word to Third World peoples. Adaptation, accommodation, and indigenization are among the initial approaches to more effective witness and proclamation of the gospel in non-Western terms. While these make use of local culture, the element of mutuality inherent in inculturation is absent. While Third World theologians may agree with the concept behind inculturation, some prefer to employ other terms. Catholic theologians tend to use "incarnation" as a synonym, whereas Protestants choose "indigenization." There are also those who find "contextualization" more comprehensive because it includes the people's socio-economic and political realities and the struggles arising from them.

Inculturation finds its model in the incarnation. Just as the Word became incarnate to reveal God's message of salvation to humankind (cf. John 3:16; Heb. 4:15), so God's Good News should also be "incarnated" in every culture, purifying and ennobling it. At the same time, the gospel read (and lived out) through different cultural lenses is broadened and enriched. This reciprocal process not only allows for pluralism but actually encourages it. Inculturation thus becomes an imperative for the church, not just for the benefit of the local community of believers, but for the universal church itself, making its catholicity more verifiable and authentic.

While nuanced variously in different parts of the Third World, inculturation addresses the following concerns. First, culture is seen as comprehensive, taking into account the tension between the influences of modernity and Westernization as well as the traditional ways of life. Second, as a dialogical process, inculturation takes into account the anti-life components in both the local culture and the gospel (its patriarchal orientation, for example), which must be critiqued and transformed. In this sense, inculturation is liberative. Third, today inculturation is mainly the responsibility of the local community and evangelizers, not of expatriate missionaries or of local experts alone. Fourth, inculturation is an ongoing process since culture is dynamic and continually evolves. Fifth, inculturation cannot be so local that the faith is no longer recognizable by others within the communion of churches. Sixth, the Holy Spirit has an essential role in the work of inculturation.

The history, current situation, and needs of a locality, be it a country or a whole continent, give rise to certain priorities in the process of inculturating the gospel. In Africa, emphasis is given to cultural values such as relationship with ancestors, rites of passage, and traditional healing services. Africans focus on the Africanization of Christianity rather than on the christianization of Africa, while recognizing that not all aspects of African culture are in consonance with the gospel. In Asia, serious consideration is given to its multireligious reality and the divergent forms of interreligious dialogue. In Latin America, the stress is on the liberating aspect of inculturation and the gospel imperative of solidarity with the poor. What makes inculturation problematic in all three contexts is the plurality of cultures and subcultures, not only on each continent but in almost every country within each continent. For authentic inculturation, however, it is not the "dominant" culture of the few but the "popular" culture of the many that should take center stage. Thus, inculturation cannot ignore the popular religion of the people.

While the work of inculturation receives the church's official support, it has barely begun. Moreover, there are those who oppose the risk involved and the undefined outcome. Without doubt, inculturation, when undertaken seriously, will produce new forms of Christianity. One Asian theologian puts it concretely: these new forms will be less structural, less dogmatic, and less juridical; more spontaneous, more experiential, and more personal. The "new" church will be a veritable and credible sign of God's reign as inaugurated by Jesus.

Virginia Fabella, MM

See also: CONTEXTUALIZATION, CULTURE, INDIGENIZATION, MISSION.

Bibliography
Michael Amaladoss, *Beyond Inculturation: Can the Many Be One?* (Delhi: ISPCK and Vidyajyoti Education and Welfare Society, 1998).
David Bosch, *Transforming Mission: Paradigm Shifts in Theology of Mission* (Maryknoll, N.Y.: Orbis Books, 1991).
Inculturation: IMBISI Study Document (Gweru, Zimbabwe: Mambo Press, 1993).
Norbert Greinacher and Norbert Mette, eds., *Christianity and Cultures, Concilium: 1994/2* (London: SCM, 1994).

INDIGENIZATION

Indigenization in the Third World is a matter of decolonization. Doing theology in the Third World is not updating theology to suit a new situation, but rather the throwing off of an imposed, alien and alienating system of doctrine and worship in order to allow Third World experiences of Jesus to find their creative manifestation in total freedom. The way to this is not to shop around for "Third World" forms of theological language. This will only lead to artificial systems of theology that may satisfy Western expectations of what Third World theology should be, but that will be as imitative and inauthentic as the alienated theologies they replace. Instead, the way to indigenization is to set the Christian community free from its colonized consciousness to spontaneously rejoin the stream of national life from within which an authentic Christian experience is to emerge.

Colonized consciousness is the most damaging legacy of colonialism, even long after overt political domination has ended. It is a second form of colonization that colonizes minds in addition to bodies and releases forces within colonized societies that alter their cultural priorities once and for all. As a result, colonized societies are cut off from their roots in order to conform to the colonizer's values. Such a colonized consciousness is found in all former colonial territories of the Third World; however, it is significantly more manifested in former colonies that have been christianized, such as the Philippines or Latin America, than in those like India, Pakistan, or Sri Lanka that have retained their traditional religions and thus have prevented the total erosion of their culture. Yet, even in such countries, a colonized consciousness is actively promoted by the Christian churches. The Christian churches continue to manifest their colonial heritage today in different ways: in the style and functioning of their bureaucracy; in the shape of their worship; in the language and content of their theology; and in the way in which all these are tightly controlled by a central authority, European in its mentality, that allows little local autonomy and is insensitive to local needs.

If that is so, indigenization today has to be affirmed as something that has, under the guidance of the Holy Spirit, been taking place among the people of God during their entire history. It is well rooted in the Bible as parts of the Bible are actual "models" of indigenization. It has a strong theological basis in the doctrines of creation and incarnation. God is the creator of all things (Gen. 1:1-31), and creation always has a God-ward direction (e.g., Pss. 8; 19; 29; 104; 148; John 1:1-4; Rom. 8:19-23; Col. 1:15-19). This is particularly true of references to creation in relation to Christ, where creation is viewed as the work of Christ and as moving toward its final destiny in Christ (1 Cor. 15:28; Eph. 1:10). The Christian doctrine of creation demands that all that is true and beautiful in the cultural and religious tradition of a nation must be gathered into the life, thought, and offering of the church to God.

With regard to the doctrine of incarnation it may be said that Jesus was *God's indigenization* in the context of first-century Palestinian Judaism. Incarnation is the ratification that what is physical and human is not inherently evil; rather, they can be the vehicles of a deeper spiritual value. The Old Testament and the New Testament may be taken as models of indigenization, not only in the matters of religious customs, practices, and expressions of faith, but also in literary forms and religious writings. The biblical writers not only employ and adapt non-Israelite ideas and terminology in composing their texts, they also employ literary forms and even adapt literary material from contemporary cultural and religious traditions. The Old Testament writers took over codes of law, wisdom literature, and folklore from non-Israelite sources. The creation story in Genesis 1 is a good example of indigenization in religious literature. It is an adaptation of a creation story from ancient Babylonian mythology. In the New Testament, the Gospel according to John is an obvious example of adaptation in faith and communication. In Acts 17:22-29, Paul is represented as adapting pagan poetical material from Epimenides the Cretan to express the Christian message for the benefit of his philosophically minded hearers in Athens. Acts 17:28 is an actual quotation from Epimenides that has become an integral part of the Christian scriptures.

Today, the term "indigenization" is more widely used by those in the Protestant tradition. Most Third World Catholic theologians prefer the term "inculturation" or "interculturation," as previously to "indigenize" referred largely to externals, such as using local languages in church hymns or replacing a largely expatriate hierarchy with a native one.

K. P. Aleaz

See also: ART, CHRISTIAN, CONTEXTUALIZATION, INCULTURATION.

Bibliography
K. P. Aleaz, *The Gospel of Indian Culture* (Calcutta: Punthi Pustak, 1994).
Michael Amaladoss, *Beyond Inculturation: Can the Many Be One?* (Delhi: ISPCK, and Vidyajyoti Education and Welfare Society, 1998).
Aylward Shorter, *Toward a Theology of Inculturation* (Maryknoll, N.Y.: Orbis Books, 1988).

INDIGENOUS THEOLOGIES

Indigenous theology is a recent phenomenon. As indigenous populations irrupted into society and the church, so all forms of indigenous theology entered the theological scene, speaking and acting in a manner unheard of previously. It was no longer necessary to mask or keep indigenous thoughts and aspirations underground.

Several factors have contributed to the rise of indigenous theologies. First, social factors. As indigenous peoples irrupted into the contemporary world, there has been movement from passive to active resistance, from a separatist struggle to joint activities with other social forces, from immediate aims to long-term objectives, from protest actions to substantive proposals. Indigenous voices and actions have begun to appear in the forefront of broad processes to transform society and the church.

Second, ecclesial factors. Considerable changes have been taking place within the church, from attitudes of suspicion and intolerance, to attitudes of appreciation and respect. Bishops have expressed their solidarity with indigenous causes. The church has moved from being the primary attacker of the religious inner world of the indigenous to becoming an ally as together they face the challenges of secularizing modernity. When the indigenous members of EATWOT, with representatives from Africa, Asia, and the Americas, met in Bolivia in August of 1997, they summarized the emerging characteristics of indigenous theologies. First of all, there are as many indigenous theologies as there are indigenous peoples and communities. These theologies are communitarian rather than focused on the individual. They are oriented toward spatial categories rather than temporal ones, so the land is the beginning point of indigenous theologies and the struggle for the land is central to the resistance of every indigenous people. As stated in the Bolivian document, "Our theologies must account for our relationship to the land where the Creator has put us and account for our sense of the aliveness of trees, rocks, rivers, mountains, birds and animals, and even the land itself."

Indigenous theologies thus reflect the interrelatedness of all creation as well as the peoples' cultures, histories, and experiences. But, necessarily a theology of resistance, indigenous theologies oppose ecclesial hegemony and cultural imposition, political and economic marginalization, and all forces of globalization.

As indigenous theologians, we recognize that our emerging theologies are more difficult to pursue than liberation theologies. Nevertheless, we believe we are witnessing an important historic moment, a *kairos* of grace, indicating God's passage through our midst. That passage will bring, if we act adequately, a substantial transformation in society, in the church, and in ourselves as indigenous peoples. Though the path is difficult, our basic attitude is plainly one of great hope.

Eleazar López Hernández

See also: ABORIGINAL THEOLOGY, AFRICAN TRADITIONAL RELIGION, ART, CHRISTIAN, PACHAMAMA, SHAMANISM, TRIBAL THEOLOGIES.

Bibliography
"Indigenous Theology: EATWOT Response," *Voices from the Third World* 21/1 (June 1998).
R. S. Sugirtharajah, ed., *Vernacular Hermeneutics* (Sheffield, England: Sheffield Academic Press, 1999).
Sabiduría indígena, fuente de esperanza, Tercer encuentro latinoamericana (Cusco: IPA, 1997).
Teología India, Primer encuentro latinoamericano (Mexico: CENAMI, 1991).
Teología India II, Segundo encuentro latinoamericano (Quito: Abya Yala, 1994).

INDONESIAN THEOLOGY

Asian liberation theology is flourishing in many places. In Indonesia, it assumes the form of a contextual theology that takes seriously the multiplicity of cultures and religions in this fourth most populous country in the world. As liberation theology, it cannot ignore the economic and political injustices suffered by the people—especially the poor, who constitute the majority of the victims. Thus Christian theology in Indonesia engages in a threefold dialogue: with the poor, the religions, and cultures—three realities whose interrelatedness has become more evident in the country's recent history. Contemporary events confirm that economic, political, and cultural injustices are interconnected. And often religion, instead of defending the poor, becomes part of the power hegemony.

Dialogue with the poor. In Indonesia, our emphasis is on *doing* theology, which, unlike religious or theological studies, requires the experience and commitment of faith. In our context, the response to the demand of Christian faith is a preferential option for the poor. Thus an integral part of doing theology in Indonesia is a contextual analysis and reflection, particularly with regard to the phenomenon of globalization. This economic system is not a neutral matter. With its practice of unfair competition and unjust relationships in all aspects of life, it has had a negative impact on the country's poor, the weak, on women, and racial, ethnic, and religious minorities, as well as on the environment. To be neutral is to support the powerful persons or groups who impose and benefit from this system of a global market. Analysis must involve the poor themselves, who may be of different cultures and religions, with the aim of common social option and action. Without the participation of the poor, there will be no real social transformation. It its threefold dialogue, especially with the poor, orthopraxis has priority over orthodoxy.

Dialogue with religions. There is but a fragile harmony of religions in Indonesia. Our multireligious reality is richness and grace, but there are also difficulties within the interreligious relationship itself as part of the broader social problems that arise from differences in ethnicity, religion, race, and class. The collective violence of the last years of the twentieth century has shown how religions have been instrumentalized by and for political interests. Learning from this experience, interreligious dialogue and cooperation become necessary for the creation of a new social and political context. Religious people are called to be committed to the common good, in which the powerless are empowered to help themselves. Interreligious harmony without common concern and struggle for justice insinuates a false and unjust harmony. Christian tradition and truth are neither inclusive nor exclusive of all other religious traditions and truths, but are related to all of them. To be religious today is to be interreligious. Crossing the boundaries of religions and beliefs, basic human communities are united in a life situation and life concern.

Dialogue with cultures. Indonesian theology has much to learn from the cosmic holistic paradigm. The holistic view of life—the Javanese, for example—has its center in the cosmos, the universe. There is no separation between the world and the divine, which has both masculine and feminine dimensions. The world is a sign of the presence of the divine, hence the immanence of the divine is more dominant than its transcendence. There is unity and harmony between the visible and the invisible in the cosmos. The duty of human beings toward the visible world is to better world welfare by seeking the guidance of the divine will. In biblical language, having been created in God's image, human beings must seek the will of God and be co-responsible for the care of the whole creation.

In the holistic or cosmic view, nothing and no one is excluded. The stories of *panakawan* (wise companion) in Indonesian shadow play show the need for the participation of the people in making correct decisions regarding the world's welfare. In such a view, the struggle for the human rights of the poor takes priority over the rights of the rich and powerful. Finally, in the holistic view, every culture and religion has its own contribution to make toward the holistic well-being of the world.

J. B. Banawiratma, SJ

See also: CONTEXTUALIZATION, COSMIC/METACOSMIC RELIGIONS, INCULTURATION, INTERRELIGIOUS DIALOGUE, LIBERATION, OPTION FOR THE POOR.

Bibliography
J. B. Banawiratma, "Christian Life in Religious Pluralism: Ecumenical Concerns in Interreligious Dialogue," in *CTC Bulletin*, 15/2 (December 1998).
A. Nunuk Murniati and I. Kuntura Wiryamartana, "An Indonesian Contribution to a Spirituality of Liberation: Two Perspectives," in *Asian Christian Spirituality: Reclaiming Traditions*, ed. Virginia Fabella, Peter K. H. Lee, and David Kwang-sun Suh (Maryknoll, N.Y.: Orbis Books, 1992).
K. Steenbrink, "Seven Indonesian Perspectives on Theology of Liberation" in *Liberation Theologies on Shifting Grounds*, G. De Schrijver, ed. (Leuven University Press, 1998).

INTERRELIGIOUS DIALOGUE

Interreligious dialogue can be described as the interactions between people who belong to different religions (or ideologies that function as religions). It is understood and practiced in two different, though related, ways. First, it is seen as a dimension of mission. Second, it is understood as dialogue in the context of believers in different religions living together in a civil society. The former understanding of dialogue is the proclamation of the good news of the reign of God. Some believe that

proclamation can only be dialogical; others, however, think that proclamation is a call to change allegiance from another religion to Christianity.

In the second understanding of dialogue, since religion is for life, not
only must believers of different religions draw inspiration from their respective religions for their public conduct, but the different religions
must actively collaborate, in a multi-religious public space, to provide a
moral-religious base for the creation of a new society of justice, freedom, and fellowship. Here, the goal of interreligious dialogue is *harmony*, which affirms pluralism in unity.

Openness to dialogue depends on the appreciation one has of other
religions. In Christian history we see a slow development from considering the church as the only way of salvation to recognizing other religions as ways of salvation. The Second Vatican Council accepted religious freedom in civil society as an aspect of human dignity. It also saw
God as the common origin and goal of all religions. In October 1986,
the various Christian churches responded to the invitation of Pope John
Paul II to come together with leaders of the world's religions at Assisi to
pray for peace. They acknowledged practically and symbolically the legitimacy of other religions as a means of divine-human encounter, since
their prayers were considered authentic and effective. In his encyclical
letter *The Mission of the Redeemer*, John Paul II accepts the presence and
action of the Spirit of God and of Christ in the other religions. This involves a willingness to listen to the Spirit of God present in other believers as individuals and groups and to enter into dialogue with them.
We find a similar openness to other religions in mainline Protestant
churches. Dialogue is between believers, not between religions.

Parallel to this growing openness to the legitimacy of other religions
there is also a deepening and broadening of the understanding of mission that makes dialogue an integral dimension of mission.

God's Good News is not an abstract message but is addressed to the
realities of the world. Mission is seen as an ongoing dialogue of the
gospel with the realities of Asia, namely, its many poor, its rich cultures,
and its great religions. Evangelization, as dialogical proclamation, is
spelled out in terms of liberation, inculturation, and interreligious dialogue. Dialogue then becomes a dimension of evangelization, and this
threefold dialogue mutually involves one another.

Interreligious dialogue can take different forms. It is customary to
speak of four of them. The dialogue *of life* refers to the ongoing friendly
exchange between different believers in the course of daily life in community. People could also participate in some way in each other's festivals and life-cycle rituals. Mutual knowledge and understanding lead to
the removal of prejudices. People learn to acknowledge and appreciate
each other as persons prior to their religious (and other) affiliations.

The dialogue *of collaborative action* urges different believers to collaborate in the defense and promotion of common human and spiritual values, like religious freedom, and human and social rights and duties. Liberation can be seen as an interreligious project.

The dialogue *of spiritual experience* invites people to share their spiritual experiences and to seek to understand each other at a certain religious depth. This may take various forms: sharing methods/forms of prayer and spiritual effort (*sadhana*), scriptures, and forms of worship. One can also evolve common forms of prayer not linked to a particular religion. Such prayer is oriented to personal and social transformation. Gandhi used such common prayer meetings to promote interreligious harmony.

The dialogue *of reflection* brings different believers together either to reflect on the common challenges they all face from other areas of knowledge or to challenge each other to clarify their perceptions and explanations of life and reality. Such dialogue can lead to a deepened understanding of oneself as well as of the others.

A look at history shows us that dialogue between religions has not been easy. Religions have been and are in conflict with each other. Each religion tends to present itself as the only true or the best religion. All religions have been missionary or proselytizing. Even when other religions are tolerated, they are relegated to an inferior status. Even today, openness to other religions needs justification. Therefore the invitation to dialogue may not be easily accepted.

Dialogue involves two partners. Therefore the prospects for dialogue may differ according to the believers with whom one is dialoguing. Dialogue with Muslims is difficult as they usually justify their openness to other religions by quoting the Qur'an: "Unto you your religion and unto me my religion" (2,109). They seem to be more open to a dialogue of life and of collaboration in action in countries where they are a minority. Islam in South and East Asia also seems more open to other believers. But just now there is a fundamentalist current everywhere and an affirmation of identity that makes dialogue very difficult, even though Islam and Christianity share a common prophetic tradition. The Sufi traditions in South Asia show the mutual influence of Islam and Hinduism.

Dialogue with Hindus seems easy. Hinduism is not an organized religion and has much internal pluralism. So the Hindus are open to dialogue at all levels, though they do not accept the absolute claims of Christians. Common prayer is easy with Hindus. Hindus seem open to Christ as a spiritual teacher, though they are critical of the missionary efforts of the Christian churches. There is also an ongoing intellectual dialogue between Hindus and Christians.

Dialogue with Buddhists is also easy because Buddhism insists more on ethical behavior and techniques of meditation and concentration than on doctrine or ritual. Though its insistence on *gnosis* (wisdom) seems to differ from the Christian stress on *agape* (love), this difference is seen as complementary rather than conflictual. Christians also promote contemplation, while Buddhists practice compassion. Adherents of both religions unite in calling for an option to *be poor*. Many Christians take easily to Buddhist methods of concentration like *zen* or *satipatana*.

Dialogue with followers of Confucianism and Shintoism takes the form of collaboration in actions for peace and/with justice.

Today there is a growing awareness of the need for dialogue with followers of cosmic or traditional religions. On the one hand, people, especially subaltern groups, are increasingly aware of their cosmic roots and, on the other, Christians appreciate their interest in the affirmation of life, their sense of community and harmony with nature.

There are an increasing number of common human communities, especially at grassroots levels, in which people belonging to different religions come together to promote common human values like justice, community, and peace. What unites them is not some abstract, rational global ethic, but an ongoing conversation that respects different identities but also strives for consensus, because the ultimate principle of community is dialogue between people who respect and appreciate each other. Diversity is then seen as richness.

Michael Amaladoss, SJ

See also: COSMIC/METACOSMIC RELIGIONS, CROSS-TEXTUAL HERMENEUTICS, MISSION.

Bibliography
Michael Amaladoss, *Walking Together: The Practice of Interreligious Dialogue* (Anand, India: Gujarat Sahitya Prakash, 1992).

S. Wesley Ariarajah, *Not Without My Neighbor: Issues in Interfaith Relations* (Geneva: The World Council of Churches, 1999).

CCA-FABC, *Living and Working Together with Sisters and Brothers of Other Faiths in Asia* (Hong Kong: CCA, 1987).

Jacques Dupuis, *Towards a Christian Theology of Religious Pluralism* (Maryknoll, N.Y.: Orbis Books, 1997).

Aloysius Pieris, *Love Meets Wisdom: A Christian Experience of Buddhism* (Maryknoll, N.Y.: Orbis Books, 1988).

J

JESUS CHRIST

(See **Christologies**)

JUSTICE

Justice is a central concept in Third World theologies; it is understood as an intrinsic element of the gospel message and, therefore, it is the goal of Christian living. Accounts of justice in Third World theologies are not intent on establishing one general theory, but, grounded in the specific reality of marginalized and oppressed peoples, they point to liberative theological/ethical praxis and are aimed at undoing oppression in relationships, structures, and societies.

The cries of the poor and the oppressed are the starting point for justice. Oppression refers to the constraints and the deep injustices that are part of unquestioned norms, habits, symbols, and assumptions present in the ordinary behaviors of people, in media and cultural stereotypes, and in the structural features of organizations, institutional living, bureaucratic hierarchies, and market mechanisms. There are different causes for, as well as different kinds of, oppression, all of them equally unjust: exploitation, marginalization, powerlessness, cultural imperialism, and systemic violence.

Using oppression of the poor and marginalized as their source and locus, Third World accounts of justice attempt to be discourses specific enough to force options and concrete enough to play a central role in devising strategies to bring about radical societal change. Third World accounts of justice articulate concrete historical projects in which oppressed people have a protagonist role, contributing to what is normative for society. In other words, because of their liberationist perspective, Third World accounts of justice are not only about rights but also about responsibilities; they are about the rights of oppressed people as moral subjects and agents as well as about their responsibilities for the social consequences of personal behaviors and institutional policies.

In Third World accounts of justice, the Judeo-Christian scriptural understanding is a key element. Justice in the Hebrew scriptures refers to righteousness (*tzedek*), not in the contemporary sense of behavior according to ethical, legal, psychological, religious, or spiritual norms, but in the sense of fulfillment of the demands of specific relationships, whether these are relationships with human beings, the rest of creation, or God. This understanding continues in the New Testament, where justice does not happen by default but has to be brought about and maintained by those involved in relationships characteristic of persons as social beings.

Instead of focusing on rights, Third World theological accounts of justice focus on solidarity with the poor and the oppressed. Solidarity moves away from the false notion of disinterestedness and is grounded instead on a commonality of interests and responsibilities that all must share for the welfare of all peoples and of the world at large. Solidarity recognizes the interconnections that exist between oppression and privilege, between richness and poverty. It also refers to the cohesiveness that needs to exist among oppressed and marginalized people and their communities of struggle. Solidarity insists on the need for oppressors to listen to the oppressed, who, precisely because they have little or nothing to protect in present structures, have much to contribute to alternative understandings and structures that will make justice possible. Dialogue and mutuality, which are not possible without a sincere appreciation and acceptance of differences and diversity, are specific practices of solidarity that lead to actions on behalf of justice.

The historicity, contextualization, and concreteness of all Third World accounts of justice make them an evolving reality. Insofar as they point to concrete, historical realities, these accounts are programmatic visions fully able to be implemented in our world. However, given the limitedness of humanity, Third World accounts of justice recognize that justice cannot be fully realized in this world. As religious-theological understandings these accounts take into consideration the fact that the unfolding and full realization of the reign of God are beyond any one realization of justice.

Ada María Isasi-Díaz

See also: Oppression, Reign of God, Solidarity, Violence.

Bibliography
Ada María Isasi-Díaz, "Solidarity: Love of Neighbor in the Twenty-First Century," in *Mujerista Theology* (Maryknoll, N.Y.: Orbis Books, 1996).
Iris Marion Young, *Justice and the Politics of Difference* (Princeton, N.J.: Princeton University Press, 1990).

JUSTIFICATION

Justification has been understood, and correctly so, as a synonym for humanization. Usually, however, only the psychological aspect of the human being has been touched: feeling oneself to be free and recognizing oneself as a finite subject without constantly needing to be affirmed before God, others, and oneself. That is not enough in a divided world in which the excluded are breaking into history. There is a deep relationship between the dehumanization of feeling, the need for approval as a human being, and bodily, cultural, and social dehumanization.

A Third World theological reading of justification in a context in which the poor are discriminated against and threatened in their existence demands that the accent be placed on the justice and grace of God, who raises the excluded to the dignity of being son or daughter of God. Rather than speaking of "reconciliation with the sinner," it speaks of God's solidarity with the excluded. The root of justification is solidarity between the Triune God and those threatened with death. It refers to the unconditional solidarity of God in Jesus Christ, which extends even to the suffering of the cross and to the solidarity of brothers and sisters. God's reconciliation with the sinner is an aspect of justification by grace but it is not the only one.

Such an act of God's solidarity has enabled the excluded to recover their dignity as free sons and daughters. When they hear the cry of abandonment on the cross, they believe that God has not only heard the crucified one and raised him but also heard their cries and offered them the possibility of resurrection. Hence, when the gift of justification is accepted, the right to live is defended.

Moreover, inasmuch as it is by faith and not by the law that one is justified, the excluded and humiliated become aware that they are agents, that they can act for themselves. No longer are they objects either of the law or of any patriarchal system reducing them to slavery. Upon being justified by the faith of Jesus Christ and by faith in him "who gives life to the dead and calls into being the things that are not" (Rom. 4:17), the excluded thereby enter with power as a sons or daughters of God into the logic of life, where the fundamental criterion is the right of all to a worthy life and to peace.

Interhuman solidarity is a sign of justification. This solidarity does not come from the words of a law that demands justice for reaching justification. Solidarity proceeds from grace and develops in grace. One who acts out of love for God in order to accumulate merits denies free justification, because such a one remains subject to the regime of law rather than that of grace.

Going beyond the traditional Protestant understanding of justification, which emphasizes individual and private sin, Elsa Tamez has reinterpreted justification from the point of view of the marginalized. She has reconceived it as humanization, whereby people are renewed and rendered worthy through the power of God, so that they can be choosers of their own history, aided by the power of the Spirit.

Elsa Tamez
(Trans. Phillip Berryman)

See also: OPTION FOR THE POOR, REIGN OF GOD, SALVATION, SOLIDARITY.

Bibliography
Barbara Rumscheidt, *No Room for Grace: Pastoral Theology and Dehumanization in the Global Economy* (Grand Rapids, Mich.: Eerdmans, 1998).
Elsa Tamez, *The Amnesty of Grace: Justification by Faith from a Latin American Perspective* (Nashville, Tenn.: Abingdon Press, 1997).

K

KAIROS DOCUMENT

The Kairos Document was a spontaneous response of faith to a life and death political crisis in the apartheid South Africa of 1985. It was signed by 153 Christians from the full range of South Africa's different church traditions. Few theological statements in modern times have had such a powerful impact.

Of particular interest is the manner in which the theology of the document was formed. In June 1985, at the height of the oppression of the apartheid regime, a small group of people met to reflect upon the significance of this political crisis for Christians. The reflection was organized by the Institute for Contextual Theology in Johannesburg. The killing and imprisonment of children, the violent suppression of all opposition, assassinations, and the recently declared state of emergency were recognized immediately as not only a crisis for politics but also for the church. "Both oppressor and oppressed claimed loyalty to the same [Christian] church," notes the document. "The church is divided against itself and its day of judgment has come."

As the discussion group included more and more people, the conviction grew that this was indeed a *kairos*, a moment of truth, a God-given opportunity, and a challenge to decisive action. What was needed was not another statement from above, but a challenge from below to the churches and to all Christians.

One of the great strengths of the document was its clear social and theological analysis of a particular moment of history. Three kinds of theology were recognized as operating in the crisis: a state theology, a church theology, and a prophetic theology. State theology simply justified apartheid, with all its repressive violence, making special use of Romans 13 to demand that Christians obey the state. *The Kairos Document* condemned this as heretical, blasphemous, and diabolical. Church theology, the kind of theology implicit in the statements of the churches about apartheid, was condemned as lacking in social analysis, calling for reconciliation without justice, appealing for reforms from above, and treating the apartheid regime as a legitimate government.

What the situation called for was a truly biblical and prophetic theology, which the document described as a concrete, confrontational, and hopeful call to action based upon an honest reading of the signs of the times. The government must be condemned as tyrannical, illegitimate, and a reign of terror. And Christians were called to act.

Inspired by the success of *The Kairos Document*, a group of black evangelicals published *Evangelical Witness in South Africa*, criticizing the indifference or neutrality toward apartheid of most evangelicals. A group of Pentecostals did the same in a document entitled *A Relevant Pentecostal Witness*. A few years later, representatives from eight countries where Christians were being oppressed by other Christians published jointly an international *"kairos* document" called *The Road to Damascus.*

Frank Chikane
Albert Nolan, OP
Molefe Tsele

See also: AFRICAN INDEPENDENT CHURCHES, APARTHEID, LIBERATION, LIBERATION THEOLOGIES: AFRICAN, RACISM, VIOLENCE.

Bibliography
Evangelical Witness in South Africa: A Critique of Evangelical Theology and Practice by South African Evangelicals Themselves (Oxford, England: Regnum Books, 1986).
The Kairos Document: Challenge to the Church. A Theological Comment of the Political Crisis in South Africa, rev. 2nd ed. (Braamfontein, South Africa: Skotaville Publishers, and Grand Rapids, Mich.: Eerdmans, 1986).

L

LAND

In many ancient cultures, there was a link between the gods, the people, and the land. It was believed that the deity or deities gave the land to the people to cultivate as a source of life and sustenance. The land became, therefore, the possession of the whole community, and any particular family inheritance must remain within it and within its extended family. In other cultures, the land was thought to have been given to the king as representing the gods, and he was entitled to dispense it to the people as he willed; he also had the right to claim it back.

In indigenous and aboriginal cultures, land is perceived both physically and spiritually as an integral part of the web of life and has an intimate relationship with human beings. In a sense, the land is sacred, which, of necessity, has ecological implications. As a result of this integral relationship between human beings and the land, various rituals and ceremonies were developed to guide the religious, social, and political life of communities in times of dearth and plenty and also to influence issues of war and peace between neighboring tribes and nations. Land is the beginning and end of all indigenous theologies.

In the biblical tradition, elaborate laws concerning the land governed the life of the people. Ultimately, land was connected with justice, because God is a God of justice. Since it was and is easy for the rich to dispossess the poor of the land, the jubilee year provided a way to restore justice (Lev. 25). Although it is impossible to know whether the jubilee provisions were ever fully implemented, they reflected God's concern for justice in the community. Generally, however, the understanding of land moved from a tribal territorial claim of a people and their god to a more universal understanding of God and the world. This universal strand was interspersed within a greater body of material that was more nationalist and exclusive (Lev. 25:27; Ps. 24:1). The movement toward greater universality was integrally connected with a growing understanding of the inclusive nature of God. At certain stages, it was believed that god/gods could only operate within their own territory and for the welfare of their own people. The integrity of the land was to be preserved and defended from the surrounding enemies. It was a sacred task to consult the gods and even take them to the battlefield. These were holy wars, and victory was perceived as a victory of the god over other gods. For the children of Israel, the experience of the exile began to shatter some of the narrower

121

concepts of God and the land. Many people had to live outside the land, and God began to be perceived as concerned about other people and lands. As God was the creator of the world (Isa. 45:18), the land must be shared with others (Ezek. 47:22-23). One of the most important books in this regard is Jonah, which expresses, through a beautiful story, the concept of God who cares even for the enemies of Israel.

This inclusive view develops even further in the New Testament where God is portrayed as a God who loves the whole world: indeed, the good news of Jesus Christ must spread to all the world (John 3:16; Mark 16: 15). There is no longer only one land or one people, but all lands and all people. The incarnation sanctifies and sacramentalizes the world, and the concept of the reign or kingdom of God replaces any narrow understanding of any land. Although this universal understanding guided the church for the first three centuries, we see, after the fourth century, a return to the particularity of Palestine as the Holy Land.

Naim Stefan Ateek

See also: ABORIGINAL THEOLOGY, INDIGENOUS THEOLOGIES, PALESTINIAN LIBERATION THEOLOGY, THIRD WORLD THEOLOGIES IN THE FIRST WORLD: NATIVE AMERICAN.

Bibliography

Geoffrey R. Lilburne, *Sense of Place: A Christian Theology of the Land* (Nashville, Tenn.: Abingdon Press, 1989).

Roy H. May, Jr., *The Poor of the Land: A Christian Case for Land Reform* (Maryknoll, N.Y.: Orbis Books, 1991).

Michael Prior, C. M., *The Bible and Colonialism: A Moral Critique* (Sheffield, England: Sheffield Academic Press, 1997).

Jace Weaver, *Defending Mother Earth: Native American Perspectives on Environmental Justice* (Maryknoll, N.Y.: Orbis Books, 1996).

LIBERATION

In the Hebrew Bible, the word for salvation also means liberation, as well as deliverance, rescue, and freedom from bondage. The term "liberation" gained additional prominence in theology and biblical studies since it was first used by two Third World theologians: James H. Cone in *A Black Theology of Liberation* in 1970, and Gustavo Gutiérrez in *A Theology of Liberation* in 1973 (which initially appeared in English in 1970 in an abridged form in *Theological Studies* entitled "Notes for a Theology of Liberation"). Each author used the term independently of the other. Gutiérrez explains that "the historical process in which Latin America has been involved, and the experiences of many Christians in this process, led liberation theology to speak of salvation in Christ in terms of liberation." It better expresses the longing that arises from the innermost hearts of the poor and oppressed, and opens them to receive the saving love of God. Gutiérrez discerns different dimensions of liberation: liberation from social situations of oppression and marginalization; liberation from all forms of inner servitude; and liberation from sin, which breaks our friendship with God and other human beings. In short, Gutiérrez equates "to liberate" with "to give life."

In his writings, Cone speaks of liberation as sanctification. To be sanctified is to be liberated, that is, politically engaged in the struggle for freedom. Sanctification does not mean substituting inward piety for social justice. Liberation, however, is not exclusively a political event but also an eschatological happening. If the oppressed, while living in history, can see beyond it, salvation or liberation is not simply freedom in history, it is freedom to affirm that future that is beyond history—God's own eschatological future.

In *An Asian Theology of Liberation*, published in 1988, Sri Lankan theologian Aloysius Pieris reviews various perceptions of liberation. In pagan Rome, stoic perception sees liberation primarily as spiritual/ personal/interior. Roman theology that christianized stoic ethics goes further and mitigates, with Christian love, social antagonisms between the various divisions of society. Structural change, however, is secondary to and a consequence of interior spiritual liberation. The minimal view commonly attributed to Marxists restricts liberation to class struggle of the poor aimed at socioeconomic justice. In contrast to these three positions, Pieris sees biblical revelation as advocating a unitary perception of liberation that admits a mutuality of dyads—personal/social, spiritual/material, internal/structural—whenever these are predicated of sin. Second, liberation is a religious experience of the poor. It is the God-encounter of the poor, the poor by choice (the renouncers) and the poor by circumstances (the *anawim* of Yahweh). Third, liberation is a joint venture of God and the people (poor) covenanted into one indivisible Saving Reality, though the final glory remains a gratuitous gift of God. And, fourth, it is not merely individuals, but also racial groupings, cultures, peoples, and nations, that are called to perfection (cf. Matt. 5:48). The crucial fact is that nations are judged by their victims, Christ himself being the "victim-judge" of nations (Matt. 25:31ff.).

Third World liberation theologies generally see liberation in a comprehensive way—as both personal and structural—though they may accentuate one or other aspect of it. Because Third World women suffer from multiple oppression, Third World women doing theology understand liberation as freedom from all bondage: from androcentric practices in society, economic inequalities, racial and ethnic discrimination, and other forms of domination and exploitation. It is the work of all. As María Pilar Aquino puts it, liberation concerns both women and men in the task of constructing new—more equal and more human—ways of living together. It is the imaginative construction of new relationships among human beings as well as human beings with the earth. Thus, in the Third World, liberation is not a mere theme in liberation theology; it is its goal.

Virginia Fabella, MM

See also: LIBERATION THEOLOGIES, THIRD WORLD THEOLOGIES IN THE FIRST WORLD, FEMINIST THEOLOGIES IN THE THIRD WORLD, THIRD WORLD WOMEN'S THEOLOGIES.

Bibliography
María Pilar Aquino, *Our Cry for Life: Feminist Theology from Latin America* (Maryknoll, N.Y.: Orbis Books, 1993).
James H. Cone, *A Black Theology of Liberation* (Maryknoll, N.Y.: Orbis Books, 1990).
Virginia Fabella, *Beyond Bonding: A Third World Women's Theological Journey* (Manila: EATWOT and the Institute of Women's Studies, 1993).
Gustavo Gutiérrez, *A Theology of Liberation* (Maryknoll, N.Y.: Orbis Books, 1988).
Aloysius Pieris, *An Asian Theology of Liberation* (Maryknoll, N.Y.: Orbis Books, 1988).

LIBERATION IN WORLD RELIGIONS

Liberation, or protest, has been the source of the origin of many religions. Judaism began with the liberation of a slave people from bondage, and the motif of liberation continues to be the heart of the theological understanding of the yearly celebration of the Passover. Buddhism began with the Prince Siddhartha's "protest" against the inability of the ritualistic and philosophic religion of his time to give answers to the concrete experience of suffering. Islam arose in the context of the Prophet Muhammad's alienation from the religious, social, and economic conditions of a time that encouraged superstition, subjugation, and economic exploitation. Jesus, coming himself from a depressed region of his country and announcing God's solidarity with the poor, the marginalized, and the oppressed, presented a serious threat to the religious and political establishments of his time. In the Indian context, not only Buddhism but also Jainism and Sikhism were religions that rose in protest against the prevailing situation. Liberation, it would seem, is at the heart of these religions.

It is important to note, however, that "liberation" within religious traditions has different levels of meaning. First, liberation has an ontological or transcendental connotation generally based on quests to understand the nature of the cosmos and human existence within it. Thus, in Hinduism, for example, in its Advaitic expression, liberation means the liberation from *avidya* or ignorance that hides the true nature of the universe and the unity of Brahman and Atman. When ignorance is removed the soul is "liberated" to find its unity with the Ultimate Reality. Similarly, in classical Buddhism, "enlightenment" liberates humans from the false sense of ego and the craving, *tanha*, which is at the heart of both suffering and the successive births that perpetuate it. Christianity, too, in its classical expressions, is dominated by an ontological understanding of sin as a human condition from which one needs to be liberated, and this liberation is understood in mystical terms as the incorporation of persons, through faith, into the salvific event of the death and resurrection of Jesus Christ.

Within all such religions there is also a second level of understanding of liberation, in which humans are liberated in order to live a more authentic human life, expressed especially in terms of the social consequences of liberation to relationships in society.

Today, a number of religions place greater emphasis on a third level of understanding of liberation, in which religion serves as the power and resource for human liberation as a concrete historical experience. In some situations the Islamic faith has functioned as a primary tool to confront and overthrow oppressive regimes, and to bring about social change. The Qur'an categorically denounces *zulum*, oppression, and seeks to protect the interests of the poor and the weak. It holds that it is within religious law for the weak and subjugated to use "liberative violence" to defend themselves, and for the faithful to use such violence to liberate those who are being oppressed. Islam also puts much emphasis on the inner *jihad*, the liberative struggle to battle the enemy within oneself, which is in fact characterized as the greater *jihad*.

Some proponents within Buddhism have begun a movement of thought and action, known as "engaged Buddhism," in the traditionally Buddhist countries of Asia. The widespread poverty, unbearable social ills, and relentless political oppression of the masses have led some Buddhist monks and lay leaders to want to change the image of Buddhism from a religion of "introspective withdrawal" to one that liberates people from all forms of bondage. "Socially engaged Buddhism" can be observed in the evolution of the Buddhist monk as a person who is deeply concerned with the socioeconomic and political predicaments of people. The aim is to mobilize the Buddhist laity to address their socioeconomic, political, and spiritual conditions, and to work toward the amelioration of conditions that produce suffering for themselves and other beings.

Engaged Buddhism is also deeply concerned with the inroads into the spiritual life of the people made by the free-market ideology and consumeristic culture. Thus the struggle against economic and sociopolitical oppression is also seen as a struggle to liberate the community from the greed and self-indulgence that hinder true spiritual liberation.

Traditions like Hinduism, Confucianism, Taoism, and Shinto are more complex than those religions that began as prophetic protests, and for centuries they have played a role in maintaining the stability, harmony, and continuity of the community. Recently, these religions have come under pressure to make a commitment to liberative justice within society.

Hinduism is a classic case of a religion in which one can discern a variety of movements at the same time. On the one hand, classical Hinduism has come under much criticism for the socioeconomic organization of the society along the lines of *varnashrama dharma* or the caste system. The division of the society according to intellectual, ruling, commercial, and labor functions is legitimized in the Vedas, the most ancient of the large corpus of Hindu scriptures. Its manifestation today into numerous *jatis*, determined by birth, strictly hierarchical, and with no room for social mobility, has been widely condemned.

In the long history of Hinduism, however, there have been repeated attempts, also by those from the "higher" castes, to challenge, reform, reinterpret, or disregard the caste system and the practices it imposes. Today many Hindu intellectuals and social activists are attempting to reinterpret the scriptures of classical Hinduism in ways that would, in their conviction, bring out the liberative intentions and potentials that have not been developed or have been suppressed. Mahatma Gandhi, in addition to contributing to such thinking, also used religion as the primary inspiration and resource for his nonviolent political struggle to liberate India from British rule.

Given the long history religious traditions have had in the human story, it would be correct to say that the attempt to link religion and liberation to the interpretation and practice of religion has only begun. Within a number of religious traditions these attempts are somewhat patchy and isolated and happen at the margins of religious life. The strengthening of the link between religion and liberation in all its dimensions—spiritual, communal, and sociopolitical—may well be the way to secure a meaningful role for religion in the future of human affairs.

S. Wesley Ariarajah

Bibliography
Ali Asghar Engineer, *Islam and Liberation Theologies* (New Delhi: Sterling Publishers, 1990).

Ali Asghar Engineer, ed., *Religion and Liberation* (New Delhi: Ajanta Publications, 1989).

Ken Jones, *The Social Face of Buddhism: An Approach to Political and Social Activism* (London: Wisdom Publications, 1989).

Aloysius Pieris, *Love Meets Wisdom: A Christian Experience of Buddhism* (Maryknoll, N.Y.: Orbis Books, 1988).

Christopher S. Queen and Sallie B. King, eds., *Engaged Buddhism: Buddhist Liberation Movements in Asia* (New York: State University of New York Press, 1996).

LIBERATION THEOLOGIES

African

Liberation as a theological category in Africa is a hermeneutic that analyzes and interprets African cultural, political, and socioeconomic realities in the light of the gospel of Jesus Christ with the goal of transforming the oppressive status quo. Liberation is, thus, Africa's acquisition of a new theological self-understanding. It has challenged Africans to discover who they are—as people in God's image—and has given them the determination to participate in God's liberative activity in history. Liberation has become the African theological choice for anthropological dignity over against anthropological poverty. It is the African quest for true humanity.

Liberation theology in Africa emerged primarily in response to white oppression and Western cultural imperialism. But it is also a response to oppression of Africans by Africans, including the oppression of women. Consequently, different approaches to liberation have given rise to different theological movements with different histories, emphases, and functions. Despite these differences, a common critical component of liberation theology in Africa is *cultural liberation*. Recent developments in African theological hermeneutics have emphasized the need to overcome the traditional separation of culture from socioeconomic and political relations. For Africans, liberation is necessarily an *act of culture*. Cultural resistance has been an effective weapon and tool in critiquing the entire colonial system.

A true revolution is evident in the great cultural movements in Africa, namely, *Négritude*, the African Personality, and the Black Consciousness Movement (BCM). These cultural movements have influenced religious thought and have also been sources of theological motivation.

In the African theological reality, culture is perceived to be holistic, embracing not just traditional symbols and customs but also every dimension that regulates societal life. Consequently, varieties of liberation theology have developed. One type addresses issues of *race* and finds expression in South African black theology. Another addresses *sex or gender* as expressed in African feminist or women's theology. A third form focuses on *culture* and finds expression in inculturation theology. A fourth form emphasizes *poverty* and attempts to redress the oppressive socioeconomic and political structures—civil and ecclesiastical—expressed in the more narrowly defined African liberation theology.

South African black theology, having drawn much theological insight from North American black theology, was the first liberation-oriented theology to appear in Africa. It took seriously the experience of black people rooted in a history of racial oppression and economic exploitation. Black theology began as a theological expression of the Black Consciousness Movement, which aimed at conscientizing blacks and arousing them to become vehicles of their own liberation. Its second phase began in the 1980s with conferences organized by the Black Theology Task Force of the Institute for Contextual Theology. This phase took seriously Marxist analyses of society and also included feminist theological perspectives. Veritably, the new post-apartheid phase, ushered in by nonracial democracy, challenges all black theologians to consider, among others, the themes of reconciliation and black empowerment in theological hermeneutics.

African women's theology is the theological articulation of African women's experiences of sexism and gender inequity in both church and society. African women theologians focus on their own specific challenges and join other women in the analysis, deconstruction, reconstruction, and advocacy that will foster the healing of human brokenness and the transformation of society. They raise questions that confront the androcentric bias that has informed the predominantly patriarchal religious traditions of Christianity. Doubtlessly, women's theology is unleashing a new dynamic that should vitalize African theological reflection.

African (Christian) inculturation theology takes culture as its point of departure. It rejects Western theological paradigms and emphasizes the African worldview and thought forms. Colonial oppression belittled African culture. Liberation, therefore, is not only political, it must also be cultural. The central theme of African inculturation theology is a theme of liberation. Correctly understood, liberation and inculturation are two names of the same process. African theology has a particular focus on inculturation as the manifestation of liberation from foreign oppression in both secular and ecclesiastical terms. This emphasis on religio-cultural liberation is what distinguishes its theological hermeneutics from Western theology.

African liberation theology sets Africa's socioeconomic and political struggle within a theological context. It defines poverty in anthropological terms and draws attention to all structures—political, economic, ecclesial, religious—that dehumanize and impoverish the African created in the image of God.

There are other currents of liberation that engage the attention of Africans. Some theologians attach great significance to spiritual healing and insist that *spiritual liberation* must be the foundation for authentic liberation, with all other components by-products of the healing process.

Emmanuel Martey

See also: APARTHEID, BLACK CONSCIOUSNESS, BIBLE: AFRICA, CHRISTOLOGIES: AFRICAN, CONTEXTUALIZATION, INCULTURATION, THIRD WORLD WOMEN'S THEOLOGIES: AFRICAN.

Bibliography

Jean-Marc Ela, *African Cry*, trans. Robert R. Barr (Maryknoll, N.Y.: Orbis Books, 1986).
Emmanuel Martey, *African Theology: Inculturation and Liberation* (Maryknoll, N.Y.: Orbis Books, 1993).
Itumeleng J. Musala and Buti Tlhagale, eds., *The Unquestionable Right to be Free: Black Theology from South Africa* (Maryknoll, N.Y.: Orbis Books, 1986).
Leonard Namwera et al., *Towards African Christian Liberation* (Nairobi: St. Paul Publications, 1990).
Mercy Amba Oduyoye, *Daughters of Anowa: African Women and Patriarchy* (Maryknoll, N.Y.: Orbis Books, 1995).

Asian

Liberation theologies in Asia emerged as a way of rectifying the earlier overly emphatic attempts to make the gospel relevant to Asia's religious traditions by shifting the emphasis to Asia's socioeconomic realities. However, the concern for the dispossessed had not been totally absent in Asian theological reflection. Long before Latin American theologians put the poor at the center of theological discourse, Asians were engaged with issues faced by the economically disadvantaged. For instance, Toyohiko Kagawa (Japan), and those who were inspired by him, like Shigeru Nakajima, were involved with the problems of labor and reflected on them theologically. M. M. Thomas (India), though not employing liberation categories, made a significant contribution to building up a theology that had political, social, and ethical consequences. Mar Osthathios, the Orthodox metropolitan, worked out a classless society modeled on the doctrine of the Trinity.

The current Asian theology of liberation differs from that of Latin America in a number of ways. First, no liberation in Asia can be simply confined to the Christian church. For liberation to be meaningful to 90 percent of Asia's non-Christian poor, one must take into account the prophetic and protest voices found in both the oral and the written traditions of Asia's religious and cultural heritage. Second, Asian liberation theology does not have a broad popular base in the Asian churches comparable to the basic Christian communities (the exception being the Philippines). Rather, it is promoted through networks, study centers, and individual theologians who opt for the poor. Third, for its social analysis it relies more on Asian folklore and stories than on Marxism. These stories are used to expose, challenge, and lament the injustices and the absurdities of the society. Finally, it does not have the function of critiquing a prevailing system that is informed by Christian values.

Besides the two significant theologies of liberation in Asia, namely the Korean *minjung* (common people) theology and the Filipino theology of struggle, other theologies of religion also have liberation as their main focus. *Minjung* theology, while clearly informed by the liberation concept, derives much of its hermeneutical resources from the historical experience of the Korean people associated with the term *han* (accumulated anger). It sees theology as a social biography of the *minjung* and encourages them to shape their history rather than be shaped by it. The second example of Asian liberation theology, the Filipino theology of struggle, emerges from political oppression, martial law, and conditions that deny a people rights and freedom. It sees struggle as the primary context of theological reflection; thus Jesus' passion and death become an important paradigm—not a passive one but a symbol of challenge and resistance. The other example is the theologies of religions that have liberation as their focus. The pioneer and prominent exponent of such theological undertaking has been the Sri Lankan Jesuit Aloysius Pieris. He has been passionately pleading for the incorporation of various liberative aspects of Asian religious traditions that advocate voluntary poverty as a way of renouncing mammon.

Asian liberation theologies demonstrate that within Asia's vast religious traditions there are resources that can be profitably utilized not only for theological illumination but also for political and social transformation. Some examples are the employment of Hindu *bhakti* (devotion), the Filipino *koreo* (liturgical-cultural performance), the Korean shamanistic ritual of *gut* (offering to gods), Gandhian principles, and even the practice of Zen Buddhism.

Recently we have seen the emergence of voices that had been excluded from mainstream theological discourse by systems imposed by culture and patriarchy. In India, the *dalits* (the name chosen for themselves by the outcastes of Indian society) are trying to bring to the fore the glaring social reality of the caste system and endeavoring to work out a theology based on the principle of equality. In Japan, the *bu-*

rakumin, the people discriminated against on the basis of ceremonial pollution, have recovered the crown of thorns as a symbol that points both to the pain of marginalization and to a future liberation. Asian women have been trying to bring together two disparate but interconnected realities—Asianness and womanness. Indigenous peoples draw upon two fundamental concepts, anti-pride and anti-greed, to work out a theology in opposition to caste pride and consumerism. These theologies, like all theologies of liberation, arise out of being wounded. Once sidelined, now the subalterns have emerged to tell their own story on their own terms; in the process they have discovered a new self-identity, self-worth, and self-validation. Teruo Kuribayashi (*burakumins*), Arvind Nirmal (*dalits*), Nirmal Minz (tribals), and Asian women such as Aruna Gnanadason, Kwok Pui-lan, Virginia Fabella, and Chung Hyun Kyung were all pioneers, not only in removing the distortion and mystification perpetuated by the reigning theologies of Asia, but in using them to reclaim their legitimate position and affirm their wish to take their place in reinvigorating Asian theologies.

At a time when the pressure of postmodernism has caused metanarratives to be viewed with suspicion in the West, liberation as a metanarrative has yet to realize its potential in Asia. Its fruition depends not only on the ability of Asian Christians to disconnect from their colonial past, but also on their willingness to divest themselves of their colonial intentions to make all of Asia Christian.

R. S. Sugirtharajah

See also: BURAKUMIN LIBERATION THEOLOGY, DALIT THEOLOGY, LIBERATION IN WORLD RELIGIONS, MINJUNG THEOLOGY, THEOLOGY OF STRUGGLE, THIRD WORLD WOMEN'S THEOLOGIES: ASIAN, TRIBAL THEOLOGIES.

Bibliography
Michael Amaladoss, *Life in Freedom: Liberation Theologies from Asia* (Maryknoll, N.Y.: Orbis Books, 1997).
Aloysius Pieris, *An Asian Theology of Liberation* (Maryknoll, N.Y.: Orbis Books, 1988).
Felix Wilfred, *Leave the Temple: Indian Paths to Liberation* (Maryknoll, N.Y.: Orbis Books, 1992).

Latin American

The core of the gospel is the proclamation of the reign of God to real people living in particular historical situations. Around the middle of the 1960s, the conviction arose in Latin America that poverty, in which

the immense majority of its population lives, is not only the most serious social issue of the continent but also the greatest challenge to the
announcement of the gospel, and, in consequence, to reflection about
the Christian faith.

To affirm this perception is by no means to neglect the economic, political, and cultural dimensions of poverty. On the contrary, this perspective leads us to pay attention to the complexity and the roots of that
situation. This is the setting for social analysis, a methodological tool
that helps us be conscious of the ultimate meaning of poverty, which,
at its deepest level, means death. Poverty is also a permanent and major
violation of the first human right—the right to life. This includes physical death due to hunger and sickness, as well as cultural death, when
people are discriminated against and despised for racial, gender, or cultural reasons. This is what we mean when we speak of poverty: while the
economic dimension is important, it is only one of the aspects of poverty.
Because poverty signifies the destruction of people and peoples, we are
not faced simply with a social problem but with something that is contrary to the kingdom of life proclaimed by Jesus.

Liberation theology has grown out of these interwoven elements.
Like any theology, it is a language about God. In the final analysis, this
language is its only theme. The question we face, then, is how to find a
way to talk about God as love to people who are suffering from poverty
and oppression. How are we to tell the poor that they are daughters and
sons of God? What words are we to use to proclaim the God of life to
men and women who die unjustly?

Liberation theology argues that in order to speak of God, one must
first contemplate God's love and then put into practice the command-
ment to love our neighbors. Together, worship and commitment to
others comprise the *first act*, the praxis. After, and *only* after praxis, are
we able to theologize. This is the *second act*, the reflection on praxis in
the light of the word of God.

When we are ready to theologize, we must first establish ourselves on
the terrain of following Jesus Christ in a stage of *silence* before God.
This will allow us subsequently *to speak*, to formulate a discourse on
God in an authentic and respectful manner. Theology will then be
speech that has been enriched by silence and by our capacity to listen to
the word of God and the sufferings and hopes of other persons.

Liberation theology tries to employ a prophetic and a mystical way of
speaking about God. This mystical language recognizes the presence of
the gratuitous love of God in our lives. The language of prophecy denounces the situation—and its structural causes—of injustice and the
marginalization of women and men. Without prophecy, the language
of contemplation risks failing to "bite" on the history in which God acts

and in which we meet God in the other, especially in the poor. And without the mystical dimension, prophetic language can narrow its horizons and weaken its perception of the gratuitous love of God, the ultimate source of joy.

These two ways of speaking about God seek to communicate the gift of the kingdom of God revealed in the life, death, and resurrection of Jesus. This communication inspires what is called the preferential option for the poor, the main and concrete expression of the theology of liberation.

Significant early works in Latin American liberation theology include *A Theology of Liberation* (1973) by Gustavo Gutiérrez and Juan Luis Segundo's *The Liberation of Theology* (1976). Ground-breaking works in christology include Jon Sobrino's *Christology at the Crossroads* (1978) and Leonardo Boff's *Jesus Christ Liberator* (1978). José Miranda's *Marx and the Bible: A Critique of the Philosophy of Oppression* (1974) was one of the earliest biblical studies and Clodovis Boff's *Theology and Praxis: Epistemological Foundations* (1987) was a major contribution in methodology. Dates refer to the English-language editions; in all cases, Spanish or Portuguese editions were published earlier.

Gustavo Gutiérrez

See also: Bible: Latin America, Christologies: Latin American, Ecclesiologies: Latin American, Hermeneutical Circle, Option for the Poor, Poverty, Praxis/Orthopraxis, Reign of God, Social Analysis, Theological Methodologies, Third World Women's Theologies: Latin American.

Bibliography
Leonardo Boff and Clodovis Boff, *Introducing Liberation Theology* (Maryknoll, N.Y.: Orbis Books, 1987).
José Comblin, *Called for Freedom: The Changing Context of Liberation Theology* (Maryknoll, N.Y.: Orbis Books, 1998).
Gustavo Gutiérrez, *A Theology of Liberation* (Maryknoll, N.Y.: Orbis Books, 1988).

M

MALAYSIAN THEOLOGY

The uniqueness of Malaysia's great diversity of peoples, cultures, religions, and languages is seen not only as an asset but also a creative challenge for Christian theology. Islam's status as the official religion has required a considerable adjustment of the Christian church, a process still going on today. Over the past three decades, Malaysian Christians have often found developments related to Islamization frightening and difficult to understand.

Malaysian Christians have an identity with many roots, a loyalty that is national, and a faith that is worldwide. Although Christianity has grown and greatly diversified in the last three decades, it has not yet become indigenous, inculturated, or contextualized. International links and influences, however, have been reduced.

Christian theological controversy has been largely stimulated by issues from the West, notably denominational doctrinal differences and, more recently, the rise of Pentecostal movements. Indigenous theological thinking emerged only recently, when Malaysian Christians were challenged by the socio-political and religious environment of its Islamic context. It must also be noted that a substantial part of the agenda of Christian theologians in Malaysia has been to liberate Christianity from its Western matrix. Malaysian Christians have also been inspired by the intellectually vigorous faith of other Christians living in religiously pluralistic situations who have fully integrated their faith with all aspects of life. The Christian community in Malaysia realizes that it needs to rely on a faith and spirituality that resonate with local sensibilities and address local challenges without losing its Christian identity.

In general, Roman Catholic theology follows mainly the official position held by the Vatican, and the Protestant side emphasizes more pietism and individual salvation. There have been, however, some prominent voices from the Catholic church in Malaysia who have taken an incarnational approach to contemporary issues and realities. One of them is Paul Tan, a senior Jesuit priest who has been actively involved in the Malaysian Consultative Council for Buddhism, Christianity, Hinduism, and Sikhism, and the Christian Federation of Malaysia.

Hwa Yung, a leading Protestant theologian, shows how many Asian theologians have failed to break out of their Western captivity. He argues that an authentic Asian Christian theology will emerge when there is a recovery of confidence in the two areas of culture and gospel. He argues for a theology of social engagement that will holistically integrate the spiritual, personal, and physical dimensions of human existence. Such an ethic should help move Asian Christianity from its tendency toward self-preoccupation within the spiritual realm into active social engagement as a Christian duty.

Similarly, Ng Kam-Weng, a theologian at the Kairos Research Centre, is developing a more realistic attitude among Christians toward Islamization. He highlights concerns arising from the dangers of Islamization, fearing that it will diminish the full participation of Christians in the government and undermine religious freedom and the full expression of the Christian faith. Both Paul Tan and Ng Kam-Weng have developed specifically Malaysian apologetics for Christianity that address Muslim theological criticisms. Their main concern has been to defend orthodox Christian doctrines: Tan from a liberal theological perspective informed by Schleiermacher, and Ng from an evangelical perspective based on scripture. S. Batumalai, an Anglican priest and formerly a lecturer at Seminari Theoloji Malaysia, has sought to interpret the gospel so as to encourage Christians to break away from narrow-minded communalism and develop a genuine love and appreciation for people of other ethnic and religious groups. The work of Batumalai follows most closely developments in the conciliar tradition.

In the last decade, a group known as Women in Theology and Ministry has sought to develop feminist theologies related to the Islamic context, dealing primarily with issues of justice for women. This group has established contact and cooperation with other women's groups, such as the Sisters of Islam, who are similarly engaged.

Malaysian theology is also emerging from the voices of people. Although not often expressed in literary form or well-articulated, theology is sometimes written and illustrated by local artists (including cartoonists), poets, journalists, human rights activists, and others—both Christians and people of other religions. Lay people, such as Tan Chee-Khoon and Cecil Rajendra, have also played prominent roles in highlighting issues related to injustice, poverty, and human rights. Cecil Rajendra, a lawyer and human rights activist, has used the medium of poetry to articulate his theology.

At the threshold of the third millennium, Christians in Malaysia are called to meet additional challenges, including a new interest in the study of Christian theology among the laity due to increasingly demanding encounters with people of other faiths. The stage has been set for a renewed interest in Christian thinking in Malaysia and for more participatory ways of theologizing that involve the laity. Theologizing in the context of multi-religious Malaysian community must be more seriously taken into account, and pro-active theologizing must be more on the agenda rather than reactionary theologizing.

Albert Sundararaj Walters

See also: INCULTURATION, INTERRELIGIOUS DIALOGUE, LIBERATION THEOLOGIES: ASIAN.

Bibliography
S. Batumalai, *A Malaysian Theology of Mihibbah* (Petaling Jaya: Batumalai, 1991); *A Prophetic Christology for Neighbourology* (Kuala Lumpur, 1988); *Islamic Resurgence and Islamization in Malaysia* (Ipoh: Seminari Theologi Malaysia, 1996).
Paul Tan, *Straight to Catholic* (Kuala Lumpur: Catholic Research Centre, 1986).
Hwa Yung, *Mangoes or Bananas? The Quest for an Authentic Asian Christian Theology* (Oxford: Regnum, 1997).

MARTYRDOM

"Martyr," a Greek word meaning "witness," describes a person who gives witness to his or her faith or convictions. It is not merely someone who is killed or who dies for a cause, but someone who "gives up life," conscious of "losing" it in order to "gain" it.

The martyrs of the first three centuries of Christianity surrendered their lives by challenging the intolerance of the Roman Empire, which confined them to a hidden existence in the catacombs. When Christianity was recognized as a legitimate religion by Emperor Constantine in the fourth century, the situation changed. During subsequent centuries, men and women, a number of them from the Third World, have died as a result of other arbitrary actions against various expressions of religion. Ninety-three Korean martyrs were recognized by the Roman Catholic Church as having died for the faith, but thousands were killed during the persecution that raged from 1839 to 1846. Between 1885 and 1887, twenty-two African youths suffered martyrdom under an impetuous Ugandan ruler. Although their individual names are recorded, they are better known as the "martyrs of Uganda," and were canonized by the Roman Catholic Church in 1964. Protestants were also put to death during the same persecution.

Starting in the 1960s, a multitude of martyrs emerged from among Christians in Latin America and elsewhere in the world's South. What is new, however, is that those giving their lives in the second half of the twentieth century did not surrender them in defense of worship or religious freedom, but in defense of the poor, people whose rights were, and are, denied them and who are killed before their time by disease, unemployment, lack of knowledge, and despair. A related new development is that these martyrs' deaths often came at the hands of "Christian" governments that felt threatened by those who proclaimed that God takes the side of the poor.

In Latin America the martyrdom of Oscar Romero, the archbishop of San Salvador who was murdered at the altar on March 24, 1980, is paradigmatic. Displaying a martyr's mind-set on the eve of his "hour" he said: "As a pastor I am obliged to give my life for those whom I love, and that is all Salvadorans. Martyrdom is a gift of God that I don't think I deserve. But if God accepts the sacrifice of my life, may my blood be a seed of freedom and a witness to hope in the future. I do not believe in death without resurrection. If they kill me I will rise in the Salvadoran people."

María López Vigil

See also: LIBERATION THEOLOGIES: LATIN AMERICAN, OPTION FOR THE POOR.

Bibliography
Robert Ellsberg, *All Saints: Daily Reflections on Saints, Prophets, and Witnesses for Our Time* (New York: Crossroad, 1997).
Jon Sobrino, Ignacio Ellacuría et al., *Companions of Jesus: The Jesuit Martyrs of El Salvador* (Maryknoll, N.Y.: Orbis Books, 1990).

MARXISM

Marxism has been at the same time an intellectual tradition of social analysis and theory, a revolutionary critique of capitalist society, aspiration for a socialist organization of society, and a ruling ideology, in the critical sense in which Karl Marx himself used that notion. While Marx has been an intellectual source and a powerful instrument in the political history of the world, Marxism can best be seen as a long and diversified process in which there have been numerous and sometimes conflicting theoretical and political interpretations (from V. I. Lenin, Leon Trotsky, and Rosa Luxemburg to Mao Zedong, Antonio Gramsci, Louis Althusser, and Georg Lukács). The relation between Marxism and the Christian religion is particularly complex. On the one hand, particularly in Marx's early thinking, it takes up the Judeo-Christian prophetic tradition and builds its own "secular theodicy of progress toward a good life"; on the other hand, it develops a critique of religion in general and of Christianity in particular as an alienating ideology.

In the Third World theologies that have developed since the 1960s, and particularly those that are commonly designated as liberation theologies,

Marxism has been understood and incorporated in different degrees and conditions as (a) an instrument of social analysis (in theories of dependence and class analyses); (b) a critique of ideology in general and of religion in particular as ideological instruments of domination; and (c) an invitation to revolutionary change (sometimes in conditions of peasant, race, or colonial oppression). Liberation theology's dialogue with Marxism has dwelt on concrete questions related to social change rather than on philosophical issues, which have been more prominent in the European dialogue. While popular movements related to liberation theology have been inclined to socialism and cooperated with Marxism in terms of social change, they have rejected Marx's atheism and have been strongly critical of "existing socialism."

José Míguez Bonino
(Trans. Phillip Berryman)

See also: DEPENDENCY THEORY, IDEOLOGY, LIBERATION, LIBERATION THE-OLOGIES, SOCIAL ANALYSIS, SOCIALISM.

MARY/MARIOLOGY

Liberation theologians in the Third World are doing a rereading of Mary that meets the demands of our time. In particular, this rereading gives witness to the privileged moment in which all of humanity is living—the awakening of women's historical consciousness.

In Latin America, certain points must be emphasized with regard to the hermeneutic used to speak about Mary. First, the cry of poor and believing people to Mary is a cry seeking hope. Mary is hope, the mother and protector who does not abandon her children. This is what makes up the spirituality of the Latin American people, and specifically their Marian spirituality. Second, the few texts about Mary in the New Testament are used by each historical period and context to construct its image of Mary. Latin American liberation theology does so from its own perspective—the option for the poor. Third, the reign of God is essential for this hermeneutic. It goes beyond the person of Jesus to affect the entirety of his movement in which men and women are actively involved. Among them is Mary, with her passion for God's justice, with her dangerous and subversive memory. Marian dogmas must be considered from the viewpoint of these hermeneutical principles and pondered in view of the ecclesial and pastoral key—the option for the poor—that has left a basic imprint on the Latin American church. Mary becomes the symbol of the people who believe and experience the arrival of God, who now belongs to the human race. Mary is thus seen in a new light.

Mary is mother of God. Beneath this title of glory, and the luxuriant images of her usually presented by traditional piety, lies motherhood as service and as inspiration for the church that wishes to be the servant of the poor.

Mary is virgin, but not in a moralizing and idealized sense. Rather, her virginity has to do with the glory of the all-powerful God, which is made manifest in the powerless and despised in the eyes of the world.

Mary is "immaculate," the pledge of assurance that the utopia of Jesus is realizable on this earth. This is a confirmation of God's preference for the humblest and the most oppressed. The so-called Marian privilege is actually the privilege of the poor.

Mary is "assumed into heaven" and so humankind and especially women have the dignity of their condition recognized and assured by the Creator. Mary's exaltation is the glorious culmination of the mystery of God's preference for the poor and defenseless in order to make God's presence and glory shine forth.

In Asia, women theologians have also reinterpreted Mary according to their emerging liberative consciousness. Together with Jesus, Mary is seen as a model of the fully liberated human being in whom Asian Christians can find their source of empowerment and inspiration. Previously, most Catholic teachings on Mary were used to justify women's subordination to men while the Protestant tradition's repudiation of Mariology may have been a way to avoid addressing the reality of women's conditions. Asian women's suffering and wisdom have contributed to the reimaging of Mary.

Mary as virgin makes Mary a self-defining woman who does not have a "derived" life as "daughter, wife, and mother," and is therefore free to respond to God's call. Mary as mother means giving birth not only to God but to a new humanity. Saying yes to becoming God's mother was saying yes to God's plan to save broken humanity.

Asian women also see Mary as sister, a woman who showed her solidarity with other women, the weak and defenseless; this was verified by her visit to Elizabeth. Mary is further recognized as a model of true discipleship who heard and accepted God's word and practiced it with courage and determination. In Asia, women's devotion to Mary is more evident than devotion to her son, perhaps because Mary is a woman who understands the plight and pain of women.

Mary is honored under many titles. As Our Lady of Guadalupe, who appeared with native features to the Indian Juan Diego in 1531, Mary has become a sustaining symbol of Latin American and U.S. Hispanic identity and spirituality, a source of fresh theological reflection on Christ and the new humanity, and a more comprehensive and open-ended concept of God as a *mestizo* God.

María Clara Bingemer
(Trans. Phillip Berryman)

Bibliography

Tissa Balasuriya, *Mary and Human Liberation* (London: Cassell; Valley Forge, Pa.: Trinity Press International, 1997).

Lina Boff, *Maria e o Espírito Santo* (São Paulo: Paulinas, 1997).

Chung Hyun Kyung, "Who Is Mary for Today's Asian Women?" (chap. 5), *Struggle to Be the Sun Again: Introducing Asian Women's Theology* (Maryknoll, N.Y.: Orbis Books, 1990).

Virgil Elizondo, *Guadalupe: Mother of the New Creation* (Maryknoll, N.Y.: Orbis Books, 1998).

MASK DANCE

The Korean mask dance is a performing art developed in the late eighteenth century in villages in Chosun, Korea. Although suppressed under the Japanese colonial rule (1910-1945), it was revived in the 1970s by the university student movement for democracy as a protest against dictatorial military regimes. Among the many forms of mask dances, the most popular is the Bong San Tal Chum (mask dance originated in the Bong San of northwestern Korea). The mask dance is staged (a) to ridicule the corrupt Buddhist monks who lost their spiritual power, (b) to make fun of illiterate literati who lost their intellectual power, and (c) to expose the plight of *minjung* women. Korean *minjung* theology understands mask dances as part of *minjung*'s cultural resistance movement.

David Kwang-sun Suh

See also: *HAN/HAN-PURI, MINJUNG* THEOLOGY.

Bibliography

Hyun Young Hak, "Theological Look at the Mask Dance in Korea," in *Minjung Theology: People as the Subject of History,* ed. Christian Conference of Asia (Maryknoll, N.Y.: Orbis Books, 1983).

David Kwang-sun Suh, "Mask Dance of Liberation," in *Korean Minjung in Christ* (Hong Kong: CCA, 1991).

MESTIZAJE CONSCIOUSNESS

Mestizaje, the biological-spiritual mixture of peoples, is as old as humanity itself. It is the natural product of human encounters and especially of the multicultural spaces of the planet. Yet, it appears that it has always been sociologically and psychologically difficult and even abhorrent, for the *mestizo* person is never certain of which humanity he or she should try to become—the mother's or the father's. Where does the *mestizo* fit in? Where does she or he fully belong? It appears that the *mestizo* will always be at the margins of full belonging, not fully accepted, fully valued, or fully trusted by either of the parent groups. This first stage is marked precisely by the lack of any *mestizo* consciousness; rather, it is the consciousness of "non-being" that predominates.

Mestizo consciousness begins as persons born of two different human groups begin to claim their own new identity, no longer trying to join one of the parent groups while rejecting the other, but working to develop the new psychology and spirituality that is at the very depths of their innermost being. *Mestizaje* consciousness begins as the new group passes from a sense of "non-being" to an excitement of "new being." In the *mestizaje* consciousness, the newly formed group gradually and creatively pulls together various elements of the parent cultures so that the new culture that emerges is neither an extension nor a denial of either parent group, but a new child coming into maturity. *Mestizaje* consciousness moves from the shame of denial to the celebration of the new humanity coming into existence.

Virgilio P. Elizondo

See also: THIRD WORLD THEOLOGIES IN THE FIRST WORLD: HISPANIC, THIRD WORLD WOMEN'S THEOLOGIES: HISPANIC.

Bibliography
Virgilio Elizondo, *The Future Is Mestizo: Life Where Cultures Meet* (New York: Crossroad, 1992; San Antonio, Texas: Mexican American Cultural Center, 1998).
Virgilio Elizondo, *Galilean Journey: The Mexican-American Promise*, rev. ed. (Maryknoll, N.Y.: Orbis Books, 2000).

MILITARISM

Militarism, a policy of aggressive preparedness, has the basic components of military organization, arms purchase, military industrialization, and outright military aggression. Beginning with the invasion of their lands by foreign colonial masters, most Third World countries have experienced a long history of militarism. After gaining independence, a great number of countries suffered the rule of dictatorships or military governments that relied heavily on military force to suppress the people's movements. When dictatorships proved ineffective, governments often resorted to low-intensity conflict by using paramilitary groups that included death squads.

After the end of the cold war in the 1990s, conflict shifted from the East-West to the North-South. At present, global militarism is increasing, which seems to be a result of worsening economic polarization of the North and South, increasing environmental constraints on economic growth and development, and increasing poverty. Many developing countries, particularly in East Asia, have increased their military buildups and even resumed nuclear testing, such as India and Pakistan. Generally, however, militarization today has shifted from the defense of political power to the defense of economic interests. Political analysts see future wars stemming from resource and environmental conflicts, from the mass movements of desperate peoples, and from violent attempts to address the increasing imbalance between the rich and the poor.

Militarism is an important concern for theology, as are the genocidal wars and ethnic conflicts present today, such as in Rwanda and Bosnia. The principle of nonviolence is advocated by many theologians, although some liberation theologians point out the inconsistency of mainstream church policies that may condemn revolutions but not violence perpetrated by the military. Theologians must emphasize the terrible effects of wars and armed conflicts on peoples, especially on women, who are always victimized and often raped, regardless of which side wins. Feminist theologians, in particular, connect sexism and militarism, both irrational realities based on the desire to dominate.

When Third World theologians question the amounts of money used for military activities, which could be better spent to alleviate poverty and provide jobs, they exercise their prophetic voices. They should call for alternatives, including demilitarization and developing a sustainable environment. They should promote conscientization to end patriarchal values and attitudes and advocate the gospel message of peace and love.

Mary John Mananzan, OSB

See also: CAPITALISM, GLOBALIZATION, LIBERATION, RECONCILIATION, VIOLENCE.

Bibliography
Gabriela, We Dare to Struggle: A Documentation Report on State Violence against Women in the Philippines (Quezon City, Philippines: Gabriela, 1992).
Sun Ai Park, ed., "Militarization and Women," *In God's Image* (March 1990).
Geoff Tansey, Kathleen Tansey, and Paul Rogers, *A World Divided: Militarism and Development after the Cold War* (London: Earthscan Publication, published in association with the World Development Movement, 1994).

MINJUNG THEOLOGY

Minjung theology is a Korean theology of liberation developed in the 1970s. *Minjung* is a Korean word for the people, the politically oppressed, economically exploited, culturally marginalized, the poor and powerless. It was born in the struggles of the Korean *minjung* for basic human rights and democratization and against the oppressive process of economic development and militarization.

Major proponents of *minjung* theology in the 1970s were Suh Nam Dong, Ahn Byung Mu, Hyun Young Hak, Kim Yong Bock, and Suh Kwang Sun (David), who actively participated in the people's movements and reflected on their experience of acting in solidarity with the struggling *minjung* of South Korea. Ahn Byung Mu articulated the *ochlos* (downtrodden) in the Gospel of Mark as the *minjung* of the time of Jesus. *Minjung* theologians share his view that Jesus was a *minjung* and a friend of *minjung*. Furthermore, the Jesus event of the cross and resurrection was a collective event of *minjung* in their struggles for liberation. Suh Nam Dong introduced the concept of *han*, a unique Korean word for the feelings of injustice imposed on the poor and oppressed. The *minjung* movement seeks to overcome and liberate the deep seated *han* of the people. Kim Yong Bock has emphasized that the *minjung* movement is a messianic political movement, and Hyun Young Hak's major contribution is the discovery of Korean *minjung's* mask dances.

The 1980s saw the emergence of two significant emphases: the *minjung* church movement, initiated by second-generation *minjung* theologians who were active in urban and industrial contexts; and the feminist *minjung* theologians, who made use of their indigenous Korean heritage, especially the shamanistic tradition. In the 1990s, the Association of Minjung Theologians was formed. *Minjung* theologians have taken up the issues of peace, justice, and the reconciliation of a divided Korea as pertinent. As Korea faces a financial crisis at the close of the century, *minjung* theology has been challenged by the plight of the *minjung*, who are faced with sudden unemployment, deprivation, and a new economic exploitation as a result of globalization.

David Kwang-sun Suh

See also: *HAN/HAN-PURI*, MASK DANCE, SHAMANISM.

Bibliography
Kim Yong Bock, *Messiah and Minjung* (Hong Kong: CCA, 1992).

Lee Jung Yong, *An Emerging Theology in World Perspective: Commentary on Korean Minjung Theology* (Mystic, Conn.: Twenty-Third Publications, 1988). David Kwang-sun Suh, *The Korean Minjung in Christ* (Hong Kong: CCA, 1991).

MISSION

Mission means "sending." One is sent with a message or task. While Christians have always felt that they were engaged in mission in the world, sent by Jesus to proclaim and witness to the good news of the kingdom of God (Matt. 28:18-20), their understanding of their task has varied in the course of the past two thousand years. In the beginning it was witnessing to a new, counter-cultural way of life. After the conversion of Constantine, when the church became closely linked to the state, the growth of the church went hand in hand with the growth of the empire. This linkage grew stronger during the period of colonization and continued until recently. Mission became almost a crusade. In the Eastern churches it had a more liturgical overtone and was centered on the celebration of the Eucharist as continuing the mysteric saving activity of Jesus Christ. After the Reformation, mission came to be identified with the proclamation and acceptance of the revealed truth about God, the world, and life (the Creed) on the one hand, and an interior response in faith to the Word of God on the other.

In the postcolonial era, amid a resurgence of the religious identities of newly liberated people everywhere, an increasingly positive appreciation of other religions became common among Christians. This led to a new understanding of mission as a deepening, a broadening, and a sharpening. One sees Godself engaged in mission in the world, seeking to share God's life with people and sending for this purpose the Word and the Spirit in various ways, in various places, and at various times. Mission therefore acquires a Trinitarian depth. Mission becomes contemplation of God's activity among a particular people and discernment of how one can best coordinate with and serve God's plan.

Mission is seen as God's good news, proclaimed and realized by Jesus, entering into dialogue through the service of the church with the whole reality of the world and seeking to transform it in the power of the resurrection. In the context of the freedom of God's Spirit, who is active among the people in ways unknown to us and the freedom of the people who respond to God, the way of mission is essentially dialogue. Mission is then seen as a threefold dialogue of liberation, inculturation, and interreligious dialogue. Our partners in dialogue are the people who are conditioned by their socioeconomic and political structures, on the one hand, and by the meaning systems offered by culture and religion, on the other. The mutual dependence of these human realities means that this threefold dialogue becomes mutually involving so that we cannot do any one of them adequately without also doing the others. However, one or another dimension might receive greater emphasis in a particular area under special historical circumstances. Latin Americans speak more about liberation, Africans are challenged more by gospel-culture dialogue, and Asians, having given rise to all the great religions, are more alive to the demands of interreligious dialogue.

This threefold dialogue is seen to have a particular structure. Jesus proclaimed the good news of the kingdom and called for conversion. He sought to free people from oppressive social and personal situations. In a world in conflict, he chose the side of the poor, the powerless, the sinners, and the marginalized of his day, promising them liberation through deed and word (Luke 4:18-21). Following Jesus, our mission is to opt for the poor, look at the world through their eyes, challenge the oppressors to conversion, and seek to transform the world, thereby ushering in God's reign. An option for the poor and the promotion of justice then become the focus around which the threefold dialogue of mission becomes structured. Thus, mission is prophecy that challenges people to conversion and transformation so that God's kingdom may come. Such a goal adds an eschatological urgency to mission.

The goal of mission, then, is the promotion of the kingdom of God and of the church as its symbol and servant. Our mission is the mission of Jesus. The church is not the ark of salvation, but a dynamic community that is called and sent to serve God in God's own mission of building up God's kingdom in the world. Such a mission is open to receive people who feel called by the Spirit to become disciples of Jesus in the church to collaborate in his project to transform the world into the kingdom of God.

Some people who still look at mission as a means of church extension set in opposition the proclamation of the good news with dialogue. But proclamation and dialogue are complementary. We cannot proclaim the good news to people who are free as humans and in whom the Spirit of God is active except by entering into dialogue with them. Dialogue will not be authentic if we do not share with people our own deep faith convictions.

In the economically and politically globalizing world that is at the same time fragmented culturally and religiously, authentic mission does not depend on the power of politics, money, the media, or the mirage of easy "salvation" from the world's ills, but on the challenging witness of counter-cultural communities that have the courage to live as disciples of Jesus, according to the gospel values of freedom and community, justice and love. In today's world this may demand a radical self-emptying.

Michael Amaladoss, SJ

See also: COLONIZATION, INCULTURATION, INTERRELIGIOUS DIALOGUE, LIBERATION, OPTION FOR THE POOR, REIGN OF GOD.

Bibliography
Michael Ali-Nazir, *From Everywhere to Everywhere: A World View of Christian Mission* (London: William Collins, 1980).
Michael Amaladoss, *Making All Things New* (Maryknoll, N.Y.: Orbis Books, 1990).
David J. Bosch, *Transforming Mission* (Maryknoll, N.Y.: Orbis Books, 1991).
Orlando Costas, *Christ Outside the Gate: Mission beyond Christendom* (Maryknoll, N.Y.: Orbis Books, 1982).
Franz-Joseph Eilers, ed., *For All the Peoples of Asia*. Vol. 2. FABC Documents from 1992 to 1996 (Manila, Philippines: Claretian Publications, 1997).
Sebastian Karotemprel, ed., *Following Christ in Mission* (Boston, Mass.: Pauline Books, 1996).
Gaudencio Rosales and Catalino G. Arevalo, eds., *For All the Peoples of Asia*. Vol. 1. FABC Documents from 1970 to 1991 (Manila, Philippines: Claretian Publications; Maryknoll, N.Y.: Orbis Books, 1997).
Thomas Thangaraj, *The Common Task: A Theology of Christian Mission* (Nashville, Tenn.: Abingdon Press, 1999).

MODERNITY/POSTMODERNITY

Among Third World theologians, Latin Americans have engaged significantly with issues of postmodernity, which have influenced many intellectuals, particularly affluent young people with global connections. Postmodernity shares some characteristics typical of times of crisis: a widespread sense of insecurity, the refusal of a particular type of life and consciousness, and a sensation of discontinuity in the common course of history.

How is postmodernity related to modernity? Two different approaches may be used to answer this question. The first understands postmodernity as a complete break with modernity. Modernity is the historical and social movement that arose in the sixteenth century, whose main subject was the emerging bourgeoisie, who pursued a project of conquering the world economically, politically, and culturally. The soul of modernity lies in the will to power (domination) based on an individual's performance. Indeed, modernity Westernized the world, destroying differences, bringing cultures and races into subjection, systematically exploiting the resources of nature, and reinforcing patriarchy. Modernity created the first world civilization based on technology, science, and Western values. Postmodernity, then, seeks to break away from this project. It reaffirms difference, proclaims the right of existence of the other, and affirms that anything can be valid with a right to exist.

The second approach sees postmodernity as the continuation and supreme realization of modernity. Individuals now enjoy full freedom and establish their own values. Every way of life has its own justification. Nothing is to be normative or prohibitive. Universal visions or meta-narratives, such as the Enlightenment, capitalism, Marxism, or Christianity, have little significance. In the Third World, however, liberation as a metanarrative is still valid. Such all-encompassing projects, say post-modern critics, have led to wars with millions of people killed. Instead, the basic principle of postmodernity calls for pluralism in all forms. Lifestyles, literary forms, codes of conduct, philosophical schools, and religious traditions are on the same level; all are equally valid.

Postmodernity, however, must itself be critiqued. The subjects of postmodern discourse and practices are most often the children of the capitalist and industrialized consumer society. They are the ones who can take an "anything goes" stance, those who do not have to struggle, those whose life is already assured. But that is not the case for most of humankind.

A second critique of postmodernity notes that because of its lack of concern for a better humankind, postmodernity does not point toward an improvement on modernity. Since its beginning, modernity has manifested destructive traces. One need only glance at Western impe-rialism, the history of violence and oppression over peoples, races, and gender, and the sick fascination with violence in social relations and in the imagery of mass media. In this sense, postmodernity continues to express modernity's *homo demens* side (which has always gone hand in hand with the *homo sapiens* side).

A third critique is that philosophical traditions have always rejected the notion that "anything goes." The torturer's destiny cannot be the same as that of the victim. If modern society is structured around individual-ism, then a tradition of solidarity and the age-old struggle for justice in so-ciety must be elaborated in order to move ahead. It is solidarity and the pursuit of ever more inclusive modalities of justice in society and more participatory communities that will constitute the seminal forces of a new order and a meaningful metanarrative. Our shared life must be structured economically, politically, and culturally so that it satisfies certain demands of humankind and ensures minimal justice for all. Only ethical norms rec-ognized by all can result in compatible institutions of human socialization.

On the positive side, postmodern discourse may signify a hope for the victims of modernity, which include the peoples of the Third World, and a hope for the end of domination, destruction, and the exclusion of al-terities and differences. Postmodernity has freed individuals and peoples from being forcibly boxed into totalitarian institutions with their rigid ethics, religions, and globalizing philosophies. For those with a com-mitment to social justice, ethics emerges as a dimension of personal au-tonomy and as a decision of responsibility toward others. Such an ethic is personal without being individualistic; it is an ethic of the human being as being in relationship, always being in the world with others. Postmodernity reveals the end of the will to dominate others and nature that was the result of modernity. It raises the urgency of a new, emerging paradigm that reconnects all with all—with the earth, with cultural differences, and with the Supreme Reality—within a planetary perspective that includes every person and every thing in creation.

Leonardo Boff

See also: JUSTICE, LIBERATION, MORAL THEOLOGY/ETHICS.

Bibliography
Leonardo Boff, "Postmodernity and Misery of the Liberating Reason," in *COELI* (Centre Ecuménique de Liaisons Internationales in Brussels, Belgium) *Quarterly 77* (Spring 1997).
K. Füssel, D. Sölle, and F. Steffensky, *Die Sowohl-als-auch-Falle* (Lucerne: 1993).

MORAL THEOLOGY/ETHICS

The terms "ethics" and "morality" are often used interchangeably to designate the judgments we make about right and wrong behavior. This is historically warranted. "Ethics" is derived from the Greek word *ethos*, meaning the "character" or "custom" of a people. The Latin word *mos*, from which our term "morality" derives, also refers to the customs or regular practices of a social group. Hence, both these terms have to do with the expected practice of a community and, by extension, its individual members and what is believed to be right or wrong in a social context.

The four major branches of ethics correspond to the various kinds of tasks undertaken. Collectively, all the branches are shaped by certain fundamental assumptions about reality or worldviews, either secular or religious. Generically, all ethical systems attempt to identify the characteristics of a life worth living, but Christian ethics undertakes this task with reference to Jesus of Nazareth. It is the disciplined attempt to explain the significance of morality for Christians and to identify those norms that should inform and guide Christians in the way they live.

The first branch, *semantics*, focuses on the logical analysis of moral terms or systems. The second, *moral epistemology*, poses questions about the foundations or origin of moral knowledge. Of these two branches, the latter is of greater interest to moral theologians, but their answers to questions about the basis of moral knowledge are anything but uniform. While all agree that the Christian tradition should be decisive in the formation of character and in judgments of moral obligation, the understanding and interpretation of the specific content of that tradition vary from place to place. Third World theologians argue, for instance, against a universalist interpretation of the insights drawn from the Bible, theology, or church practices. Moreover, they insist that these explicitly Christian sources are insufficient guides for moral insight. An ethicist must also take account of philosophical principles and methods, empirical information about the world to which ethical judgments are directed, and the experience of the people those judgments are intended to inform.

The third branch is *descriptive ethics*, which is concerned with the factual investigation of moral behavior and beliefs, without making any value judgments. It differs, therefore, from the fourth branch, *normative ethics*, which offers prescriptive directions about moral selfhood and moral action. It seeks to recommend a way of acting either to achieve certain goals or to respond to certain relationships. Precisely because of its prescriptive focus, normative ethics generates a great deal of controversy. The available Christian metaphors for articulating ethical norms, such as love, imitating Christ, and the idea of God's kingdom, are subject to a wide range of interpretations.

The distinctive contribution of Third World voices to Christian ethical discourse is their emphasis on the dynamic and dialectical relationship between norms and context, seeing the latter as the lens for understanding the issues relevant to their interests. Among the many issues at the heart of ethical analysis in Third World countries are the pervasive sense of alienation experienced by their citizens and the multiple levels of tyranny that dominate their existence. Both evils diminish and undermine the quality of life and impose harsh or impossible conditions upon their victims.

Christian ethicists from these countries argue that we should judge the validity and credibility of ethical norms by their sensitivity to these mutually reinforcing evils and by their efficacy in shaping moral visions by which to overcome them. Yet, the manifestation of alienation and tyranny has taken different forms in these countries. Where they are experienced at the cultural level, the approach has been to emphasize cultural integrity and awareness as the locus of moral development. Such a concern for culture has sometimes obscured the moral ambiguity of cultural prescriptions, resulting in the uncritical acceptance of many oppressive aspects of the dominant culture.

In places where the evils of alienation and tyranny are produced and maintained by social, economic, and political systems (whether domestic or external), liberation has been prescribed as the appropriate goal of the moral life. This goal calls for a radical realignment of the interests that constitute the collective life, with priority given to the economic and political empowerment of the poor and oppressed. Thus, the ethics of liberation challenges those who benefit from unjust structures of domination to commit themselves to and participate in the struggle to affirm the human dignity of the marginalized. It also asks the victims of such structures to view themselves as subjects rather than objects of history, thereby refusing to accept their situation as inevitable. This understanding of ethics has defined the activities of various liberation movements in Latin America, Africa, and Asia. It is also the impetus for several other issue-oriented movements, such as the Ogoni movement in southern Nigeria.

The goals of cultural renaissance and socioeconomic and political empowerment are mutually reinforcing, not exclusive. Both are predicated upon the realization that part of colonial oppression in Third World countries was the belittling of their cultural values. Underlying both visions is an inclusive understanding of freedom or liberation as an ethical good, connoting both political freedom and cultural achievement.

Ethics is not only a diverse but also a complex field of study. While its diversity results from the multiple voices that shape the discipline, its complexity stems from the very subject matter of the moral life. The appropriate moral disposition is to be aware of and affirm this diversity and complexity as constituting the organizing framework for Christian witness. Any attempt to reduce ethics to a single schema of thought and action smacks of moral paternalism with all its totalitarian implications,

Simeon O. Ilesanmi

See also: Human Rights, Liberation, Modernity/Postmodernity, Pastoral Theology.

Bibliography
José Míguez Bonino, *Toward a Christian Political Ethics* (Philadelphia, Pa.: Fortress Press, 1983).
Peter J. Paris, *The Spirituality of African Peoples: The Search for a Common Moral Discourse* (Minneapolis, Minn.: Fortress Press, 1995).

MUJERISTA THEOLOGY

(See **Third World Women's Theologies: Hispanic**)

MYANMAR THEOLOGY

It is evident that a Christian community existed in Myanmar, formerly called Burma, beginning in the early sixteenth century. Since then, Christian churches have endured through various political systems, including a monarchy, colonial rule, a parliamentary democracy, a socialist government, and now military rule. Though the churches' theologies have developed as they encountered these various sociopolitical milieus, theology in Myanmar has seldom been systemized; rather, it has been formulated and communicated orally as *pulpit theology*. A theology of *communication* used during the monarchical period became a theology of *confrontation* during the colonial period; a theology of *conquest* was used during the period of parliamentary democracy; and finally, a theology of *dialogue* begun in the socialist era continues with the present military regime.

Christian theology in Myanmar uses two different approaches to the gospel. In a primarily Buddhist culture, the traditional exclusive teachings of Christian churches are no longer found constructive. Thus, a new inclusive approach is used in encountering other religions. God is no longer depicted as a Person who has been revealed in one particular religion alone, but as a non-Person, a transcendental Reality, who is creator and preserver. Jesus Christ is portrayed not merely as a historical figure, but as the fulfillment of the Truth (*Dhamma*) discovered in all religions.

The second approach emphasizes gospel elements latent in the primal religio-cultures of various ethnic groups to express the Christian gospel in a more intelligible way. The current theological challenge, then, is not to *Christianize* the people, but rather to *Myanmarize* the gospel. Political restrictions compel Christians to take a prophetic stance and hold patiently to hope in God and to fulfill their roles of being "light and leaven" in the society.

Simon P. K. Enno

Bibliography
S. Batumalai, *An Introduction to Asian Theology* (New Delhi: ISPCK, 1991).

MYTH/FOLKTALE

Myth and folktale are collective terms used to denote some of the religious and cultural beliefs and practices of people, the origin of which is not fully known. They deal with gods, superhuman beings, and extraordinary events, and are used for symbolic communication. In the past, myths were preserved unreflectively among peoples of different cultures.

Human beings have always looked for answers to certain basic questions concerning the origin and purpose of creation, the goal of life, the mystery of death and life after death, and the phenomena of good and evil. These questions have stimulated people to search for satisfactory answers, despite their historical and cultural differences. Surveys of the world's different societies reveal that myths form a vital element of all systems of thought, both in primitive and advanced societies. An element of "sacredness" is involved in most myths.

Myths provide a holistic vision of the cosmos that includes chaos and disaster, as well as human fears and sufferings, hopes and joys. Stories of gods underscore the role of humans as responsible stewards of the universe, and they are often based on ideas of cosmic unity and synthesis. The heroes, pictured as exemplary beings, enable humankind to meet the challenges of the world. The legends of saviors help people to struggle against evil with hope and courage.

Many Third World theologians have drawn on myths and folktales as sources of theology. Particularly noteworthy are the contributions of C. S. Song, a Taiwanese theologian, whose *The Tears of Lady Meng, Third Eye Theology*, and *Tell Us Our Names* present story theology from an Asian perspective, bringing together culture, religion, history, and the suffering of the Asian people. In *Daughters of Anowa: African Women and Patriarchy*, Mercy Amba Oduyoye, a Ghanaian feminist theologian, explores her context as revealed in "folktalk"—the proverbs, folktales, and myths of the African community, showing how they perpetuate the patriarchal oppression of women within society and the church.

Myths portray both masculine and feminine elements. Different types of myths relate to a variety of cultural and religious notions. Modern scholarship on myths affirms that a meaningful assimilation of them can bring about personal and social transformation.

Leelamma Athyal

See also: CULTURE, NARRATIVE THEOLOGIES.

Bibliography
J. T. Apparoo, *Folk Lore for Change* (Madurai, India: Tamilnadu Theological Seminary, 1986).
Mercy Amba Oduyoye, *Daughters of Anowa: African Women and Patriarchy* (Maryknoll, N.Y.: Orbis Books, 1995).
C. S. Song, *The Tears of Lady Meng: A Parable of People's Political Theology* (Maryknoll, N.Y.: Orbis Books, 1982).

N

NARRATIVE THEOLOGIES

Narrative theologies employ narratives and stories as both method and resource for the theological task, and do not limit stories to illustrative purposes. Christian theology, right from its beginnings, has been a narrative theology because it is grounded in the narratives of the life, death, and resurrection of Jesus the Christ. Yet, as it developed, Christian theology has tended to be dominated more by theologies that operate on a conceptual and propositional level than on a narrative level.

In recent years there have been deliberate attempts to restore theology to its narrative character. Third World theologians have been in the forefront of this venture. They have worked out narrative theologies in three distinct ways. First, liberation theologies from the Latin American setting, *minjung* theology from Korea, and other such liberation theologies have built their theological reflection on "praxis," which is heavily informed by the stories of those who are oppressed and marginalized. Second, Asian theologains have formed contextual and inculturated theologies using the folk stories of the people of Asia. *The Tears of Lady Meng: A Parable of People's Political Theology* by C. S. Song and *Water Buffalo Theology* by Kosuke Koyama illustrate such an approach. Third, preaching as a theological exercise has operated, generally, with the primacy of narrative within the Third World context. The styles of preaching, such as Kalachebam, Harikatha, and others in India, are illustrative of this method of theologizing.

M. Thomas Thangaraj

See also: CROSS-TEXTUAL HERMENEUTICS, MYTH/FOLKTALE, THEOLOGICAL METHODOLOGIES.

Bibliography
Kosuke Koyama, *Water Buffalo Theology*, Rev. and expanded ed. (Maryknoll, N.Y.: Orbis Books, 1999).
C. S. Song, *The Tears of Lady Meng: A Parable of People's Political Theology* (Maryknoll, N.Y.: Orbis Books, 1982).
Subhash Anand, *Story as Theology: An Interpretative Study of Five Episodes from the Mahabharata* (Delhi: Intercultural Publishers, 1996).

O

OPPRESSION

The awareness of oppression and the struggle against it constitute the starting point of all liberation theologies. Oppression generally refers to the human experience of suffering due to poverty, exploitation, abuse, violence, or alienation. Liberation theology, however, views oppression as going beyond individual emotional or psychological pain to indicate social conditions that are structural or systemic. Such social, economic, and political arrangements lead to an unfair distribution of wealth and power and maintain beliefs and attitudes that perpetuate the hold of the elite on positions of power. Moreover, they generally support the interests of a dominant minority (whether local or foreign), and impose an elite or foreign set of values and way of life on the poorer majority.

Oppression takes on other forms as well, namely, systemic attempts to subordinate women, people of color, older people, people with disabilities, and homosexuals, and to deny them equal access to resources and opportunities. All forms of oppression are interconnected, designed as they are to exclude people from the normal benefits of society and to strip them of their human rights. The majority of Third World women are triply oppressed by virtue of their sex, race, and class.

Liberation theology condemns oppression as evil, as sin, and as grave injustice, and calls for the transformation of persons and structures to overcome it.

Arche Ligo

See also: MILITARISM, OPTION FOR THE POOR, PATRIARCHY/HIERARCHY, RACISM, SEXISM, VIOLENCE.

OPTION FOR THE POOR

A central dimension of biblical vision, likewise present in the other great religions, is that God has become God of the poor and the outcast and that compassionate solidarity with the poor is the decisive criterion of authentic religion and fidelity to God. This has been seen as especially significant and pressing at the end of the twentieth century among the poor majorities of the world.

In the Hebrew Bible (especially in Exodus, the Prophets, and the Psalms), God is not insensitive to suffering or neutral toward injustice, but rather feels tender compassion for oppressed people and demands that the faithful act accordingly: "I have heard the cry of my people in Egypt" (Exod. 3:7); "I desire mercy, not sacrifices" (Hos. 6:6); "may [the king] defend the oppressed among the people, may he save the poor and crush the oppressor"(Ps. 72:4).

In the Christian testament, and especially in the synoptic gospels, the option for the poor is seen as the key to the practice and message of Jesus. He presents himself as the Messiah of the poor and oppressed, as one who belongs to the lowly people and chooses his disciples from among them, and who approaches the outcast and eats with sinners (Mark 1-3; Luke 4 and 7). With deeds and words he announces "the reign of God," which is coming to change things on earth on behalf of the poor and those who suffer (Mark 1:14; Luke 6:20ff.; James 2:1-7).

For Jesus—the Son who knows the Father like no one else—the God of the reign "has hidden these things from the wise and learned and has revealed them to the simple. Because that was what he has wanted," because that has been his option (Matt. 11:25-26). As Jesus himself teaches with his parables, it is the God of Lazarus, of lepers, and tax collectors, who, in the face of the indifference and rejection of the mighty and the well fed, gives orders to go out into the highways and byways to fill up his wedding hall with "the poor, invalids, the blind" (Luke 14:21). Or, as Mary sings, it is God who "tumbles the mighty from their thrones and raises up the humble," who "fills the hungry with good things and sends the rich away empty"(Luke 1:52-53).

Hence, for Jesus, as for every authentic religious experience, love for God is validated as true only in the practical love of whoever shares with one in need (1 John 3:11-18), whoever "becomes a neighbor" of the one beaten and robbed on the roadside (Luke 10:36-37). And Jesus personally identifies with the "suffering faces" of the poor and outcast in our own history; whether we serve them or refuse to serve them, take on their cause as our own or fail to do so, will ultimately judge our entire life (Matt. 25:31-46; 7:21-23; James 2:14-17).

Therefore, Jesus calls all to be converted from the idolatry of money, to overcome the temptations of power and prestige, to serve God as the only Lord. That way, we, like Jesus, will experience the "blessedness" of "those who have the spirit of the poor," of those who voluntarily opt to take on the cause and share the condition of the poor of the earth, seeking above all the "the reign of God and his justice," and knowing that everything else—like daily work and the Father's care—"will be given you besides." Such blessedness, like that of Jesus, and with the power of the Spirit, is stronger than opposition and rejection, and is victorious over failure and death (Matt. 4-7; Rom. 8; John 16:20-24).

Today Christian churches are gradually turning back to the poor majorities of the earth—with their tremendously unjust deprivations and likewise with their reserves of humanity in solidarity and their religious faith—and they recognize there the call and hope of the Spirit of God for the world of the twenty-first century. Thus we are learning to look at life and society "from the viewpoint of the poor"; to seek the practical mediations (pedagogical and pastoral, economic, social, and political) so as to be respectfully and effectively in solidarity with them; to support the active role of the poor in the churches (out of their base communities) and in society and history.

Ronaldo Muñoz, sscc
(Trans. Phillip Berryman)

See also: JUSTICE, LIBERATION, LIBERATION THEOLOGIES, OPPRESSION.

Bibliography
Donal Dorr, *Option for the Poor: A Hundred Years of Catholic Social Teaching*, rev. ed. (Maryknoll, N.Y.: Orbis Books, 1992).
Gustavo Gutiérrez, *The Power of the Poor in History* (Maryknoll, N.Y.: Orbis Books, 1983).

ORTHODOX THEOLOGIES

Orthodox theologies center on the Holy Trinity. The Triune God gives himself freely to humanity. The Lord's Prayer affirms the Fatherhood of God (Matt. 6:9, Luke 11:2). The Incarnation of the Word, the *logos*, who is in the bosom of the Father, has made the Father known to us (John 1:14, 18). "He, indeed, assumed humanity that we might become God. He manifested Himself by means of a body in order that we might perceive the Mind of the Unseen Father," says St. Athanasios (*On the Incarnation* §54). The birth, death, resurrection, and ascension of Jesus Christ were accompanied by cosmic events. Christ reunited the whole of the Cosmos to Paradise. The Holy Spirit, sent from the Father in the name of the Son, sanctifies all those who believe in Him. The One God, Father-Son-Holy Spirit, opens up the dimension of the uniqueness of the human person, as the image of God. We are no longer individuals, but persons molded after the Holy Trinity. Orthodox theologians call this process the deification of the human person.

In the Orthodox mind, theology is not separable from the church. The church, the house of God, is the *koinonia*, the community of sharing (Acts 2:43-47, 4:32-35). Orthodox liturgy is a process in which the whole church participates: the bishop, the priest, the deacon, and all the members of the church, young and adult, male and female. Through baptism, the human person becomes a new creation in Christ. As the Christian receives the chrism, the anointing, he or she becomes partaker of the Holy Spirit (2 Pet. 1:4). The liturgy of the Eucharist unites the faithful with Christ and with one another: "through the only one body, his own, he sanctifies his faithful in mystic communion, making them one Body with him and among themselves" (St. Cyril the Great).

Orthodox theology adheres to holy tradition, which is the continuing presence of the Holy Spirit in the church. The Bible, the seven sacraments, the apostolic teachings, the ecumenical councils, the teaching of the church fathers, and ascetic and mystic life have been integrated in tradition as the living memory of the church, and represent the unity, continuity, and integrity of Orthodox theology, since the beginnings of Christianity.

The two families of Orthodox churches (the Eastern Orthodox and the Oriental Orthodox) were separated at the Council of Chalcedon (451 CE). However, through theological and official dialogue, they discovered that both families of churches follow the same spiritual tradition, but express the same faith in different terminologies and in different languages.

Maurice Assad

See also: HOLY SPIRIT, TRINITY.

Bibliography
Sergius Bulgakov, *The Orthodox Church* (Crestwood, N.Y.: St. Vladimir's Seminary Press, 1988).
Kallistos Ware, *The Orthodox Way*, rev. ed. (Crestwood, N.Y.: St. Vladimir's Seminary Press, 1995).

P

PACHAMAMA

For the Andean Aymara and Quechua people, Pachamama/Mother Earth is the source of life and is considered a divinity. These people, primarily farmers, have daily contact with the earth and observe and admire the miraculous drama of life. They maintain a dialogical relationship with Pachamama by means of rituals and a feast that begins on August 1 and ends at the carnival season in February. These rituals focus on the fertility of the fields, animals, and human life. From an inculturated Andean Christian perspective, the Andean peoples recognize in Pachamama the maternal face of God who engenders, nurtures, and sustains all forms of life.

Domingo Llanque Chana

See also: CULTURE, INCULTURATION.

PALESTINIAN LIBERATION THEOLOGY

Palestinian liberation theology addresses the Israeli-Palestinian conflict from the faith perspective of Palestinian Christians. Its emphasis is on justice as a foundation for peace. Palestinians face daily occupation, violence, and human rights violations. The Israeli perpetrators and many Christian Zionists justify these acts, not only on a historical and political basis, but on a biblical one as well. Palestinian Christians need to address these issues and interpret the Bible, especially the Old Testament, in a way that promotes justice, peace, and reconciliation. The life of Jesus Christ as a Palestinian Jew who lived under occupation presents a model of faith and praxis. His inaugural address in Luke 4, with its emphasis on justice and liberation for the oppressed, his proclamation of the jubilee, and his teachings on love and nonviolence, offer inspiration and guidance.

Perennial to this theology is a biblical theology of land that challenges Israeli exclusivity, racism, and discrimination. It confronts the narrow biblical interpretation of Christian Zionists and promotes an inclusive understanding of God and neighbor. In addition, this theology helps Christians to work for the unity and renewal of the church and for a

158

more accurate international awareness of the identity, presence, and witness of Palestinian Christians as well as their contemporary concerns. It encourages people from around the world to work for a just, comprehensive, and enduring peace informed by truth and empowered by prayer and action.

Palestinian liberation theology was first articulated in Naim Ateek's book, *Justice, and Only Justice: A Palestinian Theology of Liberation*. Ateek was preceded by a number of Palestinian Christians who expressed their theology in telling their personal stories of Israel's injustice. Notable is Father Elias Chacour's *Blood Brothers*. Some Palestinian theologians prefer to use the term "local theology" (Geries Khoury) or "contextual theology" (Mitri Raheb) rather than "liberation theology."

Naim Stefan Ateek

See also: LAND, RACISM.

Bibliography
Naim Ateek, *Justice, and Only Justice: A Palestinian Theology of Liberation* (Maryknoll, N.Y.: Orbis Books, 1989).
Elias Chacour, *Blood Brothers* (New York: Chosen Books, 1984).
Geries Khoury, *The Intifada of Heaven and Earth* (Nazareth: Hakim Press, 1989, in Arabic only).
Mitri Raheb, *I Am a Palestinian Christian* (Minneapolis, Minn.: Fortress Press, 1995).

PARADIGM SHIFT

The word "paradigm" is being increasingly used by different groups, nearly always preceded by the adjective "new." The aim is to indicate the new frames of reference that characterize our knowledge and how we understand the world. In this sense, the word paradigm does not mean the reproduction of a model or a pattern, as, for example, in studying grammar, when one verb is conjugated by using another verb as an example or model. Today, its meaning is extended to the understanding of the relations between different events and situations in human history.

A paradigm results from the movement of history and culture, and it is now regarded as important for understanding that history and culture. Thus, it can be said that the very history of human relationships gives rise to "keys" for understanding it. In this sense, a paradigm may be regarded as a key for reading and understanding history. Even so, a key cannot explain everything that happens; its function is partial but nonetheless indispensable. As a rule, new paradigms are said to arise at moments of crisis or times of great social and scientific creativity, that is, at times when the frames of reference we have for explaining our history are seen to be insufficient.

A paradigm is not only important for present history, but can also be used to reread past history in relationship to present history. Its function becomes that of a critical frame of reference having to do with certain behaviors from the past that are still quite present.

Although paradigms have always existed to some degree, as the new millennium dawns, certain authors, like Thomas S. Kuhn, have used the term to point to the most significant aspect of changes undergone by humankind, especially in the physical and mathematical sciences. The word "paradigm" has quickly taken on a broader and more general use and is now common in the social sciences, history, philosophy, and theology.

Each new paradigm leads us to adopt new instruments for understanding our reality and our ethical postures. It brings us to a better knowledge of the world in which we live and helps us change in varied ways. Thus, many scholars, particularly women, regard feminism as a new paradigm for understanding human relations in various domains of social life. Since the emergence of feminist movements in different parts of the world, the way human life is understood is no longer the same. Feminism critiques the idea and the claim that male science is universal. Through gender analysis it reveals how human relationships are constructed on the basis of hierarchical cultural behaviors that mark the superiority of the male to the female sex.

From another standpoint, ecology is also regarded as a new paradigm. It highlights the dimension of interdependence among all living beings and leads to the need for social and political projects that take into account the complex web of life and all the living beings comprising it.

This brief consideration of these two examples sheds light on the importance of the term "paradigm" as a tool for understanding our own understanding and as a tool for transforming our relationships.

Ivone Gebara

See also: ECOFEMINIST THEOLOGY, EPISTEMOLOGICAL BREAK, THEOLOGICAL METHODOLOGIES.

Bibliography
Ivone Gebara, *Longing for Running Water: Ecofeminism and Liberation*, trans. David Molineaux (Minneapolis, Minn.: Fortress Press, 1999).
Thomas S. Kuhn, *The Structure of Scientific Revolutions* (Chicago: University of Chicago Press, 1962).

PASTORAL THEOLOGY

Pastoral theology refers to a critical reflection on the presence and caring activity of God, and of human persons before God, within the social contexts of the world. It is pastoral because of its focus on the care of persons and communities. It is theological because it reflects on the activity of God as understood through the various practices and documents of faith. Pastoral theology has a strong praxis orientation.

Although there are common themes in the pastoral theological activities across the Third World, there are also regional emphases. In Africa the quest for cultural and anthropological wholeness has meant that pastoral theology has tended to engage in re-framing oppressive colonial views and depictions of African humanity while seeking more culturally appropriate ways of understanding and communicating the gospel. Traditional cultural practices of healing continue to be an important source of succor as is the struggle against institutionalized racism in the form of apartheid and its after-effects in South Africa.

Latin America has highlighted poverty and socio-economic oppression and focused its pastoral theological reflections in those areas. The quest for liberating action by and for all has been a major concern of Latin American pastoral theologians.

In Asia the context of pluralism, especially in the area of religious traditions, has set a scene in which pastoral care often includes dialogue and peacemaking between practitioners of different religions. Pastoral theologians in Asian contexts have often found ways of drawing on a vast array of religious and spiritual traditions. The many Asian texts and traditions must be taken into account and Asians often feel that those that are Christian are often more recent and not necessarily as profound as the more ancient ones. In most areas, the quest for humanity has superceded the quest for religious supremacy.

Throughout the Third World pastoral theology must face the reality of sexism although the place and role of women differs vastly from place to place. Some groups maintain matrilineal kinship structures in which lineage is traced along the mother's line. There are also matrilocal groups where the family is centered around the mother. Nevertheless, patriarchy is never far away. The struggle of women for social and sexual justice is a relevant pastoral concern. However, as has been pointed out by Third World women, pastoral theology in the Third World has been most clearly seen in the following activities: the praxis of empowering marginalized peoples; seeking just and meaningful roles for women in church and society; the struggle for economic justice and ecological harmony; reconciliation and peacemaking between varying groups; and caring for victims of war and violence, as well as for people in dire need resulting from climatic as well as human catastrophes.

Pastoral strategies adopted have included socio-economic and political analysis; hermeneutical analysis in which texts and traditions have been examined; the praxis orientation of liberation theology; the religio-cultural and anthropological analyses of African theology; working together in groups; symbolic collective action; and the nurturing of spiritualities that encourage intra-personal, inter-personal and corporate human development, while paying attention to ecological matters within the context of relationships with the Divine.

Pastoral theology in the Third World, then, has served to extend the traditional Western emphasis on pastoral counseling for individuals in their inner personal journeys. Pastoral theological praxis focuses primarily on care for the totality of the human person's experience—socially, economically, politically, and spiritually.

Emmanuel Yartekwei Lartey

See also: Basic Ecclesial Communities, Liberation Theologies, Option for the Poor, Patriarchy/Hierarchy, Poverty, Sexism.

Bibliography
Emmanuel Lartey, *In Living Colour: An Intercultural Approach to Pastoral Care and Counseling* (London: Cassell, 1997).
Masamba ma Mpolo, Jean & Daisy Nwachuku, eds., *Pastoral Care and Counseling in Africa Today* (Frankfurt-am-Main/Bern/New York/Paris: Peter Lang, 1991).
Harry W. Wilson, Judo Poerwowidagdo, Takatso Mofokeng, Robert Evans & Alice Evans, *Pastoral Theology from a Global Perspective* (Maryknoll, N.Y.: Orbis Books, 1996).

PATRIARCHY/HIERARCHY

As a term, patriarchy is composed of two Greek words: πατήρ (father, ruler, leader) and ἀρχή (beginning, origin, foundation, divine power). It translates to English as "the rule of the father" because the father figure is the foundation of the social order. The meaning of this term is traced to ancient societies in which authority was concentrated in the male heads of family and power was defined by the ability to control property and people in the household and state; it was believed that this was ordained by divine command. As an analytical category today, patriarchy refers to a global societal system maintained by powerful elites largely composed of monied, educated, Western Euro-American males who, in alliance with Third World powerful elites, control all aspects of life and rule over women, children, nature, and other males. Such a global system is characterized by unlimited competition, possession of goods, greed, and control—both physical and symbolic. Patriarchy articulates a system of privileges that benefit the ruling elites against the subordinated peoples and nature and that maintain women at systemic disadvantages. It has been identified as a system of graded subjugation that evolves and molds the roots of entire civilizations. Currently, patriarchy combines and multiplies neocapitalist exploitation, neoliberal colonization, alienating systems of meaning, controlling religious traditions, dehumanizing racism, social exclusion, cultural oppression, depredation of nature, and the sexual subjugation of women and of homosexuals.

As an intrinsic component of patriarchy, hierarchy is a term that refers to the system of elitist privileges and graded subjugation that permeates every aspect of human society, including religion and church. Hierarchy is a term composed of two Greek words, ιερός (sacred, holy) and άρχή (see above), and designates an order of things that is believed to be sacred. As an analytical category, it exposes the historical dynamics involved in the unilateral centralization of social power, the male-centered symbolic constructions (also called androcentric), the pyramidal structuring of human society, and the sacralization of androcentrism as instruments of socio-political, physio-cultural, and symbolic control. The hierarchical ordering of patriarchal society and religion is validated by androcentric ideologies, values, and traditions, and it provides support for sexism. Androcentrism is the legitimizing ideology of patriarchy as a hierarchical order. It sets forth the idea that the male is the norm for what it is to be human and it reflects the belief that social inequalities between men and women are justified on the basis of the distinct gender attributes that culture and religion have defined for each sex. Historically, gender attributes affirm higher and superior values, functions, and social roles for males to the detriment of females. Androcentrism, therefore, fails to acknowledge that gender stereotypes are unjust cultural and religious constructions that can and should be changed if the intrinsic dignity of women and men is to be honored and promoted.

As a hierarchical whole, patriarchy has been adopted and legitimized by all of the existing world religions, notably Islam, Buddhism, Judaism, and Christianity, and also by Chinese and Third World native/indigenous and Black religions. The real malice of patriarchal religion is clearly seen in the impact it has on the lives of poor and oppressed women in the Third World who suffer from physical violence as an accepted socio-cultural practice and are forced into a system of structural alienation, dependence, and self-denigration. Third World critical feminist theology denounces the contribution of patriarchal religion to the pervasive reality of violence against women, children, and nature. This theology affirms that religion cannot be used to legitimize a societal system that dehumanizes women and men, deprives women of self-worth and autonomy, and degrades nature. It also asserts that the theological enterprise cannot be used to validate patriarchal churches, androcentric theologies, and sexist relationships. Critical feminist theology in the Third World takes seriously the contributions of feminist theory and feminist movements to construct its religious vision of the Holy One, of the world, and of humanity. Such a vision understands the Holy One as essentially compassionate, just, and life-giving; it asserts that women and men are called to the wholeness of life in God; to relate to one another on the basis of justice, solidarity, and mutuality; to establish egalitarian societal models that truly reflect God's salvation and grace; and to maintain a way of living free of injustice and violence. The vision and commitment of this theology is progressively eroding the foundations of the current patriarchal church and society.

María Pilar Aquino

See also: FEMINIST THEOLOGIES IN THE THIRD WORLD, GLOBALIZATION, OPPRESSION, SEXISM.

Bibliography
Mary John Mananzan, et al., *Women Resisting Violence: Spirituality For Life* (Maryknoll, N.Y.: Orbis Books, 1996).
Elisabeth Schüssler Fiorenza and M. Shawn Copeland, eds., *Violence Against Women, Concilium* 1994/1 (1994).
Ana María Tepedino and María Pilar Aquino, eds., *Entre la Indignación y la Esperanza: Teología Feminista Latinoamericana* (Bogotá, Colombia: Ecumenical Association of Third World Theologians & Indo-American Press, 1998).

PEACE

In a world plagued by conflict and despair, it is often difficult to grasp the true meaning of peace. Broken lives, displaced and uprooted people, malnourished children, and innocent victims of war and ethnic conflict are widespread throughout the *oikoumene*, the "whole inhabited world." It is a shameful fact that at the end of the twentieth century humankind is still confronted with numerous armed conflicts involving the illegal use of military force and other forms of violence. The designation of funds from the budgets of national governments to strengthen military forces and buy arms—conducted in the name of national security—diverts resources needed for life and prosperity. Because of an unimaginable rate of genocide, summary executions, massacres, and torture, the twentieth century will go down in history scarred by the blood and suffering of the innocent.

But the people who are victims of the forces of principalities and powers of this passing age are broken but not defeated. They live in hope that lasting peace will be experienced during their lifetime and not only after their death. In such a context it is necessary to ask ourselves what the true meaning of peace is. And what is the nature of a peacemaking ministry?

In Hebrew, the word for peace is *shalom*. It refers to such things as wholeness and health, prosperity and security, political and spiritual well-being, whereas the popular notion of peace is often limited to the absence of war or to inner tranquility. These are only a part of the true meaning of peace. *Shalom* is much more than a truce or peace in one's heart. It involves ensuring that people have enough to eat, that children do not die of malnourishment, that people have opportunities for employment, and also that individuals go to bed at night without fear of being abducted or killed.

One of the fundamental tasks of peace-building is to work unceasingly to create structures, whether they be governmental, social, or economic, in which human life and human rights can be preserved and sustained. The path to peace can be found only in the struggle for justice. Working for justice automatically involves a person in peacemaking and in enacting the words of Jesus, "Blessed are the peacemakers, for they shall be called the children of God" (Matt.5:9).

Rienzie Perera

See also: MILITARISM, SALVATION, VIOLENCE.

PENTECOSTALISM

The youngest and most rapidly growing branch of world Christianity, Pentecostal churches have an estimated 450 million believers concentrated mainly in the Americas, Africa, and Asia. Contrary to the traditional view that modern Pentecostalism has its single birthplace in the 1906 revival of Azusa Street (Los Angeles, USA), recent research has shown a polycentric development with common roots in the evangelical revivals and the holiness movement of nineteenth-century Anglo-Saxon Protestantism.

Pentecostalism may be divided into three streams, all of which refer to the second chapter of Acts as the birth of the Christian church and the paradigm for Christian experience in all ages. *Classical* Pentecostalism refers to denominations that originated in the North American revival. Their main features include *glossolalia,* speaking in tongues, as necessary initial evidence of Spirit-baptism and a fourfold theological pattern: Jesus saves, baptizes in the Holy Spirit, heals, and will come again.

The *charismatic movement* describes the irruption of Pentecostal spirituality *within* traditional churches (Catholic, Protestant, and Orthodox) since the early 1960s. Recently, some of these movements have organized themselves separately in the so-called "non-denominational churches," leading to what is described as neo-Pentecostalism, some promoting a kind of "prosperity theology."

Indigenous or *autochthonous* Pentecostalism refers to movements that emerged from local revivals or from independent groups that separated from the missions of classical Pentecostalism. In general, they are more open to the influence of local patterns of religious experience.

Some typical features of early Pentecostalism—namely, oral and narrative theology and liturgy, whole body involvement, dreams and visions as ways of divine talk, cross-racial and gender pluralism, ministry *of* (not *for*) the poor, etc.— are better represented in the third stream. It is also this stream that is having the strongest impact in the poorest sections of Third World populations.

Juan E. Sepúlveda

See also: AFRICAN INDEPENDENT CHURCHES, HOLY SPIRIT.

Bibliography
Edward Cleary and Hannah Stewart-Gambino, *Power, Politics, and Pentecostals in Latin America* (Boulder: Westview Press, 1997).
Walter J. Hollenweger and Allan H. Anderson, eds., *Pentecostals after a Century: Global Perspectives on a Movement in Transition* (Sheffield, England: Sheffield Academic Press, 1999).
Karl-Josef Küschel and Jürgen Moltmann, eds., *Pentecostal Movements as an Ecumenical Challenge. Concilium* 1996:3.

PEOPLE'S MOVEMENTS

People's movements refers to groupings of people who are mobilized for empowerment and social change. Usually initiated by the poor and marginalized sectors of Third World societies, people's movements provide these groups with the vehicle, organization, network, and means with which they can address specific issues or social concerns. Examples would include indigenous people's councils resisting government projects that would destroy the environment as well as their ancestral homes, and consumer groups protesting the rising prices of basic commodities.

Regarded as representing the genuine interests of the common people and a sign of hope for the struggling poor in their quest for a fuller life, people's movements gained the support of established groups such as ecumenical and interfaith associations, peace and human rights organizations, and small ecclesial communities. As a multisectoral endeavor, the various groups came together to analyze the situation, discuss strategies, and act concertedly toward social transformation. During the last decades of the twentieth century, however, particularly with the escalation of economic globalization, people's movements (especially in certain Asian countries) became ambiguous, as they broadened out in the direction of citizens' movements (or civil society). Politically and ideologically more diverse, there is a shift in orientation and in relating to state and elite power as new groupings tackle the issues of population, reproductive health, gay rights, violence against women, ecological protection, and so on. There is a shift from the poor to middle-class consciousness, from the vision of transforming society to accommodation. Because civil society, as the new direction of people's movements, is critical of the people's movements of the past as too radical, ideologically narrow, violent, and rigid, it appears to favor the status quo.

The diversity in people's movements is their strength as well as their weakness. A greater variety of people can be included to work for the enhancement of life; at the same time, divergences point to the inherent danger of manipulation by the divide-and-rule tactics of government and capital. Third World theologies need to be critically aware of the diversity in people's movements, if they are to be truly liberating for the peoples of the Third World, particularly the majority poor, marginalized, and oppressed.

Arche Ligo

See also: CHIPKO MOVEMENT, GLOBALIZATION, JUSTICE, LIBERATION.

POPULAR RELIGION

Within the great meaning systems and the mosaic of regional traditions are semi-independent forms of popular religion. These religious forms involve beliefs and organization, ritual and celebration, worldview and wisdom. While the major teachings of the "world religions" (also referred to as metacosmic soteriologies) are generally adopted, it is the beliefs and practices inherited from the primal religion (or cosmic religiosity), deeply imbedded in the hearts and minds of the ordinary people, that give these forms their specifically "popular" character.

Popular religion arises from people's need for a symbolic relationship with what is sacred and foundational. It arises from their yearning for wholeness. As their search is done in the midst of everyday life as well as in special times and places, popular religion contains features of oppression and fatalism as well as of joy and freedom. As in the great religions and primal religions alike, there are elements that humanize while others dehumanize. For example, Christianity has been allied with racist colonialism; at the same time, it has served as an inspiration for emancipation struggles in the Third World. Primal religion has a strong reliance on magic (sometimes conjured against individuals), yet it displays an innate respect for the earth and the cosmos.

Despite its ambiguities, popular religion remains a great reservoir of the wisdom, the aspirations, and the hopes of the masses. For many millions of human beings—the majority poor of the Third World living in conditions of deprivation and neglect—popular religion is a way (often the only way they have) to manage life, that is, to find identity and meaning. It is what gives the poor, the ordinary people, the will to survive.

Yet official church teaching judges the people's religion to be natural (as opposed to divinely revealed) and superstitious, even branding it as idolatrous in the past, evaluating it on the basis of modern critical reason. Yet modernity itself has fostered opposing phenomena (e.g., fundamentalism that seeks security, and intercultural religious movements), and puts up with absolutes and idols (e.g., the individual, money, consumption, totalitarian power), which both fascinate and alienate the ordinary people.

In recent years, Christian theology and popular religion have encountered each other. Third World theology is taking seriously the spiritual and symbolic language of the ordinary people. In milieus that are multicultural and multireligious, it has engaged in interreligious dialogue that has furthered the collaboration among the different religions for the greater well-being of humanity and the integrity of creation. Third World theology has incorporated in its faith reflection the art and the healing practices, the rites and celebrations, the struggle against evil and other basic aspects of popular religion.

Theology has begun to appreciate the syncretist spirituality of the people: their rituals (e.g., the dance in black traditions, the Hindu *pūjā* offering, the Islamic *calât*, the healing rite in shamanism), the relationship with ancestors and spirits in nature, their native wisdom and ethic of reciprocity—which have their own meaning and can be regarded as mediations of revelation. Ultimately, the criterion for assessing popular religion is not orthodoxy, but love for God and neighbor. In other words, what people do together so that the abuse of the poor, the cosmos, the women and children, the neglected races and cultures, is overcome. Christian theology is being reconstructed as it interacts with popular religion. As it treats in a profound way the faith and life of the ordinary people, it will be less dogmatic, elitist, and academic. Ultimately, Third World Christian theology can be articulated in a relevant way only insofar as it takes seriously the option for the poor and their religiosity.

Diego Irarrázaval, CSC

See also: INCULTURATION, SALVATION, SPIRITUALITY, SYNCRETISM.

Bibliography
Jaime A. Belita, CM, ed., *And God Said: HALA: Studies in Popular Religiosity in the Philippines* (Manila: De La Salle University, 1991).
Jean Delumeau, ed., *Le Fait Religieux* (Paris: Fayard, 1993).
José Gonzalez, Carlos Brandão, and Diego Irarrázaval, *Catolicismo Popular* (São Paulo: Vozes, 1993).
Emefie Ikenga-Metuh, *Comparative Studies of African Traditional Religions* (Nigeria: IMICO, 1992).
Cristián Parker, *Popular Religion and Modernization in Latin America* (Maryknoll, N.Y.: Orbis Books, 1996).

POSTCOLONIALISM

Edward Said's *Orientalism* (1978) opened up the discussion on what has become known as postcolonial theory. His most critical challenge to colonialism was that the "Orient" was basically a political, ideological, and imaginative creation of European culture during the post-Enlightenment period. Orientalism was therefore a discourse of the West that controlled the nature and shape of knowledge as well as the ways it was produced and disseminated. Homi Bhabha hence defines "postcolonial" as a tool that functions to direct our attention to "bear witness" to inequities in modes of representation between the West and the non-West. In other words, the term "postcolonialism" has come to mean not only a simple periodization after Western countries dominated militarily, but also a methodological revisionism that enables a wholesale critique of Western structures of knowledge and power since the Enlightenment.

Postcolonial theory is most essential to Third World theological reflection if one understands it as a critical tool addressing primarily imperialism's general and continuing ideological roles in peoples and cultures of the Third World countries. In effect, without using the term, Third World theologies have, since their inception, already engaged themselves in a postcolonial task when they challenge the Western construction of

Christianity and reformulate contextual theologies that aim to free themselves from being a tool of the colonial masters. This engagement was based on knowledge provided by the Enlightenment. Current post-colonial theory goes beyond, among other things, binary notions and acknowledges that the contact between the colonizer and the colonized is complicated and intertwined. However, if one takes seriously the critiques raised by postcolonial theorists, Third World theologies have yet to benefit from postcolonial critics by taking on a self-critical perspective toward their strong dependence on a Third World identity. This dependence has resulted in their freezing themselves within a category of difference designed by the West. Therefore, in their continuous search for a way forward, Third World theologies must find ways to break free of the restrictive demarcation constructed by the West.

Wong Wai Ching

See also: COLONIZATION, DECOLONIZING THEOLOGY.

Bibliography

Ania Loomba, ed., *Colonialism/Postcolonialsm* (London: Routledge, 1998).
Edward W. Said, *Orientalism* (New York: Random House, 1979).
R. S. Sugirtharajah, *Asian Biblical Hermeneutics and Postcolonialism: Contesting the Interpretation* (Maryknoll, N.Y.: Orbis Books, 1998).
R. S. Sugirtharajah, ed., *Postcolonial Bible* (Sheffield: Sheffield Academic Press, 1998).
Wong Wai Ching, "Asian Theology in a Changing Asia: Towards an Asian Theological Agenda for the 21st Century," *CTC Bulletin*, Special Supplement: 1 (November 1997): 30–39.

POVERTY

One of the significant contributions of Third World theologies has been to put poverty at the center of theological discussions. Given the disparate conditions in which these theologies arise, their articulation of poverty, too, differs from context to context. It was the Latin American theologians who first took seriously the cause of poverty for theological reflection. The failure of the development decade of the 1960s, the widening of the gap between the poor and the rich, and the complacency with which the dominant theologies of the time overlooked this reality prompted Latin American theologians to re-articulate poverty as a structural issue. They saw it as a by-product of social and economic systems, rather than assigning the blame to the poor themselves. Among others, Gustavo Gutiérrez defined poverty as a subhuman existence without the basic necessities, a scandalous state incompatible with the Bible. In their view, poverty is not the fault of the poor. It can and should be eliminated, and the Bible has its own built-in safeguards such as the Sabbath laws, tithing, and the Jubilee Year of the release that offer the poor a fresh start in life.

In Africa, people face socio-economic poverty as well as another kind of poverty that the late Engelbert Mveng, a Cameroonian theologian, called anthropological poverty. This is not about exterior circumstances nor about not having material possessions. It is about the interior of African selfhood that has been affected as centuries of colonialism robbed Africans of their own ways of living and their cultural heritage. Sadly, the resulting low self-esteem has caused them to internalize the values and models of their oppressors. Deliverance from such a state is provided in the Song of Zachariah, Mary's Magnificat, and in the charter of the Beatitudes.

In the Asian context, in *God's Reign for God's Poor* (1999), Aloysius Pieris has proposed a new "covenant" christology based on two categories of poverty: the voluntary poverty of those who as followers of Jesus renounce Mammon, and the forced poverty of the masses of people who as vicars of Christ are the victims of Mammon, of organized consumerism and greed. The way to eradicate poverty is to undertake voluntary poverty, which is biblically sanctioned. The hermeneutical underpinning is provided by the biblical notion of God's active opposition to Mammon. What is important is not freedom from poverty, but the freedom that *comes* from poverty. Therefore, in Pieris's understanding, Asians struggle not against poverty, but against Mammon. Voluntary poverty does not mean leading the life of an ascetic but leading a life based on simplicity, sufficiency, and respect for both human beings and the ecological order.

While these three models are not exclusive, they are relevant and applicable beyond their contexts. All three models concur that the poor do not need charity but justice, so that instead of waiting for crumbs to fall from the master's table, they can take their legitimate place at the table.

R. S. Sugirtharajah

See also: OPTION FOR THE POOR, SOLIDARITY.

Bibliography
Rosino Gibellini, ed., *Paths of African Theology* (Maryknoll, N.Y.: Orbis Books, 1994).
Gustavo Gutiérrez, *We Drink from Our Own Wells* (Maryknoll, N.Y.: Orbis Books, 1984).
Aloysius Pieris, *An Asian Theology of Liberation* (Maryknoll, N.Y.: Orbis Books, 1988).
Aloysius Pieris, *God's Reign for God's Poor* (Kelaniya, Sri Lanka, 1999).

PRAXIS/ORTHOPRAXIS

The term praxis enters into liberation theology as a claim that theology has a new function: that of critical reflection on praxis. Initially, it means paying attention to what is done by Christians and the faith community and by using it as material for reflection. Subsequently, an effort is made to understand it more broadly, whether by giving weight to the Aristotelian tradition of connecting praxis with an ethical dimension, or by illuminating it with the light of faith.

A distinction is made between praxis and practice. Practice refers to action in a particular sector of human life, such as educational practice, while praxis is made up of the entirety of human practices in the social realm. The nature of praxis depends on its impact on reality: maintaining it (conservative practice), modifying it within the same fundamental structure (reformist practice), or radically transforming it (revolutionary practice). Liberation theology considers all human praxis to be the object of its reflection in the light of revelation. It seeks to avoid two extremes, that of alienation (theology unrelated to praxis) and that of pragmatism (action without faith-reflection).

Liberation theologians are bound to praxis in four ways: they take material from praxis for their reflection; they offer the results to those engaged in praxis; they allow themselves to be criticized by praxis; and they build their theology while being involved in a concrete praxis.

Liberation theology views historic and liberating praxis in relation to the oppression of the poor. In theological terms, theory corresponds to faith, and praxis to charity. In this sense, praxis is an integral part of faith, insofar as it is an expression of Christian activity in the pursuit of justice, solidarity, and charity.

The term orthopraxis qualifies praxis from the standpoint of Christian faith. It means that that praxis corresponds to gospel criteria and principles, interpreted in the course of the church's living tradition.

Liberation theology stresses orthopraxis not to eliminate orthodoxy, which in the past had uncontested primacy in Christian life but oftentimes merely meant adherence to an obsolete tradition or a debatable interpretation. Rather, the intent is to achieve a balanced relationship between right belief and right action to the mutual nourishment of both (Gutiérrez).

João B. Libânio
(Trans. Phillip Berryman)

See also: LIBERATION, SOCIAL ANALYSIS, THEOLOGICAL METHODOLOGIES.

Bibliography
Clodovis Boff, *Theology and Praxis: Epistemological Foundations* (Maryknoll, N.Y.: Orbis Books, 1987).
Gustavo Gutiérrez, *A Theology of Liberation*, trans. Caridad Inda, John Eagleson, and Matthew J. O'Connell, 15th anniversary ed. (Maryknoll, N.Y.: Orbis Books, 1988).

PROSTITUTION

The traditional definition of prostitution is the sale of sexual services, or the performance of sexual services for remuneration. Some feminists think this definition focuses exclusively on the used and fails to mention the abuser. An alternative definition is the use of a person for sexual satisfaction in exchange for money or other mercenary consideration. There are many types of prostitution, ranging from the *geisha* type of entertainers to street "hookers." Prostituted persons are mainly women and girls although some males, especially young boys, may also be prostituted. In the context of the Third World, mail-order brides and overseas contract workers, especially entertainers, who are considered victims of women-trafficking may not necessarily become prostitutes but are often in situations that can lead to prostitution.

In contemporary times, many factors have arisen to promote prostitution, such as tourism, the presence of foreign military bases, and massive developmental projects, particularly when these exist in a context of perennial economic crises. The main reason for persons to engage in prostitution is economic need. A contributing factor is the cult of virginity existing in many traditional societies that makes women feel totally worthless when they lose their virginity. Thus, many prostitutes are victims of incest, rape, or sexual harassment in the workplace.

Feminist theorists have analyzed prostitution uncompromisingly as "the ultimate in the reduction of women to sexual objects which can be bought and sold and forms the foundation of women's oppression." Prostitution is also a form of male sexual violence against women. Prostitution sends the message that women are sexual objects and that sexual harassment is an acceptable way to treat women and girls when men pay for it.

In the last two decades, advocates for prostituted women have increasingly maintained that prostitution is sex work and should be legalized to protect the rights of the women sex workers. Without diminishing the urgency of protecting prostituted women, many feminists still maintain that prostitution in itself is oppressive, that the "choice" of women to work as prostitutes is so limited by formidable constraints as to put into question the reality of choice. This is particularly true in Third World countries.

Third World theology, which takes as its starting point the struggle of peoples against oppression, considers prostitution an important concern. Having in mind Christ's attitude toward prostitutes, theologians refrain from having a moralistic attitude toward the prostituted women. Rather, they consider the socio-economic and gender factors that drive them to prostitution. Condemned instead are the oppression and exploitation exercised by greedy people and the market system that takes advantage of economic need to lure women and children to a life fraught with the dangers of physical violence, disease, drug abuse, and degradation as human beings.

While there is yet no fundamental solution to prostitution, there is a continuing struggle to give emergency help and to rehabilitate prostituted persons, and there are also militant moves to defend their rights. A fundamental solution includes revamping economic policies and structures on a national and global level and bringing about a radical change in patriarchal consciousness and relationships.

Mary John Mananzan, OSB

See also: HUMAN RIGHTS, OPPRESSION, PATRIARCHY/HIERARCHY, SEXISM, VIOLENCE.

Bibliography

Rita Nakashima Brock and Susan Thistlethwaite, *Casting Stones: Prostitution in Asia and the United States* (Minneapolis, Minn.: Fortress Press, 1996).
Sheila Jeffreys, *The Idea of Prostitution* (Melbourne: Spinifex Press, 1997).
Aida Santos, ed., *Awake 2: Migration and Sex Tourism* (Manila: Wedpro, 1992).

R

RACISM

Racism is a concept based on the assumption that an aggregate of descendants of a common ancestral origin have innate superior characteristics, coupled with a belief in their right to dominate others who differ decisively from their own distinct identity traits. In other words, racism can apply to any group of immanent relations (family, tribe, people, nation) who possess the power to define rights, duties, and liberties; to legitimize ideologies, theologies, and systems of value; to assign myths to various members of the human family, which, in turn, invariably divide human ontology between persons and non-persons.

From antiquity to the present time have come traditionalist hierarchal paradigms of phenotypical, genealogical, and/or geographical determinism. Supposedly, reliable signifiers of measurable dimensions exist among the human species, to the least advanced, barbaric savage categorization, to those positioned at center-stage as the most highly evolved subjects in all areas. In short, the historical conditioning surrounding racism reinforces certain bodies of humans as being relegated to physical, moral, intellectual, and cultural inferiority, while members of the mainstream population use narrow and rigid codes to bestow upon themselves privileged classifications as the inherently superior embodiment of normative humanity.

Racism gained wide currency under the aegis of European expeditions of conquest. As a serious moral evil, racism grew dramatically as a way of justifying brutal, exploitative, and oppressive structures of domination and subordination. People in the Third World were defined as inferior heathens, objects of conquest in so-called just wars for the glory of kings and God. Due to the great spectrum of Eurocentric hegemony—slavery, apartheid, imperialism, colonialism, genocide—racism is now commonly referred to as being synonymous with white supremacy, the alleged divinely ordained "rightness of whiteness."

Katie G. Cannon

See also: APARTHEID, OPPRESSION, VIOLENCE.

Bibliography
Katie G. Cannon, *Katie's Canon: Womanism and the Soul of the Black Community* (New York: Continuum, 1995).

Robert E. Hood, *Begrimed and Black: Christian Traditions on Blacks and Blackness* (Minneapolis, Minn.: Fortress, 1994).
Charles W. Mills, *The Racial Conflict* (Ithaca, N.Y.: Cornell University Press, 1997).

RECONCILIATION

Reconciliation refers to a process of restoring a broken relation between different parties. In Africa, as in most parts of the world, there are as many different processes of reconciliation as there are cultures. But the aim is always to ensure that the shattered relationship is repaired and re-established on solid and lasting grounds. It is worth noting that the communal dimension of reconciliation is highly valued in many Third World societies.

In Rwanda, for example, the traditional judicial system called *Gacaca* is an effective means for solving conflicts and reconciling people involved in litigation. The *Gacaca* system functions as an unofficial court whose decision is binding on everyone in the community. The senior elder serves as prosecutor while some members of the community volunteer as witnesses on behalf of both defendant and plaintiff. After a thorough examination of all the facts, the senior elder asks the defendant if he or she acknowledges those facts and if he or she is willing to ask for forgiveness. When the defendant apologizes, the harmed party and the community always forgive him or her. In consultation with the community, the elders determine the punishment of the wrongdoer. Very often people agree on material compensation, such as an animal, a piece of land, or simply some beer to be drunk by all present in the *Gacaca* as a sign of harmony, which is now restored.

Since the 1994 genocide, the Rwandan judicial apparatus has confronted thorny practical problems posed by insufficient human and material resources while thousands of people await trial on charges of genocide. As a result, the government has decided that villages should use the *Gacaca* system to deal with those charged with simple crimes such as looting or destruction of properties during the genocide. In some provinces, the *Gacaca* system has already borne fruits leading toward reconciliation.

Efforts toward national reconciliation have also been undertaken in South Africa. In May 1995, the Parliament created the Truth and Reconciliation Commission (TRC) in order to bring about unity and reconciliation after the horrors of apartheid. Amnesty was offered to those who would tell the truth about "gross human rights abuses" committed during apartheid. During the TRC hearings, public acts of forgiveness proved to be the most powerful way to free victims of apartheid from their tormented past.

The practices of *Gacaca* in Rwanda and the TRC in South Africa provide structures for rebuilding the society, but they do not guarantee forgiveness or the healing of memories. This is why people seek help from religions, which can provide a spiritual dimension to deal with broken lives and produce social reconciliation.

From a Christian perspective, reconciliation starts with God's initiative and is, first and foremost, God's work. God begins this process with victims by restoring their humanity. Reconciled with God and with self, a victim is enabled to bear the suffering and forgive the wrongdoer. Thus, repentance on the part of the wrongdoer and forgiveness on the part of the victim are not conditions for reconciliation but consequences of it. Reconciliation appears to be a matter of grace that must be sought and accepted.

Sacrament and rites of reconciliation are practiced by some Christian churches. For instance, for the Catholic church, the sacrament of reconciliation is very important for healing. But it still remains a personal and private affair. The practices of reconciliation in the churches would be more beneficial if the churches integrated cultural elements that stress the communal aspect of reconciliation.

Anicet Setako, SJ

Bibliography
Gregory Baum and Harold Wells, eds., *The Reconciliation of Peoples: Challenges to the Churches* (Maryknoll, N.Y.: Orbis Books, 1997).
Daan Bronkhorst, *Truth and Reconciliation: Obstacles and Opportunities for Human Rights* (Amsterdam: Amnesty International, 1995).
Laurenti Magesa, *African Religion: The Moral Traditions of Abundant Life* (Maryknoll, N.Y.: Orbis Books, 1998).
Robert J. Schreiter, *The Ministry of Reconciliation: Spirituality & Strategies* (Maryknoll, N.Y.: Orbis Books, 1998).
Stef Vandeginste, "*L'approche vérité et réconciliation du génocide et des crimes contre l'humanité au Rwanda,*" in *L'Afrique des Grands Lacs. Annuaire 1997-1998* (Paris: Harmattan, 1998).

REIGN OF GOD

The concept "reign of God" signifies God as creator, sovereign, sole authority, and controller of the universe, as manifest in God's relationship with humanity and all creation. As a political metaphor, the kingdom of God in the biblical tradition points to God as ruler of history, protecting and liberating people from pain, injustice, and oppression. Though kingdom of God is still used, many theologians prefer to use "reign" because the former has connotations of male overlordship and superiority. Reign also incorporates "kindom," which encompasses the ideas of group and relationship, shared by all people. In many parts of the Third World, reign of God is expressed through the indigenous names and attributes of God, many of which imply the invisible but present reality of a gender-neutral God. A major concern in the Third World, confronted by rampant anti-life forces, has been whether God is present and why God allows such evil. The reign of God presupposes social justice, freedom, fulfillment, healing, restoration, reconciliation, community, communality, and, indeed, life.

Mary Getui

See also: JUSTICE, LIBERATION THEOLOGIES, SALVATION.

Bibliography
John Fullenbach, *The Kingdom of God: The Message of Jesus Today* (Maryknoll, N.Y.: Orbis Books, 1995).

REVELATION

Revelation is a central idea that pervades all facets of Christian thought and practice. It is a free gift, a grace, and its purpose is human salvation. It refers to God's self-disclosure to and interaction with human beings, and the appropriation of that disclosure by human beings. The idea of revelation is rooted in the Bible. From the very beginning, the Bible presents God as disclosing Godself to human beings in various ways and entering into covenant relationships with them. In creation, we have God's primary and fundamental self-disclosure to humanity (Rom. 1:20). Human beings are not passive recipients of God's self-disclosure but active participants in the process (Gen. 8:20-22; Exod. 19-20). The religion of Israel, for example, is a response to God's self-disclosure to Israel's ancestors. Yet it is God that makes such a response possible. Only those enabled by God can recognize and appropriate God's self-disclosure in the world. However, the appropriation of revelation is often mixed with human imperfection, even in the case of Israel's history. We are, therefore, to discern what in history belongs to genuine revelation and what to human imperfection.

Revelation is an on-going process. In Christianity, the people of God mediate it in the Old Testament, while in the New Testament revelation reaches its fullness in Jesus as mediator (Heb. 1-2). In the incarnation whereby Jesus represents the entire humanity, God disclosed and continues to disclose Godself to humanity in Jesus. Jesus' life and personal interaction with people during his earthly ministry constituted the highest form of God's redeeming self-disclosure to humanity and reached its fullness in the resurrection. Now, in his risen state, Jesus' revelatory-redemptive activity *continues* in the world through the Holy Spirit (Matt. 28:20). Individuals or groups may be enabled by God to appropriate the disclosure. While, in some cases, such disclosures may be for the spiritual nourishment of individuals only; in other cases, they may be for public dissemination. It is the teaching authority of the church that has the competence to discern between the two.

God's self-disclosure to humanity does not take place in a vague general way but within specific situations in the normal course of history; nor is it restricted to Christian history but is experienced by non-Christians as well. Though most of the human race lives in the Third World and is poor and exploited, the revelation of God in the history of this two-thirds of humanity has been mostly ignored. Most non-Christian religions in the Third World today show elements of divine truth in their tenets, such as belief in the divine. Some of these religions have scriptures while others do not. The presence of divine truth in these religions indicates divine self-disclosure to these people and their appropriation of it. This becomes understandable considering God's covenant with Noah (Gen. 9:8-17) that involved all humanity and was not abrogated by the covenant with Israel. Furthermore, Third World theologies have called attention to the biblical emphasis on God's preferential option for the poor and Jesus' identification with them: God today makes the poor and oppressed people of the world and their history a preferential way of revealing who God is, what God is like, and where God is to be found. It is the work of Third World theologians to help to uncover this revelation.

Justin S. Ukpong

See also: OPTION FOR THE POOR, RECONCILIATION.

Bibliography
Juan Luis Segundo, *The Liberation of Dogma* (Maryknoll, N.Y.: Orbis Books, 1992).

RITUALS

(See **Worship/Rituals**)

S

SALVATION

In the Judeo-Christian tradition, salvation is the story of the journey of humankind and the world—from the first creation (Gen. 1:1) to the new creation (Rev. 21:1-5). It encompasses the story of Israel's beginnings (Gen. 12-Judges), the subsequent story of the Israelite people (1 Sam.-Ezra), and the perceived story of prehistorical beginnings (Gen. 1-11).

The original core of this story is Israel's confessional story of the patriarchs through Moses to Joshua (Deut. 26:5-9), later expanded forward to include the story of the kings (Samuel and Kings), still later backward expanded to include the "story" of the beginnings in prehistory (Gen. 1-11), until eventually it takes the final form as we have it in some of the psalms and the historical books of the Hebrew Scriptures. The overarching theme is not, as is sometimes believed, the spiral of humankind's sin and the hope to be redeemed from it. Rather it is about the drive for *life* and life-blessings: land, progeny, liberation from slavery, alliance with God, harvests, secure homes, and so on (see, for example, Deut. 7:12-16). Because the Exodus is the key event, the most significant life-blessing in this story is justice (Deut. 24:17-22).

The classical prophets carry the story further by planting seeds of hope for a better and definitive story in the future. Again, that history is about life-blessings and justice (Isa. 65:17-25). It is the prophets who moved the story toward expectations of eschatological salvation. Salvation— eschatological salvation—in the New Testament is about the coming into being of a new world and a new history with life-blessings. Jesus' preferred name for it is the reign or kingdom of God. The reign or kingdom of God, according to Jesus, based on his re-contextualization of Isaiah, is a new earth with such life-blessings as health for the sick (blind, lame, lepers, deaf), life for the dead, good news of liberation to the poor, release to captives, liberty to the oppressed, a jubilee year, and justice to the nations (Matt. 11:2-6, 12:18-21; Luke 4:16-21, 6:20-21, 7:18-23; Mark 1:14-15).

The second part of each beatitude in Matthew provides another window to the biblical meaning of the reign or kingdom of God or eschatological salvation. Again, the beatitudes speak of a new earth with a new history, where the following blessings are envisioned: divine filiation (5:9), seeing God (5:8), experiencing compassion (5:7), inheriting the earth (5:5), laughter and joy for the sorrowing poor (Luke 6:21b), food for the hungry (in Luke 6:21a, satiation of real hunger; in Matthew 5:6, of hunger for righteousness), liberation of the '*anawim*, the poor and oppressed (Luke 6:20). Salvation also encompasses the destruction of satanic powers (Matt. 12:28; 1 Cor. 15:24-28); resurrection from death (Luke 20:34-36); and the unity of all things in Christ (Eph. 1:9-10), where "God is all in all" (1 Cor. 15:28).

Other significant names for eschatological salvation are: the "new heaven(s) and new earth" of Revelation 21:1 (a new world or a new creation) and the "age to come" of Mark 10:29-30 (a new and different alternative history in the future).

Biblical salvation is seen as having both a *future* aspect (Luke 13:29) and a *present* aspect (Luke 17:21). As a future reality, the reign or kingdom of God will be realized at the "close of the age," that is, at the end of our present history. Although, therefore, there is a life soon after the death ("going to heaven") of each individual, our *ultimate* destiny is not heaven but rather that new world and new history at the close of the present time. As a reality in Jesus' time, salvation took the form of life-giving blessings through Jesus' actions. In our time, it should likewise take the form of life-giving blessings enfleshed in a humane social order. Such a social order would include, for example, employment, job security, the right to organize for workers, land for peasants to cultivate, liberation from oppression for women and children, rights to ancestral lands for indigenous peoples, a healthy mother earth, and humane alternatives to neo-liberal globalization.

The reign/kingdom of God is associated with four principal Christ events. The first is the *ministry/practice* of Jesus when he first proclaimed the reign/kingdom of God (Mark 1:14-15). The *death of Jesus* was a consequence of his conflictive kingdom proclamation (Mark 14:1-2). Its mystical meaning is reconciliation and atonement for sin, a life-blessing par excellence in the Christian economy of salvation (1 Cor. 15:3-5; Col. 1:20). The *resurrection of Jesus* was a vindication of Jesus' kingdom practice and death (Phil. 2:5-11). The risen Jesus is the first fruit and the first born into the reign/kingdom of God (1 Cor. 15:20). He has become the indwelling Spirit that guarantees our own resurrection in the final kingdom (Rom. 8:9-11). Jesus is the cosmic Christ that binds together all things (Eph. 1:9-10). Finally, the *parousia of Jesus* is the sign that the reign/kingdom of God will have come in its fullness (Luke 21:25-28).

Biblical salvation, therefore, is not for souls but for persons, for the natural world (Rom. 8:19-23), and the universe. The blessings of salvation encompass everything that gives life, including, but not limited to, divine life, sanctifying grace, or beatific vision. It is not narrowly limited to the private sphere of the individual person but also has to do with the social, political, economic, and other dimensions of life. If the contemporary term "liberation" is taken to refer principally to the social (economic, political) sphere, then such liberation is part of salvation. One may not limit the Christ-events to the paschal mystery (death and resurrection); rather, they must encompass his whole career, beginning with the ministry and culminating in the *parousia*.

Carlos H. Abesamis, SJ

See also: ATONEMENT, BIBLE, CHRISTOLOGIES, ESCHATOLOGY, JUSTIFICATION, LIBERATION, OPTION FOR THE POOR, REIGN OF GOD.

Bibliography
Carlos H. Abesamis, *A Third Look at Jesus: A Guidebook along a Road Least Traveled*, 3rd rev. ed. (Quezon City, Philippines: Claretian Publications, 1999). Ched Myers, *Binding the Strong Man: A Political Reading of Mark's Story of Jesus* (Maryknoll, N.Y.: Orbis Books, 1988).

SEXISM

This term can be defined as an analytical category that serves to examine the historical reality of distorted understandings and uses of social power in relationships between men and women. Sexism has been present in all the social models created by humans throughout the world, including modern historical socialism and capitalism. Its roots are found in the system of patriarchal domination and exploitation of women on the basis of sex. Patriarchal societies are characterized by the privileged position granted to men against the subordinate position of women in all areas of life. Sexism enforces both the unequal power relationships between men and women and the cultural behavior that controls and disempowers women. As such, sexism is the historical manifestation of androcentric ideologies, cultures, and religions. As a patriarchal religion, Christianity has been a major contributor to the preservation of sexist social relationships, theologies, attitudes, and behavior.

Sexism is a major component of Third World societies, cultures, and theologies, due to the strong dominance of the patriarchal system throughout the Third World. Nonetheless, it is only recently that Third World theologians, especially liberation theologians, have been open to examine sexism as a distinct component of the global patriarchal system. The neglect of these theologians to analyze critically the role of sexism has only contributed to deepen the causes that maintain poor and oppressed women and children in unjust conditions of living. Although the major world religions have been born in the Third World, they are permeated by patriarchy and have been unable to challenge sexism. Critical liberation theology, especially feminist theology, is committed to the eradication of patriarchy and considers sexism to be a sin because it damages the inner being of women and men. Feminist theologians agree that sexist attitudes and beliefs are conducive to violence against women. Therefore, insofar as Third World theologies accept and tolerate sexism, they are responsible for the many forms of violence to which Third World women are subjected. The struggle against the sin of sexism is not optional for Third World liberation theologians, feminist or not-feminist. Involved in this issue is the authenticity of liberation as the historical expression of God's justice and salvation.

María Pilar Aquino

See also: FEMINIST THEOLOGIES IN THE THIRD WORLD, OPPRESSION, PATRIARCHY/HIERARCHY, THIRD WORLD WOMEN'S THEOLOGIES, VIOLENCE.

Bibliography
M. Shawn Copeland, "Difference as a Category in Critical Theologies for the Liberation of Women," *Concilium* 1996/1 (1996), 141-151.
M. Shawn Copeland and Elisabeth Schüssler Fiorenza, eds., *Violence Against Women. Concilium* 1994/1 (1994).
Alma M. García, *Chicana Feminist Thought. The Basic Historical Writings* (New York: Routledge, 1997).
Elisabeth Schüssler Fiorenza, *Jesus: Miriam's Child, Sophia's Prophet. Critical Issues in Feminist Christology* (New York: Continuum, 1994).

SHAMANISM

Shamanism is a set of magico-religious practices found in various areas of the world, usually among nonliterate peoples. Since it antedates the coming of metacosmic religions such as Buddhism and Christianity, it is considered an indigenous religion; and because certain shamanistic elements have been incorporated in world religions, it is also considered a form of popular religiosity. One of the vital elements of shamanism is its cosmology, which assumes that the entire cosmos is inhabited by a multiplicity of spirits (including those of dead ancestors) that have the power to affect the lives of human beings.

Still practiced in both the First and Third Worlds, shamanism retains its vitality in some regions, for instance, in South Korea. Although it is looked down upon by elitist intellectuals as a "primitive" religion that provides a facile form of escapism, South Korean people (particularly the *minjung*, that is, the struggling, oppressed masses) have discovered in it a source of inspiration and power. With its ethos of harmony rather than competition, its place for playfulness in prayer, its deep-rootedness in the rituals of daily living, and its sensitivity to the cosmic forces that pervade our world, shamanism is a powerful cultural resource for the South Korean people in their struggle for liberation.

Shamanism is of special significance to Korean women. In striking contrast to the male-dominated Buddhism and Christianity, in which women play a passive and secondary role, shamanism gives them a dominant place. Fully 90 percent of the active shamans in South Korea are women. Shamanism has also had an important influence on Korean women's theology. Their methodology follows steps similar to the shamanistic ritual to assuage women's pain: first, *speaking* and *hearing* women's experience of suffering and oppression; second, *naming* the source of their oppression; and third, *changing* the unjust situation by action leading to individual and collective healing and liberation.

Chung Hyun Kyung

See also: HAN/HAN-PURI, MINJUNG THEOLOGY, THIRD WORLD WOMEN'S THEOLOGIES: ASIAN.

SIN

Sin signifies not only any word or deed or thought that is a transgression of religious law, but also the self-conscious disregard of God's will for each person to become a responsible social-self. The first understanding gives attention to serious offenses in the personal sphere that cause individual estrangement from God, and the second focuses on socio-cultural factors of oppression that tamper with the communal *imago Dei*.

Of particular interest to the Third World theological context is how sin is defined. In some contexts sin is perceived as embedded in the structures of society. Latin American theologians focus specifically on the class structure and economic oppression of society, while Third World feminist theologians explore the multiple social evils of gender, class, race, and culture. Some point out that oppressed people are not only the "sinners," but also the "sinned against."

In the African-American perception of sin, of particular interest is the work of Howard Thurman. Thurman does not begin with original sin, the reference to the universal and hereditary sinfulness of humankind since the fall of Adam and Eve. Rather than focus on formulated doctrines that connect all people with rebellion against the order of creation and subsequently dividing into distinct typologies mortal and venial sins, Thurman is more concerned with the general development of God consciousness or lack thereof.

Thurman argues that sin moves in two concentric circles. The compact inner circle is the individual sin of shirking the responsibility to be in right relation with God, and the surrounding supervening circle is the communal sin of violating the inherent relatedness of inclusive well-being for the society.

In Thurman's thought, sin is reshaped in the religion of Jesus, a technique of survival for the oppressed. All interactions either encourage wholeness or brokenness. All experiences either nourish religious exposure to truth or snuff it out. How this is determined is clearly stated— sin is anything that fragments, prohibits, or interrupts the progress from outward life to inward life and to outward life in a justice-making world.

Katie G. Cannon

See also: MORAL THEOLOGY/ETHICS, OPPRESSION, VIOLENCE.

Bibliography
James H. Cone, *God of the Oppressed* (Maryknoll, N.Y.: Orbis Books, 1997).
Marjorie H. Suchocki, *The Fall to Violence: Original Sin in Relational Theology* (New York: Continuum, 1994).
Howard Thurman, *Jesus and the Disinherited* (Richmond, Ind.: Friends United Press, 1981).

SOCIAL ANALYSIS

Liberation theologians working with Third World impoverished urban and rural workers soon realized the importance of social analysis for doing theology. Social analysis is defined as a deliberate team effort to investigate and evaluate the conditions of life (economic, political, cultural, etc.) of one's own community, or the community one is committed to, in order to transform such conditions in accordance with God's liberating plan.

A basic presupposition of social analysis is that transformative pastoral action inspired by the Christian faith requires serious research into the social conditions from and for which such action has arisen. In other words, faith and good intentions alone are never sufficient to make ours a better world. Many of the real, albeit oft-overstated, linkages of (Christian) social analysis to (secular or atheist) Marxist social theories stem from this presupposition, as well as from the fact that contemporary Third World liberation movements have often experienced convergences with, if not direct influences of, socialist groups.

Nonetheless, the sense and practice of social analysis among Third World Christians have deep roots both in the tradition of Roman Catholic social teaching and in the history of the Catholic Action movement, both in Europe, where it originated and from where in the 1940s and 1950s a large percentage of Roman Catholic missionaries carried the movement to the Third World, and in Latin America, where the first forms of liberation theology emerged in the 1960s among clergy linked to Catholic Action. Of crucial importance is the "see-judge-act" methodology of life revision, particularly as it was conceived and practiced in the Young Christian Workers' branch of Catholic Action. This methodology required an effort to understand life in its own right, before and as a prerequisite to any theological reflection about reality. It was also indispensable to pastoral decision-making. The "see-judge-act" approach decisively favored a heightened regard for the use of the social sciences (sociology, anthropology, history, economics, etc.) by pastors and theologians, often pairing such use with a more critical stance toward the traditional understanding of philosophy as the foundational discipline of theology. This new perspective was decisively impressed upon dozens of Third World clergy and lay leaders in the latter third of the twentieth century through the decisive mentoring of François Houtart, the noted Belgian sociologist of religion.

This methodology became somewhat "canonized" in Roman Catholicism through a process marked by the new papal social encyclicals, above all John XXIII's *Pacem in Terris* and Paul VI's *Populorum Progressio*, as well as by *Gaudium et Spes*, the most influential document arising from the Second Vatican Council. This methodology played a significant role at the Second Latin American (Roman Catholic) Episcopal Conference held in 1969 in Medellín, Colombia, and was not entirely irrelevant to Protestant developments in the 1960s and 1970s, as expressed, for instance, in the positions of the World Council of Churches toward Third World liberation movements. The noted "hermeneutical circle," at least as understood by Third World theologians, is a critical extension of the "see-judge-act" method of pastoral action, and social analysis is one of its key elements. Similarly, the adult literacy method of "conscientization," developed by Paulo Freire and pioneered in Brazilian Catholic Action movements, contributed most to the understanding and centrality of social analysis in Third World liberation theologies.

Social analysis, while inextricably linked to the social sciences by its consistent attention to the latter and its propensity to legitimize itself by reference to them, distinguished itself from the so-called social sciences by its attachment to the Christian faith; its rejection of "objective," "neutral" research done "on" the poor without their proactive participation; and its overt option for the conscious self-liberation of the oppressed (as main agents and beneficiaries of both social analysis and social change). These latter two characteristics contributed to significant, albeit implicit, collisions between practitioners and proponents of social analysis, on the one hand, and Marxist groups and theories, on the other. Likewise, the last two traits have repeatedly pitted Northern/ Western Christian groups and understandings against the grasp and practice of social analysis by Third World liberation theologians.

Otto Maduro

See also: HERMENEUTICAL CIRCLE, SOCIAL LOCATION, THEOLOGICAL METHODOLOGIES.

Bibliography
Joe Holland and Peter Henriot, *Social Analysis: Linking Faith and Justice* (Maryknoll, N.Y.: Orbis Books; Washington, D.C.: Center of Concern, 1983).
Anne Hope and Sally Timmel, *Training for Transformation: A Handbook for Community Workers* (Gweru, Zimbabwe: Mambo Press, 1985).

SOCIAL LOCATION

Social sciences have defined "socialization" as the process through which "individuals internalize the values, standards, and mores of society at large." Such internalization will inevitably condition the way in which people understand and express their views on religion, ethics, politics, or economics. One's social location has to be taken into account in the interpretation of texts, ideologies, and attitudes. This practice, also called a "hermeneutics of suspicion," has been applied to biblical texts, to theological texts, and to decisions, behaviors, and attitudes of Christian individuals and institutions by liberation and feminist theologians. A person, group, or institution, can, however, take a critical view of their own location and voluntarily position themselves differently, as in, for example, making an option for the poor.

José Míguez Bonino

See also: BIBLE, HERMENEUTICAL CIRCLE, IDEOLOGY, SOCIAL ANALYSIS.

SOCIALISM

There is no universally accepted definition of "socialism." It can be understood as a political movement that has as its goal the overcoming of a capitalistic ordering of society and greater social justice in the distribution of income and property—if necessary by socializing the means of production. It tends to put the interests of society as a whole before those of the individual. Argentine socialist Juan B. Justo (1865-1928) defined socialism as "the struggle to defend and elevate the workers (*pueblo trabajador*) which, guided by science, tends to achieve a free and intelligent human society, based on a collective means of production."

The concept of "socialism" is a relatively young one. In 1827 an English trade union publication used the term, and since that time it has been linked to the idea of the workers' struggle for emancipation. Early socialism, which developed especially in France after 1789 in opposition to individualistic liberalism, was critical of private property and favored production cooperatives for the self-help of the workers. This type of early socialism, sometimes labeled associationism, was promoted quite early in Latin America by thinkers such as Esteban Echeverría. Marx and Engels opposed their own "scientific socialism" to this type of early "utopian socialism."

As of the Second World War, various socialist movements and ideologies began to crystallize throughout the Third World, largely as a manifestation against colonial or neo-colonial dominance. They blend elements from indigenous cultural and religious traditions that reject capitalistic egoism and materialism and emphasize community and solidarity, with particular interpretations of Marxism (e.g., Islamic or Arab socialism; Buddhist socialism; the Ujamaa movement in Tanzania; Cuban socialism). For many Third World Christians, socialist political options seem those most akin to the biblical imperative of justice.

Nancy E. Bedford

See also: CAPITALISM, IDEOLOGY, MARXISM.

SOLIDARITY

Solidarity is the process-action of being united with the cause and political project of a person or a group. To be in solidarity means to share solidly the other person's struggle for justice, peace, and harmony. Solidarity is built on mutual respect and trust, sustained by accountability, and strengthened by one's spirituality.

Solidarity is particularly significant to people in the developing countries and to Third World theologies. First, international solidarity calls world attention to their struggles and moves people to action. Second, national and sectoral solidarity strengthens the power of the people's movements. Finally, women's groups and women's ways of doing theology experience solidarity as a living and sustaining spirituality. Solidarity among women is "beyond bonding," to use a phrase of Virginia Fabella. It means creating together a safe space, shared power, strategic linkages, and action toward social transformation.

True solidarity can transcend the barriers of race, class, gender, age, and creed. It is both a gift and a responsibility.

Elizabeth S. Tapia

See also: FEMINIST THEOLOGIES IN THE THIRD WORLD, JUSTICE, OPTION FOR THE POOR, THIRD WORLD WOMEN'S THEOLOGIES.

SPIRITUALITIES

Spirituality is our connectedness to God, to our human roots, to the rest of nature, to one another and to ourselves. It is the experience of the Holy Spirt moving us and our communities to be life-giving and life-affirming. Throughout the Third World, spirituality is celebrated in songs, rituals, and symbols that show the energizing Spirit animating the community to move together in response to God.

Spirituality is a cry for life and for the power to resist death and the agents of death. It provides the strength to go on, for it is the assurance that God is in the struggle. It fulfills the quest for self-discovery, self-affirmation, and self-inclusion, so the whole human community can live fully as human beings created by God.

Different cultures and contexts in the Third World enrich all of Christian spirituality. African peoples call Christians to a life-force that is earthed and efficacious, where life is celebrated through myths and symbols in a spirituality that creates and sustains community. An emphasis on the importance of balance and harmony is brought by Asian Christians who draw on traditional Asian religious practices. From Latin America comes an awareness of the blessedness of the poor and the necessity to analyze those conditions that lead to and sustain poverty. From indigenous peoples flow respect for the land, a sense of community and of close communion with God, and new sources of spiritual energy. The marginalized peoples of the First World bring gifts of self-naming and identity and a sense of the importance of human dignity and human freedom.

Christian spirituality in the Third World is rooted in the Jesus of the gospels, the Jesus who experiences conflicts, undergoes suffering, shares in joys and sorrows, and who remains faithful to his mission even when it brings him death on the cross. Following Jesus means being critical of power within the structures of society when they engender injustice and oppression. It means working for a just society, feeding the hungry, and fighting for the liberation of those who are oppressed.

Christian spirituality in the Third World is also rooted in the Bible, the same Bible that was formerly read *to* the people and that was used as an instrument for the spiritual conquest of America, Africa, and Asia. Now the people read it for themselves. It has been necessary to free the Bible from wrongful, oppressive readings and to recover its text, its history, and its inspiration on the basis of local traditions of revelation and salvation. God's self-revelation is, first of all, present in our created world and in other peoples' cultures and religious traditions from the beginning. The Bible, then, is a second book of revelation, revealing the fullness of God's word as it is interpreted and appropriated by the community in a spirit of prayer, faith, and celebration.

The goal of spirituality is to support the fullness of life. Spirituality is that which permits us to make sense of life. In the words of Indian theologian Samuel Rayan, "As our method is incarnate in our theology, so our spirituality is enfleshed in our commitment to and work for the liberation of the oppressed." To be committed to the people's struggle for life is to be committed to a world where there shall be justice, freedom, and new respect for all of creation. Commitment varies with the particular context of struggle. To a Ghanaian it might mean speaking for the rights of women in church and society. For a Mexican American it might involve leading a group of poor men and women to demonstrate against the policies of a local bank. For a Filipino, perhaps mobilizing to protest the renewed U.S. military presence. To a South Korean it might mean working toward the reunification of the Korean people and for peace. Commitment might lead to harassment, marginalization, ecclesiastical sanctions, arrest, torture, or even death. To be committed means there is no cost too great when one joins God's mission to make the world a place where life is valued for all of God's creation. Faith in Jesus Christ and love of neighbor must lead the Christian to a concrete commitment to the struggle for the liberation of the oppressed and the transformation of the world.

Various EATWOT Members

Bibliography
K. C. Abraham and Bernadette Mbuy-Beya, eds., *Spirituality of the Third World: A Cry for Life* (Maryknoll, N.Y.: Orbis Books, 1994).
Virginia Fabella, Peter K. H. Lee, and David Kwang-sun Suh, eds., *Asian Christian Spirituality: Reclaiming Traditions* (Maryknoll, N.Y.: Orbis Books, 1992).

Engelbert Mveng, ed., *Spiritualité et libération en Afrique* (Paris: L'Harmattan, 1987).

Jon Sobrino, *Spirituality of Liberation: Toward Political Holiness* (Maryknoll, N.Y.: Orbis Books, 1988).

SYMBOLS

The term "symbol" is from the Greek noun *symbolon* whose verb form *symballein* means literally "to throw together." The term is derived from an ancient Greek practice whereby a contract or agreement between two people was often sealed by breaking a coin, a piece of pottery, or a ring into two pieces and each partner keeping one half. The two pieces, called *symbola*, when brought together, served to identify the legitimate partners in the contract. The word later came to mean a sign that bound members of a group together. In ecclesiastical usage it designates the profession of faith, the creed, that binds Christians together, and the images and instruments through which aspects of that faith are expressed. For example, the fish is an ancient Christian symbol for Christ.

In modern usage symbol means something in which a reality expresses itself. It may be natural, as smoke is a symbol of fire, or socially constituted, as a dove is a symbol of peace. Socially constituted symbols are chosen based on their natural qualities in relation to the realities they are intended to express. Symbols are rooted in human experience, and are essential to human interaction. All communication uses symbols. Human beings spontaneously identify with, respond to, and let their behavior be guided by symbols.

In Third World cultures where, in general, most people live very close to nature and do not separate the sacred from the secular, and where the spiritual realm is seen as a dimension of the material, symbols play a crucial role in social relations and in religion. An animal, fish, or tree may be the symbol of identity and unity of a clan. Rituals heavily loaded with symbols make up the center of religious worship, and sacrifice, which involves the slaughtering of animals, is a high point in these rituals. Sickness or any evil threatening the life of the community is cast away by symbolic gestures in rituals. For example, in the traditional religion of the Ibibio people of southern Nigeria, to heal an illness thought to be caused by the water goddess, a white hen is offered in sacrifice. A hen is offered because a female deity is involved, and the white color symbolizes the purity and beauty of the water goddess. The offering is made at a riverside, which symbolizes the dwelling place of the goddess. The hen is waved over the head of the patient and then thrown alive into the river to symbolize giving the hen's life to the goddess in exchange for that of the patient.

Religious symbols are polysemous and guide the mind to encounter the ultimate. Because theology deals with the ultimate reality, theological language is highly symbolic. In inculturation theology in Africa, for example, Christ is symbolized as Ancestor or Elder Brother; the church is symbolized as family; and the communion of saints as the assembly of ancestors. The Christian religion centers on Jesus the Christ as the symbol of God's renewal of creation, and Christian theology has to do with God's continued renewal of creation in Christ through the Holy Spirit. When Third World theology describes Christ as liberator, this is symbolic language pointing to the liberation movement as a process of the renewal of creation in Christ.

In every age, theological symbols respond to the needs of the age, which, in turn, change according to societal situations. Inculturation and liberation motifs have become basic theological symbols of our age in the Third World. The struggle of Third World people today for identity and liberation symbolizes concern for cultural diversity and justice in the world. That Third World people make up the majority of the Christian population and are the most vibrant Christians today and yet are at the margin of Christian history symbolizes God's saving hand in human history calling for the abolition of boundaries that exclude and divide the human community.

Justin S. Ukpong

See also: INCULTURATION, LIBERATION, LIBERATION THEOLOGIES, WORSHIP/ RITUALS.

Bibliography
Ranjini Rebara, *A Search for Symbols: An Asian Experiment* (Manila: CCA Women's Concerns, 1990).
Elochukwu E. Uzukwu, *Worship as Body Language: Introduction to Christian Worship: An African Orientation* (Collegeville, Minn.: Liturgical Press, 1997).
Justin S. Ukpong, *Sacrifice—African and Biblical: A Comparative Study of Ibibio Sacrifices and Levitical Sacrifices* (Rome: Urbaniana University Press, 1987).

SYNCRETISM

Syncretism continues to be a critical and controversial issue in global theological discourse, partly accentuated by the increasing number of voices from the Third World. However, many Third World theologies, particularly those born out of liberatory praxis, tend to reject the notion of syncretism as the indiscriminate mixing of religions. Rooted in a vision of an "oppression-and-exclusion-free" reign of God, they insist upon the need for vigilance against any betrayal of the Christian faith, but they also hold that cultural interaction and symbolic transformation of the gospel are critical for the gospel to be liberative and relevant in diverse contexts. In fact, syncretistic processes may be seen within the biblical corpus itself and in the whole of the history of the church.

Attitudes to syncretism depend upon the social location of the theologian. In the past, pronouncements of syncretism have been made by those in privileged places of power within the church, defenders often of institutional knowledge and integrity. Power has been a critical issue in any re-evaluation of syncretism. Further, syncretism appears to be unsettling and pejorative when seen from an essentialist, static, and binary mind-set, which is often characteristic of colonial or Eurocentric worldviews. Within such a world, religious identities and truth are often seen as fixed, sealed, and once-for-all delivered entities. Syncretism is seen as an external and primarily intellectual process of "amalgamating" two or more incompatible religions.

In contrast, most Third World theologies are formed within a postcolonial framework in the midst of conflict and struggles. Religious identities are not seen as fixed. Religion and culture are seen as nothing if they do not concern *people*. As people-centered, religious identities are relational, dynamic, and integrative. Religious meaning emerges within a process of communal interaction and social judgments. Therefore, syncretism, the process of integrating the gospel into cultural codes, is seen as an inevitable part of living the faith within the matrix of the Third World. Consequent diversity and difference are held as significant. One can live with partial understanding and in liminal situations. Synthesis and hybridity need not be feared; instead, they may point to creative new ways of being in the world.

As all growth necessarily involves mutation, formation of new religious identities also involves syncretism. There is life-generating as well as death-dealing syncretism. Unwitting accommodation of the gospel to individualism and capitalist consumerism among many Christians in the West is clearly a form of death-dealing syncretism, as is the uncritical acceptance of the attitude of patriarchal cultures toward women in the life of the churches. Therefore, it is critical that Christians across cultures commit themselves irrevocably to mutual accountability and critique, and that together they identify the signs of authenticity of Christian faith and life as they engage in liberating praxis for a domination-and-fragmentation-free human community in the perspective of the reign of God as manifested in Christ Jesus.

Christopher Duraisingh

See also: CONTEXTUALIZATION, CULTURE, INCULTURATION, SOCIAL LOCATION.

Bibliography

Leonardo Boff, *Church, Charism and Power: Liberation Theology and Institutional Church* (New York: Crossroad, 1985).

Gerald D. Gort, H. M. Vroom, et al., eds., *Dialogue and Syncretism. An Interdisciplinary Approach* (Grand Rapids, Mich.: Eerdmans, 1989).

Robert Schreiter, *The New Catholicity: Theology Between the Global and the Local* (Maryknoll, N.Y.: Orbis Books, 1998).

Charles Stewart and Rosalind Shaw, *Syncretism/Anti-syncretism: The Politics of Religious Synthesis* (London: Routledge, 1994).

T

TAIWANESE THEOLOGIES

Contemporary Taiwanese theologies draw upon the history and cultures of Taiwan for their resources. Similar to other Third World theologies, Taiwanese theologies concern the social, political, and economic well-being and, most particularly, the identity problems of the Taiwanese people. Generally speaking, they are constructed upon the missionary experiences of the churches as well as the historical and cultural experiences of the people.

Christian mission in Taiwan occurred in three separate waves. The first took place in the seventeenth century when Dutch missionaries from the Reformed Church accompanied the Dutch East India Company to southern Taiwan and began evangelizing the aborigines. Several years later the Spanish arrived in northern Taiwan, establishing the Catholic church. The second wave began in the middle of the nineteenth century, when Catholic and Presbyterian missionaries rekindled Christian evangelism. After the end of World War II, the third wave began, consisting primarily of the arrival of mainstream Christian denominations from the Chinese mainland, along with the defeated Chinese nationalist government. The particularity of its historical experiences, especially colonization, has heavily influenced the development of its contextual theologies.

During the 1970s, the Presbyterian Church in Taiwan expressed its concerns with socio-political issues, domestic oppressions, and dictatorial domination. Then in the late 1970s, the Commission for Theological Concerns of the Christian Conference of Asia (CTC/CCA) initiated a series of consultations to search for motifs for contextual theologies in Asia. Two themes proposed by Taiwan's consultation were Homeland theology and *Chhut Thau Thin*. Both themes emphasized the historical experiences of suffering, including colonization, martial law, and the confusion and distortion of identity caused by the policies of the colonizers, especially contemporary threats of imperialism that might deny the rights of self-determination of the Taiwanese people.

Wang Hsien Chi, a former professor at Tainan Theological College and Seminary, is known as a founder of Homeland theology. He has examined issues relating to the ethnic, cultural, and political identity of the Taiwanese people. Huang Po Ho has investigated the themes of *Chhut Thau Thin* ("to raise one's head out of darkness to see the blue

195

sky and breathe the spring air"), a traditional proverb of Taiwan that he interprets as a hope for liberation. *Chhut Thau Thin* theology is based on the historical experiences of the struggle for self-determination of the Taiwanese people by means of an analysis that intersects the gospel and culture. These two theologies differ primarily in their methods, with Homeland theology more of a political theology, and *Chhut Thau Thin* a theology that relates culture and gospel.

During this same period of time, the Catholic Church focused more on issues of inculturation based on the traditional cultures of China.

Huang Po Ho

See also: COLONIZATION, CONTEXTUALIZATION, INCULTURATION, INDIGENOUS THEOLOGIES.

Bibliography
Huang Po-Ho, *A Theology of Self-determination* (Tainan: Chhut Thau Thin Theological Study Center, 1996).

THAI THEOLOGY

Thailand, called Siam until 1939, is a country in Southeast Asia. Thailand, or *Muang Thai*, means "the Land of Free Men." Thai people have always been proud of their freedom as Thailand is the only Southeast Asian country that has not been colonized by the West. Today, it is governed by a democratic system with a prime minister as the elected head of government. However, the king still plays an important role and is highly respected as a spiritual leader by all Thai people. When Thailand was hit by an economic crisis in 1997, it was the king who advised the Thai people on how to cope with the crisis.

Even though Buddhism is the main religion in Thailand, religious freedom does exist and the Thai government recognizes Christian organizations and churches. The first Christian missionaries to arrive in Thailand were the French Jesuits in 1665. The first Protestant missionaries reached Bangkok in 1828. Two major contributions made by both Roman Catholic and Protestant missionaries were Western forms of education and health care. Many Christian schools acted as agencies to propagate Christianity to students, irrespective of their religious background.

The most challenging task for Thai Christians is communicating the gospel to Thai Buddhists. Thai Christians have followed the Western Christian teaching of belief in eternal life. The Lord Buddha taught that the cause of suffering derives from human desire. For many Buddhists, eternal life can mean long-lasting suffering. Many Thai Buddhists understand that their suffering derives from the law of *karma*. Thai Christians, by contrast, believe that suffering derives from human sin, which causes guilt in those who have done wrong. This Christian teaching poses a problem in Thai culture, where wrong-doing leads to feelings of shame rather than guilt.

Thai Buddhists believe that a person can do nothing but accept one's birth, age, illness, and death. Thai Christians emphasize grace and the salvation offered to all through the life, death, and resurrection of Jesus. While Buddhism and Christianity in Thailand move in different directions, the book of Ecclesiastes in the Old Testament contains teachings that are able to bridge the gap between Christianity and Buddhism.

Seree Lorgunpai

See also: INTERRELIGIOUS DIALOGUE.

THEOLOGICAL METHODOLOGIES

The awareness that theology can and must be regional has taken shape in recent decades. Most Third World theologians, that is, theologians of the world's South, now realize that it is impossible to speak about a general and universal theological method without taking into account that it is inevitably situated historically and socially. One cannot speak about a particular and regional theological methodology without connecting it in its basic foundations with the more general type.

Faith, which is theology's object, has one dimension that is universal and perennial, and another that is particular and historical. Accordingly, theological method must also encompass these two dimensions. In this sense, there is no separate method for liberation theology or women's theology; what exists is an overall theological method into whose *organon* the respective liberating or feminist apparatus must be integrated. Theological methodologics of the Third World must always be situated within the general horizon of fundamental theological methodology; otherwise, they will lose their radical identity and originality.

Object and perspective of theological method. The object of theology is God in God's own mystery, the God of revelation. The revealed God, however, is the God who liberates the oppressed people and who has sent Jesus as messiah of the poor and sinners. Therefore the very notion of the biblical God includes the idea of liberation, understood in its concreteness and in its full radical sense. The mystery of God will always be the central theme or the subject of theology. Theology sees everything with God's eyes and theology's proper perspective is the faith perspective.

While the mystery of God is the formal object of theology, its material object is everything: God and the world, the church, and society.

Inasmuch as faith is the inheritance of the entire church, theology is always ecclesial. It must make its own the patrimony accumulated by the great tradition of the people of God, such as the teaching of the church councils, theologians, lives of the saints, and popular piety.

Faith, the deriving principle or source of theology, has three fundamental dimensions.

The *experiential dimension* corresponds to the *fides qua*. Faith is first the experience of mystery. All authentic theology is based on an experience of faith, a spirituality. Hence, in the world's South, we speak of the experience of God in the poor. Indeed, the poor constitute a privileged place, albeit not the only one, where God is manifest. The Bible and experience both justify speaking of a spiritual and epistemological privilege of the poor.

The *cognitive dimension* is the *fides quae*, faith that becomes doctrine and that seeks to be true. The primordial witness of Christian faith is recorded in sacred scripture. Here, likewise, the perspective of the poor provides a particular inflection. From that perspective, which is lived out especially in base communities, the biblical texts and the data of faith acquire a particular resonance, made up of concreteness, solidarity, and hope.

The *practical dimension* is the *fides formata*, that is, faith informed by love and its works. It is only when it is practiced that faith becomes truly intelligible. If faith sheds light on praxis, praxis likewise sheds light on faith by means of a dialectical return. The theologies of the South have highlighted the practical or liberating dimension of faith.

Secondary perspectives. Besides the clearly delimited topics within theology, other *problématiques* or approaches run through theological reflection and are significant. There are five in particular.

The *social or liberating perspective* takes up the dramatic question of the poor and the outcast, massively present in the South of the world. Liberation theology has arisen and become established around this *problématique*.

The *ethnic or cultural perspective* spells out the *problématique* of ethnic groups and of those who are different, including the issue of inculturation. That has been the starting point for black theologies and indigenous theologies.

The *feminist or gender perspective* discusses the patriarchy that has existed for millennia and types of women's emancipation. Out of this concern has emerged the now flourishing feminist theology, which has particular connotations in the South of the world, stressing the synergy of gender and socio-structural change.

The *ecumenical perspective* strives to take into account the riches of other Christian confessions and the truth of other religions. In the world's South, this twofold exchange emphasizes grassroots work and commitment to justice.

The *ecological perspective* strives to overcome a strictly anthropocentric worldview by considering human beings in their organic connection to nature. The South's ecological theology seeks to connect the "cry of the earth" to the "cry of the poor" (Leonardo Boff).

These perspectives are not all situated on the same level. The social-liberating perspective seems to run through everything so extensively and intensively that it tends to affect all theology, no matter how general or particular.

In order to take into account the *problématique* that underlies the different perspectives, theology makes use of analytical mediations. These are the theoretical instruments that theology borrows from the existing culture and uses as "auxiliary sciences." A socio-liberatory theology, for example, makes use of the social sciences, such as sociology or economics; theology from an ethnic perspective employs anthropology, history, and so forth. However, the appropriation of other sciences within theology is done under the critical governance of faith. In the field of social sciences, this is valid not only for the Marxist tradition, but for the liberal one as well.

Philosophy, for its part, enters in a constitutive manner into theological discourse insofar as the latter presupposes the question of being and of existence. The South seeks to give due appreciation to popular wisdom, the spontaneous philosophy of the people.

All these particular perspectives do not in any manner replace the primary and general perspective of theology: the perspective of faith. Rather, they connect with it.

Proper language of theology. Theological language is necessarily analogical: it speaks through comparisons. There are two types of analogy: conceptual (God as being, goodness, and so forth), which is preferred by scholarly theology; and metaphorical analogy, which uses images and symbols (God as Father, and so forth), which is preferred by the Bible and the people, and in pastoral activity. The theologies of the South particularly emphasize metaphorical language, because of its evocative and mobilizing power.

A theologian, however, must be very aware that no language is adequate to the ineffable Mystery. There is a growing awareness in the world's South that the ultimate language of theology is non-language: the silence of adoration, of course, but also the silence of committed love.

Goals of theology. Three goals have been proposed: knowledge of God (the theoretical end), experience of God (the affective end), and obedience to the will of God (the practical end). This latter is the basis on which the theologies of the South, anchored in the practice of faith, articulate these goals. Theological knowledge does not have itself as its own end, but rather it is aimed as its mediate and indirect end at experience of God.

Theological knowledge must end in the practice of faith. Such is the ultimate end of theology on earth: serving faith as it is experienced and practiced. The theologies of the South insist on this, fully aware that a theology devoid of critical seriousness renders poor service to both experience and practice.

Three moments of theological method. We need to distinguish between the method by which theology is produced, the theoretical-epistemological viewpoint; and the method by which it is presented, the practical-expository viewpoint. From the strictly theoretical-epistemological standpoint, it must be said that the process of theological construction takes place in three moments. The starting point is the positive moment. It is the memory of what God has said or done on behalf of the world. It is a hermeneutic, and therefore critical, reason. In theological practice, that means that the Bible must be the first and most important book in all theology, inasmuch as it is the "soul of all theology."

In the theoretical or speculative moment, theological reason strives, insofar as possible, to clarify the mysteries of faith, by analyzing and systematizing data and raising new questions.

The practical or operational moment, largely ignored in classical and modern theology, is the privileged function in the theologies of the South for which "acting" represents a constitutive moment of all true theology.

However, from the practical-expository standpoint (whether pedagogical or pastoral) that is preferred in the South due to the committed nature of its theology, the theological and methodological process follows a rhythm that is different but also threefold, namely the method of see (analytical mediation), judge (hermeneutical mediation), and act (practical mediation).

If the starting point of one method or another seems to be different, that is simply because of their concern, which is theoretical-epistemological on one side and practical-expository on the other. Even so, there is an underlying epistemological correspondence between them. Whether one process or another is used is entirely a matter of convenience: the important thing is that faith and life be brought into confrontation; the entry way does not matter. Placing the pole of life as constitutive of theological method is one of the greatest strengths of the theologies of the world's South.

Clodovis Boff

See also: EPISTEMOLOGICAL BREAK, FEMINIST THEOLOGIES IN THE THIRD WORLD, HERMENEUTICAL CIRCLE, LIBERATION THEOLOGIES, OPTION FOR THE POOR, PARADIGM SHIFT, SOCIAL ANALYSIS, SOCIAL LOCATION.

Bibliography
K.C. Abraham, ed., *Third World Theologies: Commonalities and Divergences* (Maryknoll, N.Y.: Orbis Books, 1990).
Clodovis Boff, *Theology and Praxis: Epistemological Foundations* (Maryknoll, N.Y.: Orbis Books, 1987).
Leonardo Boff and Clodovis Boff, *Introducing Liberation Theology* (Maryknoll, N.Y.: Orbis Books, 1987).
Jon Sobrino, *The Principle of Mercy: Taking the Crucified People from the Cross* (Maryknoll, N.Y.: Orbis Books, 1994).

THEOLOGY OF STRUGGLE

The theology of struggle is a name for the theology that has emerged in the Philippines. It received its name in the 1970s, especially at the height of the Filipino struggle during the years of martial law, when some theologians reflected on their involvement in the national struggle. But it has deep historical roots, for Filipino Christians have reflected on their struggle against foreign and domestic forces ever since Spanish colonization.

It may be said that the theology of struggle belongs to the genre of liberation theology, but its distinctive emphasis is on the struggle even as it aims for liberation. The struggle is not simply the process that is directed toward the goal, because the struggle itself is constitutive of the goal. When the struggle is seen as a journey that is in itself an experience of a transformed life, it makes sense that the theologians of struggle speak simultaneously of the spirituality of struggle. Struggle is an expression of a deep spirituality.

While the theology of struggle focuses on the transformation of individual lives and society, it points not only to a struggle outside of theology, but to theology itself as a domain of struggle. The theology of struggle is not only an interpretation of the struggle, but is at the same time a struggle for interpretation. Theology is an arena of struggle, and Filipino theologians know that they must reclaim their right to theologize.

Moreover, as a theology that is expressive of the people's plight and faith, the theology of struggle can only be a theology of the people. It is for this reason that some Filipino theologians prefer to speak of "people's theology." Not to be forgotten in the use of the generic term "people" is the significant and active role that women have played in the struggle and in the articulation of a people's theology. A people's theology can only claim to be truly expressive of the people if it is informed by the oppression, struggle, and vision of women. In short, the theology of struggle is a political, epistemological, and theological necessity.

Eleazar S. Fernandez

See also: FEMINIST THEOLOGIES IN THE THIRD WORLD, LIBERATION THEOLOGIES.

Bibliography
Currents in Philippine Theology, Kalinangan Book Series II (Quezon City, Philippines: Institute of Religion and Culture, 1992).
Eleazar Fernandez, *Toward a Theology of Struggle* (Maryknoll, N.Y.: Orbis Books, 1994).

THIRD WORLD

The term "Third World" is understood in various ways, from a purely geographical sense to a sociopolitical description. It was originally used in 1952 by the French demographer Alfred Sauvy, who saw similarity between the nations moving toward independence from colonial powers and the Third Estate in France demanding freedom and equality during the French Revolution. The term soon became a useful designation of the international reality: the "First World" referred to the powerful, capitalist nations, mostly of the West; the "Second" to the socialist countries of the East; and the "Third" to the non-aligned "underdeveloped" and "developing" countries in the rest of the world.

Currently "Third World" is used as a self-designation of peoples who have been excluded from power and the authority to shape their own lives and destiny. As such it has a supra-geographic denotation, describing a social condition marked by social, political, religious, and cultural oppressions that render people powerless and expendable. Thus Third World also encompasses those people in the First World who form a dominated and marginalized minority.

For many years, the term "Third World" has been widely used, but toward the last years of the twentieth century, it has been called into question, especially after the demise of the Second World in 1989. Substitutes have been forwarded (such as "South" or the "underside of history") but a term such as "two-thirds world" seems to indicate numbers rather than a quality of life.

Theological groups in the Third World, for example, EATWOT, affirm the term as valid and significant for their self-identification, and maintain it for its theological and evangelical relevance as an alternative voice.

Virginia Fabella, MM

Bibliography
Kofi Buenor Hadjor, *Dictionary of Third World Terms* (London: Penguin Books, 1993).

THIRD WORLD DEBT

Third World debt refers to the massive borrowing, which has remained largely unpaid, undertaken by Third World governments in the 1970s. Oil-rich countries produced an excess of petrodollars that were deposited in commercial banks in the First World. Hence, money became easily available at attractive interest rates to developing countries, most of which were under dictatorial rule at that time. Due to corruption and faulty development projects, funds that could have alleviated poverty and served national interests were often misdirected, with most ending up in dictators' private coffers.

Although onerous debts are not confined to the Third World, the problem is not so much the amount owed but the capacity of the debtor country to service the loan and to pay back the principal. In 1992, for example, Mexico publicly announced its inability to do either, which triggered the "debt crisis." The increase in oil prices and in interest and currency exchange rates, together with falls in commodity export prices and low levels of inflation, caused foreign debts to skyrocket. Mexico's problem was not unique.

The World Bank and International Monetary Fund (IMF) have initiated structural adjustment programs (SAPs) that entitle debtor countries that comply to receive new loans in order to pay off old ones. SAPs not only ensure that loans are repaid but they also accelerate the integration of local economies into the global economy. Aggravated by the flight of capital and misguided priorities, SAPs have neither decreased Third World debt nor improved the economic well-being or social condition of the people, especially the poor.

As debts piled upon debts, there was no way out, especially for the low-income, highly indebted countries. The need to reduce the debt burden became evident, but none of the proposed strategies for debt relief went far enough. Concerned groups in both the First and Third Worlds see debt cancellation, rather than just debt relief, as the only pragmatic and moral solution. It is on record that Third World debtors have already paid back much more than they had originally borrowed. Concerned Christians initiated the Jubilee 2000 campaign, an ecumenical, worldwide movement "to cancel the crushing international debt of impoverished counties by the new millennium." The movement takes its inspiration from the book of Leviticus in the Hebrew Scriptures, which describes a year of jubilee every fifty years to correct social inequalities and cancel debts. The movement calls for a definitive debt cancellation not conditioned on policy reforms that perpetuate poverty or environmental degradation, but which would benefit ordinary people and facilitate their participation in determining the priorities of their national and local economies.

Virginia Fabella, MM

See also: CAPITALISM, COLONIZATION, GLOBALIZATION, POVERTY, THIRD WORLD.

Bibliography
Pat Adams, *Odious Debts* (Toronto: Earthscan, 1991).
Susan George, *A Fate Worse Than Debt* (New York: Grove Weidenfeld, 1990).
Dale Hidelbrand, *To Pay Is to Die: The Philippine Foreign Debt Crisis* (Davao City, Philippines: Philippine International Forum, 1991).
Sergio Schlesinger, "External Debt, A Third World Perspective," *SEDOS Bulletin* 26/11 (December 15, 1994).

THIRD WORLD THEOLOGIES IN THE FIRST WORLD

Introduction

There are four major groups of racial-ethnic minorities in the United States who are doing theology: Native Americans, African Americans, Hispanic Americans, and Asian Americans. People of African, Asian, and Caribbean descent in Britain, as well as some other groups, are also undertaking theological reflection. Each of these groups has complex and different histories and cultures that have influenced the origin and the development of their theological discourse. Theology is always made when people seek to understand the ultimate meaning of their existence in relation to their neighbors and their God. Who are we? Why were we created? What is our purpose in the world? *How* a people answer these questions and the *sources* from which they derive the answers define the nature of their theological discourse.

To be oppressed means that a people's answers to questions about their identity have been imposed upon them. In the United States, racial-ethnic minorities live in a society whose religio-cultural and sociopolitical values have been defined by an ideology of white supremacy. The English Puritans who landed at Plymouth Rock in 1620 believed that they were God's chosen people, the New Israel, elected by God to civilize and christianize the "New World." Their idea of Christianity emphasized not only the Calvinist theme of the absolute sovereignty of God but also a similar rule of the white Anglo-Saxon race over others. The dominant expression of Christianity in the United States has been primarily Protestant. However, the Catholic Church, though a minority denomination and often itself persecuted, supported the white Protestant ruling class in their justification of the right of whites to exterminate, enslave, and segregate non-Europeans. Protestants and Catholics not only provided religious justification of the government's exploitation of minorities, they also oppressed them within their own communions. The indigenous people, Blacks, Hispanics, and Asians were defined as the "Other" who either had to be converted to the "white Christian way of life" by willingly accepting their inferior status, or they did not deserve to exist. "The only good Indian is a dead Indian" was the expression of this value in the popular mind of white America in relation to the original people of the continent. Similar dehumanizing characterizations were made in regard to minorities from Africa, Latin America, and Asia. To be "colored" in the United States meant to be only partly human—"three-fifths" was the portion set for African slaves by the Founding Fathers in the Constitution of 1787.

As long as racial-ethnic minorities accepted their assigned places in the society as defined by the dominant white race, they were often allowed to exist. Many minorities, however, resisted the white definitions of their humanity and fiercely asserted their right to define the terms of their existence. The history of America is also the history of their resistance. It is a history from the *underside* of the American story, largely invisible to others who do not share or identify with its legacy.

To understand the rise of liberation theologies among racial-ethnic minorities in the United States, it is necessary to know something of the history of their struggle to be recognized as human beings in a land that defined them as non-persons. Our liberation theologies have not been borrowed from Latin America, Africa, or Asia, even though we have been greatly stimulated by our brothers and sisters of the Third World and have learned much from them. Our thinking about God, however, has been initiated by and created out of our different cultural histories and our continuing struggles for freedom in the United States.

Liberation theologies among U.S. minorities cannot be correctly interpreted by using the historical and theological categories of white people. Neither can they be placed in one general theological framework, as if they shared the same cultural history and perspective on God. As the liberation theologies in Latin America, Africa, and Asia are different, so are the theological reflections among minorities in the United States. We are not only different; our differences sometimes clash. Racial-ethnic minorities often live in separate communities and the white ruling classes are often quite successful in dividing us from each other, thereby creating animosities between our communities. Many of us, however, are determined to overcome the barriers that separate us so we can make a common cause in our struggle for freedom. But we cannot forge a genuine solidarity with each other unless we show mutual respect and appreciation for the uniqueness of each other's cultural history.

James H. Cone

Asian American

Asian American theology refers to the theology articulated by those Asian Americans who address theological issues from Asian American perspectives. Asian American theologians include all Asian descendants, whether born in the U.S. or naturalized, as long as they grapple with Asian American theological issues. From the beginning, Asian American theologies have voiced theologies for their churches rather than for academia.

Japanese American. In the early 1970s before his election as bishop of the United Methodist Church, Roy Sano envisaged an apocalyptic role for Asian American Christians. His apocalyptic understanding was of a sudden collapse of the unjust and racist power structures. If such an apocalyptic ending would not come about on its own, he suggested that we make it possible. In the same period, Paul Nagano developed an Asian American indigenous theology. Its strategy was called "AI Power." In Japanese, AI stands for Asian identity and love. It involves the humanness of the people as well as participation, belongingness, and independence. In addition, Nagano considered theology as an agent of change in society. Since the early 1990s, Rita Nakashima Brock has articulated her poignant christology from an Asian feminist perspective. Opposing the unilateral interpretation of divine power projected in patriarchal christologies, she proposes an erotic, relational power of God based on Asian sensibilities and process theology. Since the mid-1990s, Fumitaka Matsuoka has sought unity in the effort of liberating minority groups and has explored an alternative way of understanding race relations. Through truth-telling, reconciliation, and interracial community-building, he works to achieve a new form of race relations.

Chinese American. In the 1970s, Chinese American Wesley Woo asserted that theology is our integrity of faith in God who calls us to full and authentic humanity. For Woo, it must be founded on the Scriptures, insight-action, and the corporate context of Asian American experiences. His theological methodology consists of prophetic confrontation, the debunking of dehumanizing realities, and the understanding of corporate salvation. In the 1990s, David Ng advocated a sojourner theology of Asian American churches. He treated sojourners as pioneers—people on the Way (Christ and Tao) to the community of hope and vulnerability. His visions moved toward diversity, unity, and solidarity.

Korean American. Since the 1970s, Sang Hyun Lee has developed his "pilgrim theology" to comfort and guide Korean American churches. Introducing "pilgrimage" as a theological paradigm, Lee interprets Korean immigrants' marginality as a sign of a sacred calling and finds its ultimate form in Jesus. In the 1990s, based on the yin-yang philosophy, Lee Jung Young worked on the creativity of marginality. Rather than moving a group from a margin to the center, he redefined the meaning of margin as the place of creative matrix. In the throes of the Los Angeles eruptions in 1992, Andrew Sung Park developed his theology of transmutation based on the Asian, particularly Korean, culture. He sees *han* (the long-accumulated suffering of a victim) as a critical problem and offers the virtue of seeing of Asian culture as its method of social transformation. Genuine seeing elicits mutual enhancement (transformity) that surpasses the unity and diversity of the multicultural society. In contrast with feminism and womanism, Young Hertig uses the term *yinism* for Asian American feminism. *Yinism* seeks to overcome the false dichotomy deriving from a dualistic paradigm: margin against center, male against female, and humans against nature. Through the holistic and dynamic principles of *yin* and *yang, yinism* seeks to heal the problematic relationships of gender, class, and race. Ai Ra Kim stresses the role of religious institutions within Asian-American churches. By using the authority of the Bible, the Korean American church perpetuates institutional sexism at home and in the community. She calls for reform in the church. In a similar vein, Jung Ha Kim is concerned about the role of religious institutions within ethnic communities and the relative importance of gender and race/ethnicity in shaping the identities of women of color. By examining the interrelationships among religion, gender, race/ethnicity and social status, she brings her socio-theological insight to women's studies, race/ethnicity studies, and the Asian American church.

Although diverse, Asian American theologies have grappled with the issue of ethnic identity and have pursued ecclesiastical and social transformation through an evolutionary rather than a revolutionary vision.

Andrew Sung Park

See also: *HAN/HAN-PURI*, CHRISTOLOGIES: ASIAN AMERICAN, THIRD WORLD WOMEN'S THEOLOGIES: ASIAN AMERICAN.

Bibliography
Rita Nakashima Brock, *Journeys by Heart: A Christology of Erotic Power* (New York: Crossroad, 1988).
Lee Jung Young, *Marginality: The Key to Multicultural Theology* (Minneapolis: Fortress Press, 1995).
Fumitaka Matsuoka, *Out of Silence: Emerging Themes in Asian American Churches* (Cleveland, Ohio: United Church Press, 1995).
David Ng, ed., *People on the Way: Asian North Americans Discovering Christ, Culture, and Community* (Valley Forge, Penn.: Judson Press, 1996).
Andrew Sung Park, *Racial Conflict and Healing: An Asian-American Theological Perspective* (Maryknoll, N.Y.: Orbis Books, 1996).

Black Liberation Theology in Britain

Black liberation theology in Britain is a means by which black people of African, Asian, and Caribbean descent have made sense of the ideas of God, and humanity made in the image of God. It is also the interpretive instrument by which they oppose all attempts to justify the denial of black humanity. British black theology, then, is a contextual response of Third World people who, by design or default, find themselves living in the First World.

The contextual realities of black people in Britain are shaped by many factors, including the influences of the slave trade, imperialism, colonialism, and neo-colonialism. In addition, there are the historic and contemporary inequities in economic, political, and socio-cultural spheres. Confronting these challenges are the tenacity and outright determination of black people to insist upon their dignity as human beings made in the image of God, and therefore endowed with the right and responsibility to so live. Increasingly, too, the challenge of the young black is for respect, not as immigrant, but as full citizen.

In the midst of and in response to these realities, black liberation theology in Britain has followed two clear routes. First, the sheer presence of black Christians in Britain has led to an assumptive and prophetic theology that is legitimized by a theological anthropology based upon humanity made in the image of God. Because God has created every person from the same physical and spiritual substance, all are of equal value in their God-given diversity. This theological premise insists simply and profoundly that "I am"; it does not so much *seek* liberation from oppression as *take* it, without regard for those who appear to deny this reality.

Second, black liberation theology in Britain reacts and protests against the scandalizing injustice of racism, white elitism, and black exclusion. The reality is that black people exist in Britain—socially, economically, and politically—as weak minorities who are constantly oppressed by personal and institutional racism based upon a white supremacist ideology.

Even within the church, black Christians find persistent attitudes of elitism in white-led churches, resulting in attempts at excluding blacks. This attempt at exclusion is prevalent from the church pews to the corridors of ecclesiastical power.

Britain has a rich tradition of black theologizing dating back at least to the slave trade epoch, including explicit and implicit forms, expressed orally and through writing. In the Middle Ages, literary forms were used as in, for example, the works of Olaudah Equiano and Ignatius Sancho. During the post-1950s period, believers engaged in both oral and activist forms. Today, as we enter the twenty-first century, literary and activist theologizing as means of engagement have become more dynamic.

A number of developments in praxis stand out, particularly since the 1950s. One of the most significant expressions of theological praxis has been the establishment of black-led (African, Asian, and Caribbean) churches across Britain. These have acted as seedbeds for the development of black self-worth, and as places to nurture black Christians for wider participation in all spheres of life in Britain. These black-led churches command community-wide respect and encourage black people belonging to "mainline" white-led denominations to take their rightful place within them. As a result, black caucuses have established themselves within these churches as instruments of empowerment. During the 1970s the demand for respect and the search for cultural and spiritual identity led to a form of black consciousness that resonated with the U.S. model, but which expressed itself in Britain in the form of Rastafarianism, an Afrocentric religion. By the 1990s this had given way to an embrace of Islam, in its black expressive form, particularly among younger black people. Other significant developments include the formation of black-led church agencies, ecumenical projects, social and economic initiatives, and increasing political involvement. Publications by black theologians appear with greater frequency in academic studies and reports of research. Three primary centers for training, research, and publication are the Black Theology in Britain Forum at The Centre for Black and White Christian Partnership, Birmingham; the Institute of Black Theology at the Urban Theology Unit, Sheffield; and the Black Faith in Britain Project at the University of Birmingham.

Joe Aldred

See also: BLACK CONSCIOUSNESS, RACISM, THIRD WORLD THEOLOGIES IN THE FIRST WORLD: BLACK THEOLOGY IN THE UNITED STATES.

Bibliography
Joe Aldred, *Preaching with Power: Sermons by Black Preachers* (London: Cassell, 1998).
Selwyn Arnold, *From Scepticism to Hope* (Nottingham: Grove Books Ltd., 1992).
Robert Beckford, *Jesus Is Dread: Black Theology and Black Culture in Britain* (London: DLT, 1998).

Black Theology in the United States

The term "black theology" first appeared as a description of a theological movement in the United States with the publication of James H. Cone's *Black Theology and Black Power* in 1969. Its meaning was derived from a community of African American clergy and lay persons who were struggling to understand the meaning of their identity as *black* and *Christian* in the white racist society of the United States, which also claimed to be Christian and the leader of the free world. If the Christian faith has nothing to do with black people's struggle for justice, as implied in the silence of America's white theologians regarding slavery and oppression, how then is it possible for African Americans to affirm their identity as being both black and Christian? What has the gospel of Jesus Christ to do with the black struggle for freedom in a society that refused to acknowledge African Americans as human beings? These were the questions that initiated the development of a black theology of liberation.

As a theological discipline, black theology arose out of the Civil Rights and Black Power Movements of the 1950s and 1960s, as defined by the life and work of Martin Luther King, Jr., and Malcolm X. The meaning of the word "black" in black theology was derived from the black nationalist philosophy of Malcolm X. The meaning of the term "theology" in the phrase was derived from Martin King. The idea of a black theology came into being as black clergy political activists attempted to reconcile Christianity and Black Power, Martin King and Malcolm X.

The historical roots of black theology, however, go back to the beginning of African slavery in the United States and the founding of black independent Baptist and Methodist churches in the late eighteenth and early nineteenth centuries. The central theological claim of black theology is that the God of the Exodus, prophets, and Jesus can be known only in the struggles of the poor for liberation. Christian theology, therefore, is language about God's liberating activity in the world on behalf of the freedom of the oppressed.

Because the public meaning of the Christian gospel has been almost exclusively identified with the dominant cultures of white Americans and Europeans, who are primarily responsible for the victimization of blacks and other colored peoples throughout the world, African-American theologians of the 1960s concluded that many Christian symbols had to be radically transformed and redefined in the light of the struggles of the poor for freedom. That was why they began to speak of a *black* theology of liberation, referring to God and Jesus as black in order to emphasize God's solidarity with the oppressed. Instead of turning to the white theologians of America and Europe for an analysis of the gospel, African Americans began to re-read the Bible in the light of their own history and culture, as well as the contemporary black liberation struggles.

James Cone published *A Black Theology of Liberation* in 1970 and *God of the Oppressed* in 1975. Other important interpreters of black theology in the U.S. included J. Deotis Roberts and Gayraud S. Wilmore.

During the 1980s and 1990s, black theology developed in three important directions: the rise of womanist theology; the emergence of new voices in biblical studies; and the return to the religion of African slaves.

Since African American women were invisible in the black male liberation theology, black women broke their silence and began to speak of "womanist theology." They derived the term "womanist" from Alice Walker's *In Search of Our Mothers' Gardens* (1983), where she defined it as "a black feminist" who is "committed to survival and wholeness of entire people, male and female." While black male theologians emphasized the biblical theme of liberation as defined by the Exodus, prophets, and Jesus, womanist theologians emphasized the theme of survival as defined by the biblical character, Hagar, whom God, in contrast to the Israelite slaves, did not liberate. Womanist theologians do not deny the importance of liberation as a biblical theme in the African-American community. Rather they claim that liberation is not the only theme in the Bible and the African-American community. Also present, especially among women, in scripture and in the black experience is the theme of survival. Womanist theology critiques black liberation theology for failing to take African-American women's experience seriously in their discourse about God. Prominent interpreters of womanist theology include: Delores Williams, Jacquelyn Grant, Kelly Brown Douglas, and Katie G. Cannon.

Although the biblical message of liberation defined the center of black theology from its beginning, academically trained biblical scholars were few in number. But since the publication of Cain H. Felder's groundbreaking work, *Troubling Biblical Waters: Race, Class, and Family*, African-American biblical scholars have begun to re-read the Bible in the light of the themes of liberation and justice and the "racial motifs in the biblical narratives." *Stony the Road We Trod: African American Biblical Interpretation*, edited by Cain H. Felder, represents five years of collaboration among African-American biblical scholars. They are challenging the Eurocentric focus of biblical scholarship and are discovering an African presence in the Bible that white biblical scholars either ignored or marginalized.

The third development in black theology is being shaped by a second generation of young black theologians who are seeking to deepen black theology by returning to its sources in the slave narratives, sermons, prayers, songs, and folklore. *Cut Loose Your Stammering Tongue*, edited by Dwight Hopkins and George Cumming, is their major text. Hopkins has also published *Shoes That Fit Your Feet: Sources for a Constructive Black Theology*. Both books identify the religion and culture of African slaves as the most important starting point for shaping the future direction of black theology.

Black women and men in all theological disciplines have begun a creative conversation and are working together for the improvement of the quality of life in the African American churches and community. Black theology arose out of black churches and continues to be closely linked with them. In the African American community, the struggle for liberation and survival is not alien to the black religious community but rather is an essential part of it.

James H. Cone

See also: BIBLE: AFRICAN AMERICAN, CHRISTOLOGIES: AFRICAN AMERICAN, THIRD WORLD WOMEN'S THEOLOGIES: AFRICAN AMERICAN.

Bibliography
James H. Cone and Gayraud S. Wilmore, eds., *Black Theology: A Documentary History, Vols. One and Two: 1966–1979, 1980–1992,* rev. ed. (Maryknoll, N.Y.: Orbis Books, 1993).
Delores Williams, *Sisters in the Wilderness: The Challenge of Womanist God-Talk* (Maryknoll, N.Y.: Orbis Books, 1993).

Hispanic

U.S. Hispanic (or U.S. Latino/a) theology emerged in the United States in the 1980s. For a number of years, Latin American liberation theology had influenced the pastoral and theological reflections of Latino/a Christians in the United States. Eventually, however, these pastoral workers and theologians felt the need to contextualize their reflection in the particular experience of the U.S. Latino/a community. They recognized that the sociohistorical context of Latinos/as living in the United States was distinct and, in significant ways, different from the Latin American context. Thus, to be true to the method they adopted from Latin American liberation theology, they would need to reflect explicitly and systematically on the praxis of the U.S. Latino/a community. The "fathers" of this theological movement were Virgilio Elizondo, among Catholics, and Justo González, among Protestants.

One salient characteristic of the U.S. Hispanic context is its complexity and diversity. The U.S. Latino/a community is diverse not only with respect to economic class, gender, race, and religious affiliation, but also with respect to country of origin, language (some U.S.-born Latinos/as grow up with little or no knowledge of Spanish), and tenure of residency in the United States. Many commonalities do exist: e.g., most U.S. Hispanics are poor. Nevertheless, any analysis of "the" U.S. Hispanic community should keep in mind the great diversity underlying the similarities.

Within this diversity, U.S. Hispanic theologians have pointed to certain key characteristics of the U.S. Hispanic sociohistorical context: the historical experience of *mestizaje*, racial-cultural marginalization, and popular religion. Drawing on his own experience as a Mexican American growing up in San Antonio, Texas, Virgilio Elizondo has written extensively on the experience of *mestizaje*, or racial-cultural mixture, as a locus for theological reflection. Reading the Christian tradition and scriptures through the "lens" of that historical experience, he has underscored the social and theological significance of Jesus Christ's Galilean Jewish identity. Coming from Galilee, a borderland of mixed races, cultures, and religions, Jesus was rejected by the elite of his time. Yet it was precisely among the *mestizos/as* of Galilee that God chose to become incarnate. Through the person of the *mestizo* Jesus, those persons who are racially and culturally marginalized are revealed as privileged witnesses to God's salvific action in the world (Elizondo).

The history of *mestizaje* in the "New World" remains forever marked by the violence and conquest that gave birth to the *mestizo* people of the Americas. A first *mestizaje* resulted from the attempt to impose European cultures on indigenous and African peoples; this second *mestizaje* involves the ongoing attempt by the dominant U.S. culture to impose its own values and worldview on Hispanics. Yet, paradoxically, it is among these victims of history that God's love and power are made manifest.

God's solidarity with U.S. Hispanics and all marginalized peoples is affirmed, above all, in popular religion. Elizondo and other U.S. Hispanic theologians have examined, for example, the theological, racial-cultural, and social significance of Our Lady of Guadalupe. As that aspect of U.S. Hispanic culture most treasured by the community and, thus, most immune to assimilation, popular religion remains an essential source of identity in the face of a dominant culture that encourages and, indeed, demands assimilation. As a constant reminder of God's love for all peoples, especially the poorest, and as an affirmation of the inherent dignity of U.S. Hispanics, popular religion is the birthplace of U.S. Hispanic liberation in a culture that is alien and alienating.

Within the larger U.S. Hispanic theological movement, women play an increasingly important role. Ada María Isasi-Díaz has systematically elaborated a *mujerista* theology that takes as its methodological starting point the lived experience of U.S. Latinas. As such, *mujerista* theology distinguishes itself both from Euro-American feminist theologies and U.S. Hispanic theology insofar as the latter reflects the experience and interests of Latino males.

Though most U.S. Hispanic theologians identify themselves as Roman Catholic (as does the majority of the Latino/a population), the number of Latino/a Protestant theologians continues to grow, along with the number of Protestants in the larger Latino/a community. While acknowledging the Catholic historical roots of Latino/a culture in general, Protestant Hispanics like Justo González have emphasized, especially, the scriptural bases for Latino/a theology. At the same time, they point to similarities between Latino/a popular Catholicism and Latino/a popular Protestantism, such as the shared values of family, community, and celebration.

U.S. Hispanic theology remains a diverse historical movement that, as such, continues to evolve. By according a central role to culture, *mestizaje*, and popular religion in the development of a comprehensive, historical liberation project, U.S. Hispanic theologians have already made important contributions to Third World theologies.

Roberto S. Goizueta

See also: CHRISTOLOGIES: HISPANIC, *MESTIZAJE* CONSCIOUSNESS, PRAXIS/ ORTHOPRAXIS, THIRD WORLD WOMEN'S THEOLOGIES: HISPANIC.

Bibliography
Virgilio Elizondo, *Galilean Journey: The Mexican-American Promise* (Maryknoll, N.Y.: Orbis Books, 1983).
Orlando Espín, *The Faith of the People: Theological Reflections on Popular Catholicism* (Maryknoll, N.Y.: Orbis Books, 1997).
Justo González, *Mañana: Christian Theology from a Hispanic Perspective* (Nashville: Abingdon Press, 1990).
Ada María Isasi-Díaz, *Mujerista Theology: A Theology for the Twenty-First Century* (Maryknoll, N.Y.: Orbis Books, 1996).

Native American

American Indians first encountered Christians under colonialism; every discussion of this relationship must begin, but by no means end, with this catastrophic context. While Native peoples have certainly been victimized by the racist and culturecidal agenda of Euroamerican Christianity, they have also creatively appropriated the white man's religion on their own terms. The voices of Native American theology demand justice, reparation, and even the redefinition of theology itself.

Edna Chekelelee, a traditional Cherokee storyteller, tells a tale about "Jesus before Columbus Time" in which she constructs a definition of Jesus through the sacred directions orienting each Cherokee village and the colors associated with each direction. Jesus is red, the color of east, because of his purest blood and success; he is white, the color of south, because he makes peace; he is black, the color of west, because he honors the dead; he is blue, the color of north, and green, the color of Earth, because he loves wisdom and respects his Mother. When Columbus asks how the narrator knows this, Mrs. Chekelelee responds that long before the arrival of Europeans the Cherokee knew the presence of God in their hearts. This story embodies what Kiowa novelist N. Scott Momaday describes as "a long outwaiting"—a resistance and overcoming in which Indian people assume the names and even religion of their enemies, but still manage to preserve their innermost souls.

Edna Chekelelee's story braids the meanings of Jesus together through the strands of space and color, which possess sacred connotations for virtually all Native peoples. The importance of space to Native theologizing sharply distinguishes "Fourth World" liberation theologies from their "Third World" counterparts. George Tinker (Osage) argues that the way many liberation theologies reduce nationness to classness remains inappropriate to the struggles of American Indians for self-determination. Because Indian selves and communities are so closely tied to particular places, subsuming these land-based identities under economic categories "promise[s] no better than the continuing cultural genocide of indigenous peoples." Tinker alternatively offers the biblical concept of *basileia* (kingdom), which he reinterprets through a spatial understanding that places humans and all other forms of life firmly within the circle of creation. Other Native inflections of Christian theology include the assertion of multiple Old and New Testaments, and imagining salvation as the restoration of balance and harmony.

Some American Indians have preserved their souls by calling Christians back to true biblical principles. For instance, William Apess, a nineteenth-century Pequot and itinerant Methodist preacher, strongly rebuked the Euroamerican theological establishment for preaching that God meant Indians to be destroyed and replaced by white Christians. He also refused to excuse individuals for being misled by religious leaders. Apess declared that these Christians could (and should) have read the Bible for themselves; if they had, they would have discovered that Indians were not made to be the objects of manifest destiny's wrath.

Steve Charleston (Choctaw) has articulated a Native People's Christian theology in which he attempts to find common ground between traditional and Christian Indians and to promote nothing less than Christianity's second reformation. Acknowledging an "Old Testament of Native America" affirms that American Indians are not "just footnotes for Western colonial expansion" (Charleston, in Treat, p. 73). It also recognizes that because indigenous peoples possess a radically different history than that of Europe or the Mediterranean, they possess their own distinctive covenants with God.

Some Native theologians have suggested the possibility of multiple New Testaments as well. For instance, William Baldridge (Cherokee) perceives profound parallels between Selu, the Corn Mother, and Jesus. Their stories proclaim the good news that Selu, the Daughter of God, and Jesus, the Son of God, feed the hungry, love their children, and die sacrificially for the continuing good of their communities. They are relatives rather than enemies. As theological constructs, the Old and New Testaments of Native America emphasize the refusal of Indian Christians either to relinquish their past or assent to Christianity's often imperialist monoculturalism.

Finally, American Indians have re-imagined Christian theology through their interpretation of salvation as the restoration of balance and harmony. For Native North Americans, the maintenance of balance, or the dynamic interrelationship that structures the world and prevents dominance by any one entity, is both a core cultural value and a sacred responsibility. Disrupting this balance through neglect or disregard entails negative, and sometimes catastrophic, consequences for individuals and communities: suffering, illness, injustice, and environmental degradation. Salvation as the attainment of balance demands that Christians orient themselves to the world not only through a spirituality but also through an ethic of reciprocity.

Indeed, this spirituality and ethic of reciprocity also describe the larger Native American engagement with Christian theology. In what exists as a parable of this process, Rosemary McCombs Maxey (Muscogee), the first Indian woman ordained by the United Church of Christ, reminisces about the Sunday afternoons she spent at Weogufkee Indian Baptist Church. It was here that non-Native missionaries "condemned us to hell, then offered a way back with an altar call. In return, we would sing them songs, feed them, and laugh a lot. When the missionaries weren't there, we imitated them, and told their stories with our own embellishments and endings." It is through just such acts that American Indians have not only survived five hundred years of colonialism, but also forged theological perspectives with profound implications for the future of Christianity.

Laura E. Donaldson

See also: CHRISTOLOGIES: AMERICAN INDIAN, THIRD WORLD WOMEN'S THEO-
LOGIES: NATIVE AMERICAN.

Bibliography
Vine Deloria, Jr., *God Is Red: A Native View of Religion*, 2nd ed. (Golden,
Colo.: North American, 1992).
George Tinker, *Missionary Conquest: The Gospel and Native American Cul-
tural Genocide* (Minneapolis: Fortress Press, 1993).
James Treat, ed., *Native and Christian: Indigenous Voices on Religious Identity
in the United States and Canada* (New York and London: Routledge, 1996).
Jace Weaver, ed., *Native American Religious Identity: Unforgotten Gods* (Mary-
knoll, N.Y.: Orbis Books, 1998).

THIRD WORLD WOMEN'S THEOLOGIES

Introduction

Third World women's theologies entered the theological scene during the last quarter of the twentieth century. Since then, Third World
women have been making their presence increasingly felt and their
ideas heard in a world that had rendered them invisible and voiceless
in the past. The movement began slowly. The early generation of Third
World women theologians was schooled in Western theology, which
they accepted, though some had a gnawing sense it did not fit their
situation.

Their encounter with the emerging liberation theologies in the 1970s
altered their theological viewpoint. They found themselves in agreement with the analysis of the Third World reality of poverty and oppression, the new articulations based on context and rooted in praxis,
and the general critique of the so-called "universal theology." Though
the women admittedly gained much not only from the Third World liberation theologies but also from the feminist (liberation) theologies
coming from the West, they gradually recognized the inadequacies of
these theologies: the former as male-dominated and the latter as white-
oriented. Moreover, as Third World women delved more deeply into
their context, culture, and experience, they realized they had a different
word to say about God than their Third World brothers or First World
sisters. And that word would be different even among themselves.

The earliest attempt to "be different" was by Indonesian theologian
Marianne Katoppo in 1979. Her *Compassionate and Free: An Asian
Woman's Theology* was based on her experience in her own country as
the "other," a woman from Minahasa. In the following decade, Third
World women made a conscious effort to do theology from their own
perspective. This involved two important components: first, a critical
understanding of women's multiple oppression and their secondary

and subservient role in both the church and society; and second, active involvement in the struggle toward a new world of just and reciprocal relationships.

Doing theology from a Third World women's perspective became a concerted endeavor, particularly in the Women's Commission of the Ecumenical Association of Third World Theologians (EATWOT), which initiated a program precisely for this purpose, inviting non-members to its consultations. To begin the process of theological reformulation, dialogues were organized with women from the grassroots, for they constitute the majority of Third World women. Our theologies are primarily accountable to these women. To lend credibility to our statements, we favor quoting a poor woman from a depressed urban area or a miner's wife in contrast to the First World practice (including that of Western feminists) of citing scholars or experts. To be relevant to Third World women, our theologies must necessarily be inclusive, contextual, and liberational, besides being pluralistic and ecumenical.

The work of reformulating theology from the perspective of Third World women entails both reworking classical themes such as christology and ecclesiology, as well as reflecting on current concerns, such as the growing violence against women and the ecosystem. Today more women are writing on Third World women's spirituality, and some have begun to work on hermeneutical principles and methodology. The Bible is important to women, and their efforts include fresh interpretations of biblical texts that take into account gender issues and also differing multicultural and multireligious milieux. They do theology with "passion and compassion," which they may express in poetry and song and through art and story-telling. Life is central and women affirm their solidarity with all who struggle for life. Although Third World women's theologies strive for the empowerment of women, their ultimate aim is the full humanity of all. Third World women hope that their experience and perspective will be incorporated (not just subsumed) in all liberation theologies. Without women's contributions as an integral part, no theology in the Third World can be truly life-giving or liberating for the church or for society.

Virginia Fabella, MM

Bibliography

María Pilar Aquino, *Our Cry for Life: Feminist Theology from Latin America* (Maryknoll, N.Y.: Orbis Books, 1993).

Virginia Fabella, MM, *Beyond Bonding: A Third World Women's Theological Journey* (Manila, Philippines: Ecumenical Institute of Third World Theologians and the Institute of Women's Studies, 1993).

African

In Africa, women's theological discourse consists not only of words but of transformative action. Participants come from all walks of life, disciplines, and educational backgrounds. Not all read or write, but all talk, pray, and sing. The appearance of women on the theological scene in North America opened African women's lips to say their own words publicly. Before then, the voices of African theologians were not gender specific; women merged their voices with men's and they were often indistinguishable. Gender and sexuality were repressed except when women were chided on moral or theological grounds. Although African women wrote on mission and other theological themes, they did so with scant reference to women, or not at all.

The situation changed in the mid-1970s as *women-centered* theology began to deliberately portray women's lives and thoughts on theological issues. It set forth women's visions and strategies for attaining more wholesome living. It was and is a theology that strongly critiques those aspects of African culture that dehumanize women, and it searches for those aspects that are empowering. This approach to human life represents a healing theology intended to eliminate the stereotyping of men and women. It is intentionally dialogue-oriented and consciously invites and honors all voices. The theology emphasizes the dignity of the human-woman as a being akin to the Divine and aids women in their struggle to transform negative myths surrounding women's bodies and capabilities into a theology of the resurrection of the body. It seeks to replace hierarchy with mutuality.

African women's theology also attempts to be *inclusive*. While there is an effort to include all of Africa, a deliberate focus is directed on individual ethnic groups rather than nations, as national boundaries served only the purposes of colonizing Europeans. We prefer to highlight the diversity that constitutes Africa, not shying away from the fact that varying theologies arise within different religions or faith families.

In 1989 The Circle of Concerned African Women Theologians was inaugurated to allow women of differing religious traditions to come together to create an atmosphere for multi-religious discourse, to build solidarity among women, and to identify the most critical areas for dialogue and action by the whole community. It is to this end that women seek to enrich gender-related language about God because the predominantly male image has tended to result in a world and theology that are androcentric rather than theocentric. A more inclusive image of God reflects more accurately our experience of God because the source of both female and male being. It also reflects more accurately the mixed images that appear in ethnic concepts of God. This chosen path is necessary for a theology that can nourish people who live daily in multi-religious encounters. It is a theology that takes Africa seriously as a location of many religions and many cultures. In this sense, we can say it is *culture-sensitive*.

African women's theology, particularly the forms presented in The Circle, is intentionally *liberative*, although there are African women who adhere to dogmatic theologies, including theologies that are deliberately dismissive of African culture. Such theologies are often Bible-centered and oriented toward traditional theology taught from the pulpits, showing little concern for the historical circumstances that produced it. The Circle begins doing theology with theological discourse and dialogue, which then nurtures liberative and transformative thinking. Such reflection urges action. Action leads to further reflection, which then flows back into praxis. This emphasis on and sensitivity to praxis in the community and society emphasizes how transforming structures within communities can be a means of changing women's lives and consequently the lives of men and children.

In forming their liberative theology, many African women employ a "narrative" theology, utilizing their life-experiences and sharing their reflections in the form of stories, thus extending the study of theology beyond the academic realm. They also express theology in poetry and lyrics in an attempt to heal the dualistic breaches that have been imbibed from Western education. They struggle to make religion a dynamic, relevant, and liberative force that will enhance human life and sustain the ecosystem. This community approach to human life, based on relationships among human beings and between humans and the Divine, is necessary to nourish people who experience daily multi-religious, multi-cultural, and multi-racial encounters.

This women-affirming theology seeks the shalom of all creation, conscious that it is one body and that when one part hurts eventually all will be hurt. Through this approach to theology, people are encouraged to work for transformation and development of the societies in which they find themselves and the faith communities to which they belong.

In sum, this genre of African women's theology seeks the transformation of individuals as well as the societies and structures they create, a re-reading of the scriptures of African religions, Christianity, Islam, and other ethno-cosmic religions, and to reconfigure sexist myths and the culture of male-entitlement and female self-abasement. We who contribute to this theology believe that God demands life-giving creativity of the whole human race, especially of those whose voices are yet to be heard.

Mercy Amba Oduyoye

See also: BIBLE: AFRICA, CHRISTOLOGIES: AFRICAN, FEMINIST THEOLOGIES IN THE THIRD WORLD, LIBERATION THEOLOGIES: AFRICAN.

Bibliography

Elizabeth Amoah, *Where God Reigns: Women in the Commonwealth of God* (Accra: Sam-Woode Publishers, 1996).

Musimbi Kanyoro and Nyambura Njoroge, *Groaning in Faith: African Women in the Household of God* (Nairobi: Acton Publishers, 1996).

Mercy Amba Oduyoye, *Daughters of Anowa: African Women & Patriarchy* (Maryknoll, N.Y.: Orbis Books, 1995).

Mercy Amba Oduyoye and Musimbi Kanyoro, *The Will to Arise: Women, Tradition, and the Church in Africa* (Maryknoll, N.Y.: Orbis Books, 1992).

African American

Women of African descent in the United States continue to exist as women of the Third World, albeit in a First World country. They have been and continue to be marginalized and oppressed because of the multiple impact of their race, gender, and usually economic status. As a result, they have developed a liberating theology that emerges from their historical experience, which they name "womanist." Although based on the original definition of womanist developed by Black novelist Alice Walker, they have moved beyond Walker to encompass their particular oppressions as black, female, and usually poor as a critical aspect of their self-definition. In doing so, they have created a new language and a renewed self-identity.

Womanist theology emerged as women of African descent in the United States engaged in the study of theology realized that their presence was taken for granted. It seeks to affirm their roles as women who have been full and active participants in the history of black Americans and the United States itself. Both feminist and black (male) liberation theologians have erred historically in claiming to speak inclusively, while basing their theologies primarily on the respective experiences of only white women or black men. Womanists assert that full human liberation can be achieved only when all forms of oppression are equally addressed. Thus, their emphasis is on the building of community by relying on the resources of all, male and female, young and old.

A major resource has been the linking of their historic experiences as slaves without control over their lives or bodies with the biblical figure of Hagar, the concubine of Abraham. Hagar, the only one to speak to God face to face, and her experience are seen by womanists not only as affirming their efforts to survive in a hostile world but also indicating that they can thrive, keeping the black family and the black community intact. Womanists challenge the negative stereotypes that still abound around women of color with regard to their sexuality (seen as overtly promiscuous or neutered) and also leadership roles within the black family and society (seen as emasculating and unfeminine). They seek ways to heal and be healed. At no time do they accept a restricted role in working for a better future for their people.

Leading womanists such as Katie Cannon mine the lives of black women as a resource for identifying the ethical values and assumptions of the black community, while Jacquelyn Grant explores the significance of Christ's life, death, and resurrection for that same community, acknowledging that his maleness is not the issue but that his divine co-suffering as shared with the black community is of critical importance. Delores Williams condemns the historical surrogacy of black women and seeks a way of affirming their strength in the face of social and structural evil. She has called for an emerging dialogue that is liturgically effective, morally grounded, and also confrontational. She seeks to engage the black church to confront the issues of sexism, homophobia, and classism that serve to undermine its message of liberation.

Other womanist theologians, Protestant and Catholic, are engaged in exploring ways in which black women have been made invisible in both church and secular society. They call for new ways of speaking and seeing, a new language that shows forth the critical role of women as "bearers of culture" in both church and society. They also explore the lives of black women who came before them, and are reclaiming them as challenging and true role models for all women to follow.

Womanist theologians seek a better world for all of God's people, regardless of race, gender, ethnicity, class, or sexual orientation. Their immediate goal is to reclaim the voices of black women in order to help strengthen and rebuild the black community. Their ultimate goal is the development of a theology that liberates all people.

Diana L. Hayes

See also: BIBLE: AFRICAN AMERICAN, CHRISTOLOGIES: AFRICAN AMERICAN, FEMINIST THEOLOGIES IN THE THIRD WORLD, THIRD-WORLD THEOLOGIES IN THE FIRST WORLD: BLACK THEOLOGY IN THE UNITED STATES.

Bibliography
Emilie Townes, ed., *A Troubling in My Soul: Womanist Perspectives on Evil and Suffering* (Maryknoll, N.Y.: Orbis Books, 1993).
Emilie Townes, ed., *Embracing the Spirit: Womanist Perspectives on Hope and Salvation* (Maryknoll, N.Y.: Orbis Books, 1998).
Delores Williams, *Sisters in the Wilderness: The Challenge of Womanist God-Talk* (Maryknoll, N.Y.: Orbis Books, 1993).

Asian

In the late 1970s, Asian women began to do theology consciously from the perspective of women as they related the Bible and their faith to Asia's socio-political and religio-cultural realities. Many of their writings appear in the theological journal *In God's Image*. Theologically trained women formed associations in Korea, Taiwan, Indonesia, India, and the Philippines, among others, and ecumenical networks that facilitated mutual exchange and critical dialogue. Some of the important figures include Marianne Katoppo (Indonesia), Mary John Mananzan, Virginia Fabella, and Elizabeth Tapia (Philippines), Cho Wha Soon, Chung Hyun Kyung, Lee Oo Chung, and Sun Ai Lee Park (Korea), Kwok Pui-lan (Hong Kong), Hisako Kinukawa (Japan), Nantawan Boonprasat Lewis (Thailand), and Aruna Gnanadason and Stella Baltazar (India).

Several important issues emerged. First, the relation between gospel and culture is significant because Asian women theologians recognize there are both oppressive and liberating elements in the Asian and Christian traditions. Second, since the Bible occupies a pivotal place in church life, the interpretation of the Bible from women's perspective is crucial for theology. Third, women theologians have engaged in dialogue with women of other religious traditions to discuss feminine representation of the divine, the use of inclusive language, and strategies for transforming society. Christian women theologians have also reinterpreted Christian doctrines, including christology, Mariology, and ecclesiology, and developed a spirituality for affirming life.

Many Asian women emphasize the liberating heritage of the Bible by lifting up such women as Ruth and Naomi, Hannah, Miriam, Deborah, Mary Magdalene, and Mary the mother of Jesus as role models. Others have reclaimed the tradition of oral interpretation of scriptures in Asian cultures to retell, dramatize, and perform stories of biblical women, giving them voice and subjectivity. Reading the Bible through the lenses of socio-political analyses and cultural anthropology, Asian women theologians demonstrate the commonalities of struggles between biblical and Asian women. An emerging approach uses the insights of cultural studies and postcolonial theories to understand how biblical texts and their transmission have been influenced by empire-building and colonization.

Asian women live in a religiously pluralistic world, with enchanting gods and goddesses. Their religious imagination is influenced by the expansive religious language and metaphors of the divine in Asia and the symbolic structure in the cultural environment. Some women theologians have recovered feminine images and metaphors of the divine in both the Asian and biblical traditions. They point out that many Asian religious traditions emphasize the interplay between the feminine and the masculine, *yin* and *yang*, and heaven and earth, and challenge the predominant usage of male metaphors and images in liturgy, theology, and preaching in Asian churches.

A critical question for women theologians is, "Who is Jesus Christ for Asian women?" Mananzan and Fabella understand Jesus as a fully liberated human being whose prophetic ministry challenged the status quo and transgressed the religious and ethnic boundaries of his time. Chung and others turn to their shamanistic tradition and reinterpret Jesus as a priest of *han*, a feeling of hopelessness and indignation against unjustifiable suffering. Gnanadason and Baltazar speak of Jesus as the embodiment of *Shakti*, the creative feminine principle in Hinduism, and Kwok has begun searching for organized models for Christ that provide alternatives to anthropocentric and colonialist interpretations of Christ.

Women in the Catholic tradition have reclaimed Mary as a co-redeemer for human salvation and a fully liberated human being, instead of a docile, obedient, and sanctified mother. She accepts the challenge of the Holy Spirit and has a profound historical sense of the destiny of her people. As a self-defining woman, she defies cultural customs of her time, follows Jesus to the cross, and continues his ministry after his death. As a model of discipleship, she symbolizes a woman who yearns for liberation from oppression and who nurtures the hope of new humanity. In the Philippines, for example, the dark-skinned Madonna becomes a patron for women's resistance against colonialism and oppression.

More and more Asian women are becoming aware of the misogynist teachings and patriarchal and hierarchal structures of the churches. They challenge the churches to recognize women as full members of the body of Christ and equal partners in ministry. They maintain that the church needs to challenge its own sexism before it can serve as a beacon of hope for society. Instead of a body-denying and other-worldly form of Christian spirituality focusing on prayer and meditation, Asian women theologians develop a life-affirming spirituality that integrates body and soul, inner and outer worlds, and contemplation and social action. This spirituality affirms the creative power of women, the interrelatedness of all things, and the sacredness of earth. Such spirituality will enable Asian women to struggle against the exploitation of the global economic order, sex tourism, militarism, classism, and gender oppression.

Kwok Pui-lan

See also: BIBLE: ASIA, THIRD WORLD WOMEN, CHRISTOLOGIES: ASIAN, FEMINIST THEOLOGIES IN THE THIRD WORLD, *HAN/HAN-PURI*, SHAMANISM.

Bibliography

Chung Hyun Kyung, *Struggle to Be the Sun Again: Introducing Asian Women's Theology* (Maryknoll, N.Y.: Orbis Books, 1990).

Virginia Fabella and Sun Ai Li Park, eds., *We Dare to Dream: Doing Theology as Asian Women* (Maryknoll, N.Y.: Orbis Books, 1989).

Kwok Pui-lan, *Discovering the Bible in the Non-Biblical World* (Maryknoll, N.Y.: Orbis Books, 1995).

Asian American

Asian American women defy all forms of simple categories that homogenize. They include women from continental Asia and the Pacific Islands and their descendants who were born and/or raised in North America. They occupy various social locations as (im)migrants, refugees, citizens, and un-/under-documented aliens who speak fluent, limited, or no English. In spite of the vast diversity in their walks of life, two self-conscious commitments have enabled Asian American women to coalesce and do theology together: first, they define North America as their own "home base," and, second, they attempt to resist all forms of domination. Reflective of their own social locations and commitment to end domination, their theologies unpack the interlocking relationships between race, ethnicity, gender, heterosexism, class, and (neo-)colonialism. As such, their theologies point to Christianity as the locus of both patriarchal oppression and potential liberation.

Further, due to the varying degree of their exposure and affinity to cultural and religious "Asian" traditions, Asian American women's theologies challenge much of what Christian traditions are based on: the mutually exclusive binary opposition between the sacred and the profane, life and death, women and men, and the East and the West. As exemplified in the proliferation of Asian American women's works, especially in the past two decades, doing theology that is both contextualized and liberating requires multi-religious sensitivities as well as interdisciplinary methodologies.

Since Asian American communities are so diverse, theological reflections from Asian American women take different routes. Rita Nakashima Brock has constructed a christology through the lens of the abused child and has studied prostitution in Asia and the United States. Jung Ha Kim and Ai Ra Kim study how Korean American women in immigrant and ethnic churches negotiate their identities and the role of religion in cultural passage from Asia to America. Greer Anne Wenh-In Ng has written on inclusive language in worship and Asian festivals. Naomi Southard examines the Asian goddesses as resources for empowerment, and Young Mi Angela Pak recovers early history of immigrant women and their autobiographies to understand their religious experience.

Jung Ha Kim

See also: THIRD WORLD THEOLOGIES IN THE FIRST WORLD: ASIAN AMERICANS.

Bibliography
Ai Ra Kim, *Women Struggling for a New Life: The Role of Religion in the Cultural Passage from Korea to America* (Albany, N.Y.: SUNY Press, 1996).
Rita Nakashima Brock, *Journeys by Heart: A Christology of Erotic Power* (New York: Crossroad, 1994).
Jung Ha Kim, *Bridge-makers and Cross-bearers: Korean American Women and the Church* (Atlanta, Ga.: Scholar's Press, 1997).
Women of South Asian Descent Collective, *Our Feet Walk the Sky: Women of South Asia Diaspora* (San Francisco, Calif.: Aunt Lute Books, 1993).

Hispanic

To name oneself is a powerful act. A name provides identification as well as a conceptual framework, a point of reference, and a mental construct for understanding and relating to persons, ideas, movements. This is the main reason why a group of Latina women in the United States who are keenly aware of how sexism, ethnic prejudice, and economic oppression subjugate them call themselves *mujeristas*. The explanations of their faith and its role in their struggle for liberation are articulated in *mujerista* theology. This theology enables them to have a protagonist role in the women's movement, a role they had not hitherto had within the feminist movement controlled by the dominant women's group.

Important understandings of *mujerista* theology are the following. First, liberation is not an individual but a community struggle that enables the development in Latinas of a strong sense of moral agency. Second, following St. Anselm's understanding of theology as "faith seeking understanding," the source of *mujerista* theology is the lived experience of Latinas, in which religion plays an important role. This does not preclude church teaching and traditions, biblical understandings, or religious understandings and practices labeled "popular religion" that are mainly a mixture of Christianity, African, and Amerindian religions. Third, *mujerista* theology is a communal theology: the materials developed in this theology are gathered primarily during reflection sessions of groups of Latinas meeting for this purpose in different parts of the United States. Fourth, *mujerista* theology has learned much from Euro-American feminist and Latin American liberation theology, but it adds a critique of Latino culture as well as of the dominant culture in the United States and denounces racism and ethnic prejudice.

The first publication dealing with *mujerista* theology—then called Hispanic women's liberation theology—appeared in 1987.

Ada María Isasi-Díaz

See also: FEMINIST THEOLOGIES IN THE THIRD WORLD, THIRD WORLD THEO-LOGIES IN THE FIRST WORLD: HISPANIC.

Bibliography
Ada María Isasi-Díaz, *Mujerista Theology: A Theology for the Twenty-First Century* (Maryknoll, N.Y.: Orbis Books, 1996).
Ada María Isasi-Díaz, *En la Lucha—Elaborating a Mujerista Theology* (Minneapolis, Minn.: Fortress Press, 1993).
Ada María Isasi-Díaz and Yolanda Tarango, *Hispanic Women: Prophetic Voice in the Church* (Minneapolis, Minn.: Fortress Press, 1992).

Latin American

Women theologians in Latin America have discovered their vocation and mission through their involvement with women in poor areas who have become organized. They have become spokeswomen for these women, whom they regard as their sisters and companions. They have made it their aim to reflect upon, organize, and make heard what these women from poor communities share—though in an unsystematic and unpolished way—as they gather in Bible circles, mothers' clubs, and in other settings. Imbued with their faith experience, these poor women carry out responsibilities for various struggles which they assume on behalf of their people. The resulting theological discourse is therefore an incarnated theology, done in solidarity and in feminine plurality, fundamentally collective and communitarian. Above all, it is an engaged and committed theology.

This theology is not based on the purely rational; it involves both feeling and reason, sensibility and reflection. It is a theology where contemplation and gratitude find fulfillment in thinking and speaking of topics that are perennially reflected upon and elaborated, and constitute the treasury of God's revelation to God's people.

Theology done by Latin American women is therefore closely connected with spirituality. It arises from a spiritual experience that is thought out and explicated. It is organized on the basis of a desire that arises from minds and hearts yearning for liberty and struggling for liberation.

There are women's groups that focus on feminist theology and spirituality, and ecofeminism. Among them is the Chile-based women's collective more commonly known by the name of the journal it publishes,

Con-spirando. The members participate in rituals and workshops incorporating Pachamama ceremonies, and reflect on the theological implications of matters and events affecting Latin American women.

On the whole, Latin American women theologians, as interpreters of and spokespersons for experience that is lived and suffered, do not limit themselves to issues related to gender. Rather, they speak about and reflect on all the themes in theology, doing so from their particular perspective as women. In so doing, theology is enriched and becomes more human and more broadly theological. Most women theologians in Latin America do not do theology apart from men. Rather, theologizing with men, they desire to build God's reign, the dream of Jesus realizable in this world.

María Clara Bingemer

See also: BASIC ECCLESIAL COMMUNITIES, BIBLE: LATIN AMERICA, FEMINIST THEOLOGIES IN THE THIRD WORLD, LIBERATION THEOLOGIES: LATIN AMERICAN.

Bibliography
María Pilar Aquino, *Our Cry for Life: Feminist Theology from Latin America,* trans. Dinah Livingstone (Maryknoll, N.Y.: Orbis Books, 1993).
Elsa Tamez, ed., *Through Her Eyes: Women's Theology from Latin America* (Maryknoll, N.Y.: Orbis Books, 1989).

Native American

Since American Indian women were often special targets of evangelization, it seems especially appropriate that they are now engaging Christian theology on their own terms. However, Native women speak in very different theological dialects than those enunciated by non-Natives. For example, many American Indian languages possess no pronouns. Because of this, Native women tend to imagine God in much less sexually differentiated terms than Euro-American theologies. Another dialect emerges through the use of oral tradition and storytelling, which, in American Indian cultures, provides the people with moral, religious, and intellectual instruction.

Some American Indian women have created indigenous christologies by linking the story of Jesus with particular stories of their own peoples. The realm of literature has also offered a powerful forum for Native women's theologizing. In Linda Hogan's (Chickasaw) novel, *Solar Storms,* four generations of fictional women living in the community of "Adam's Rib" rewrite the book of Genesis and, in so doing, transform the meaning of covenant by including animals, plants, land, and water as equal participants. Perhaps the most unique dialect comes from the fact that, historically and spiritually, Native women were and are at the social and spiritual center of their societies, and their religious discourse reflects this status. Walking in balance, loving in connection, and speaking in their own tongues: these actions constitute the transformative and dynamic heart of American Indian women doing theology.

Laura E. Donaldson

See also: CHRISTOLOGIES: AMERICAN INDIAN, FEMINIST THEOLOGIES, THIRD WORLD THEOLOGIES IN THE FIRST WORLD: NATIVE AMERICAN.

Bibliography

Juanita Little, OSF, "The Story and Faith Journey of a Native Catechist," in *Native and Christian: Indigenous Voices on Religious Identity in the United States and Canada*, James Treat, ed. (New York and London: Routledge, 1996), pp. 209-218.

Nancy Shoemaker, ed., *Negotiators of Change: Historical Perspectives on Native American Women* (New York: Routledge, 1995).

Andrea Smith, "Walking in Balance: The Spirituality-Liberation Praxis of Native Women," in *Native American Religious Identity: Unforgotten Gods*, Jace Weaver, ed. (Maryknoll, N.Y.: Orbis Books, 1998), pp. 178-198.

TRIBAL THEOLOGIES

Tribal people are regarded as distinct from the main line national society in many nations of the world. They claim their indigenous status in many modern nations today. Tribals understand the world in terms of relationships. Nature, human beings, and spirit are dependent on each other as organisms. Land, forest, water, and air are God-given with no ruler or national government having proprietary ownership of them. Human beings are custodians of everything around them and must relate with everything as a relative and friend and live in harmony with them.

Love, truth, and justice are ordained by God and are administered in society through the customary laws. The tradition of "gift child" (India) and "peace child" (Papua New Guinea) enables them to resolve conflicts and restore peace and harmony in human life.

The *Ashur Kahani* among the tribals of Chotanagpur (India) shows tribal concerns for environment and provides a method to deal with environmental issues in the modern industrial age. God intervenes in human affairs to maintain an earth that is pollution free and balanced.

Space is more important than time for tribals. Land is life and without land life is not possible. Colonial governments and modern independent nations have been instrumental in destroying the inalienable tribal rights over land by implementing modern concepts of development. Tribals are among the communities suffering most in the world and continually face questions of survival. Theology must address both the tribal context and concepts.

Nirmal Minz

See also: INDIGENOUS THEOLOGIES, LAND.

Bibliography
Nirmal Minz, *Rise Up, My People, and Claim the Promise: The Gospel among the Tribes of India* (Delhi: ISPCK, 1997).

TRINITY

To speak of the Trinity within the Christian tradition means speaking of God or of one God in three different persons: Father, Son, and Holy Spirit. It is a "concept" for making explicit the understanding of the notion of God as experienced by the first Christian communities. At that time, Christian theologians wanted to connect the Greek notion of God as "unchangeable substance" with the presence of God in the Son Jesus, Emmanuel, God-with-us. They spared no intellectual effort in passing on a doctrine that has stood for centuries. As this millennium draws to a close a number of critical studies, especially by feminist theologians, have opened up historical, philosophical, and theological discussions on different portions of Trinitarian theology.

The doctrine on the Trinity is marked not only by a sexist vision of the divine reality, inasmuch as the three persons are expressed historically in the masculine, but also by a vision that includes a particular understanding of the human person stamped by Greek philosophy. This conception projects onto God the idea that a being can be unique and personal and, at the same time, multiple; that is, three persons acting independently and connectedly. This notion of *person* plainly bears the imprint of an idealistic philosophy that is the product of a particular moment in the history of Christianity.

Some contemporary theologians are not simply criticizing the philosophy present in this idea, but they are trying to "re-imagine" different routes toward a more just and equitable understanding. Some of these theologians stress that the relationship between unity and multiplicity is part of everything that exists: God is the expression of everything existing and everything is the expression of God. There is another "intuition" of the divine mystery, which holds onto its aspect of oneness and, at the same time, is comprised of multiplicity. Thus, "all" can be said to live in God and God in "all." Each being in its own way shares in oneness and multiplicity. This approach retrieves the *relational* character of the ancient Trinitarian doctrine. God is not a powerful being in isolation but is captured in human relationships and in relationships with nature and with the cosmos. We leave behind an abstract and metaphysical concept to touch the level of common human experience. That is the point at which the beauty and complexity of life becomes palpable for us. Such relationality is synonymous with the connectedness and interdependence of all lives. In this sense, the Trinity suggests above all else the relational reality that constitutes us. Re-reading the Trinity entails a philosophical and ethical posture of emerging from individualism and moving out of the hierarchical relationships found in social institutions and especially in religious institutions. Such a perspective avoids fixation on male images and becomes open to the male and the female and, indeed, far beyond them. It also opens us to an understanding of the relationship with God as "something vital" in which we exist, are, and grow. This conception of the Trinity leads us to think that we are simply "in God," that we are in the "greater mystery" with our good or bad actions and beyond them.

While it is true that various contemporary theologies have explored various paths toward "re-imagining" the Trinity, it is also true that relatively few have taken this path. At this end-of-century moment, conservative and fundamentalist forces are seeking to restore traditional doctrines, which means security, order, and hierarchical obedience. Such attitudes are regarded as crucial for maintaining fidelity to a certain Christianity and for maintaining a society that privileges small groups.

Only the future will be able to tell us which understanding of the Trinity will be most widespread. What is certain is that we can no longer hold onto a single and dogmatic understanding, while ignoring cultural differences and the specific problems being raised by different human groups.

Ivone Gebara

See also: CHRISTOLOGIES, GOD, HOLY SPIRIT, THEOLOGICAL METHODOLOGIES.

Bibliography

Leonardo Boff, *Trinity and Society*, trans. Paul Burns (Maryknoll, N.Y.: Orbis Books, 1988).

Ivone Gebara, *Longing for Running Water: Ecofeminism and Liberation* (Minneapolis, Minn.: Fortress Press, 1999).

Elizabeth Johnson, *She Who Is: The Mystery of God in Feminist Theological Discourse* (New York: Crossroad, 1993).

Catherine Mowry LaCugna, *God for Us: The Trinity and Christian Life* (San Francisco: Harper San Francisco, 1991).

U

URBANIZATION

The process of the concentration of populations in urban centers is linked closely to the processes of economic, political, cultural, and religious change. Since the industrial revolution and the development of capitalism, the phenomenon of urbanization has taken on a universal character, although, today, the most densely populated cities are located in the Third World, while the major urban centers of the developed North have seen their growth slowed as their inhabitants escape to suburbs and satellite cities.

Most Third World cities have colonial origins whose culture and interests are reflected in their locations—as ports or strategic intersections of overland routes—and in their urban design. Throughout the Third World, most of the world's population is tending to concentrate in cities in which poor migrants have given shape to multiple kinds of "informal economies," while only a portion of them have obtained steady work. Spatial and cultural segregation, growing irregular self-employment, and the poverty associated with criminal violence, drug traffic, and consumerism have caused the inhabitants of large cities to feel less secure and more fearful. Extensive and often corrupt police bodies aggravate such feelings and result in a situation that impedes the development of persons and the human community. Meanwhile, the poor have created their own houses and their neighborhoods, driven by increasing migration from countryside to city, with only feeble support from their governments. They often maintain their own traditions and values and with scarce resources they challenge the norms of the city of the elites, usually while occupying spaces little suited for human habitation.

Against this background, governments attempt to pursue decentralization and social policies aimed at reducing the gap between rich and poor, but with little success. More hope-inspiring are the many practices of solidarity that, with great effort on the local level, the "marginalized" themselves are undertaking to deal with the daily challenges of survival, minimum housing, and a lack of basic services, including space for shared life and recreation, popular education, and culture. In all of this, we can recognize the action of the Spirit, who "breathes where she will" to "infuse life" in the midst of the many forces of death and to prepare in the midst of the poor a "new city" where justice will dwell.

232

Certainly, poor city dwellers need the support of governments and of the "developed" sectors of the citizenry—but on the condition that they be refashioned to serve the processes of liberation and development set in motion by those poor inhabitants. Similarly, Christian churches must increasingly recognize that their base communities or small congregations contain the initial "cells for the building up of the church . . . and [are] a primordial factor for human promotion and development" (Medellín, 1968). It is there that the poor gradually discover themselves as persons in communities that are "sign and ferment" of a new city, with the mission of bringing the reign of God and God's justice to all. For its mission in the large city, churches undoubtedly need other spaces, lay movements, and mass media. But, most of all, they need a deep conversion and reform from the gospel standpoint of the poor majorities—a conversion in parish ministries, in the services provided by communities of religious men and women, and in the ministry of priests and bishops.

Ronaldo Muñoz, sscc, and Mario Garcés
(Trans. Phillip Berryman)

See also: BASIC ECCLESIAL COMMUNITIES, COLONIZATION, POVERTY, SOLIDARITY.

Bibliography
Phillip Berryman, *Religion in the Megacity: Catholic and Protestant Portraits from Latin America* (Maryknoll, N.Y.: Orbis Books, 1996).
José Comblin, *Called for Freedom: The Changing Context of Liberation Theology*, trans. Phillip Berryman (Maryknoll, N.Y.: Orbis Books, 1998).
Jorge Hardoy and David Satterthwaite, *La Ciudad legal y la Ciudad ilegal* (Buenos Aires: Grupo Editor Latinoamericano, 1987).
Aylward Shorter, *The Church in the African City* (Maryknoll, N.Y.: Orbis Books, 1991).

V

VIETNAMESE THEOLOGY

Christianity appears to have entered Vietnam in the first decades of the sixteenth century. An edict of 1663 mentioned that in 1533 there had been a prohibition of the diffusion of the Christian religion. In the following decades, sporadic attempts to evangelize Vietnam were carried out by mostly Portuguese Dominicans and Franciscans, but their efforts bore no long-lasting fruits. It was only with the arrival of the French Jesuits in Cochinchina in 1615 that Christianity began to take root. From 1615 to 1659 the bulk of missionary work was done by the Jesuits, of whom the most famous was Alexandre de Rhodes. Missionary work in the next two centuries, though highly successful, met with grave difficulties caused by the political strife between Tonkin and Cochinchina, the *padroado* system, the Rites Controversy, and above all by repeated and bloody persecutions, during which some 130,000 Christians were killed. In spite of these severe difficulties the church expanded rapidly. In 1933 the first Vietnamese bishop was consecrated. In 1960 Pope John XXIII established the Vietnamese hierarchy, dividing the church into three ecclesiastical provinces.

One political event that traumatized the church was the decision by the 1954 Geneva peace conference to divide the country at the 17th parallel, resulting in the formation of the Democratic Republic of Vietnam (communist North Vietnam) and the Republic of Vietnam (anti-communist South Vietnam). Shortly afterwards, some 900,000 people, mostly Catholic, emigrated from the North to the South. Again, in 1975, following the defeat of the South by the North, several hundred thousand South Vietnamese, most of whom were Catholic, left the country to seek refuge in the West.

It is against this historical background that Vietnamese theology should be understood and assessed. In the second half of the twentieth century, church activities in the North were severely restricted; no serious theological training was allowed and no theological scholarship was possible. In the South, on the contrary, from 1954 to 1975, conditions for church life and theological development were highly favorable. Not only did the church benefit from a massive influx of Christians from the North, but it also underwent the renewal generated by Vatican II.

The development of Vietnamese theology was greatly facilitated by the opportunities, mainly for priests and religious, of studying abroad,

234

primarily in Rome and Paris. Doctoral dissertations have been written on the history of mission in Vietnam, inculturation, Vietnamese ancestor veneration, Vietnamese indigenous religions, Vietnamese philosophy, and various aspects of Vietnamese culture, themes that contribute to an elaboration of Vietnamese theology. It must be said, however, that to date there has not been developed a Vietnamese theology comparable to those of Korea, Japan, or the Philippines. In general, Vietnamese theology can be elaborated only by means of a reflective encounter between the Christian faith and traditions of various religions in Vietnam, the *tam tai* philosophy (heaven, humanity, and earth), the worship of ancestors, and the struggle for integral liberation.

Peter C. Phan

See also: INCULTURATION, INDIGENIZATION, INTERRELIGIOUS DIALOGUE.

Bibliography
Peter C. Phan, *Mission and Catechesis: Alexandre de Rhodes and Inculturation in Seventeenth-Century Vietnam* (Maryknoll, N.Y.: Orbis Books, 1998).

VIOLENCE

Violence, a challenge to all of creation, takes many different forms: the violence of natural disasters such as earthquakes and floods; violence against the environment caused by exploitation and pollution; the violence of racism; the violence of disease, including HIV/AIDS; the violence of poverty, hunger, and economic dependence; the violence of crime and unemployment; violence against women; and the violence of militarism, war, and genocide. As the twentieth century ended in an explosion of violence, thousands were killed in Central America, Sri Lanka, Rwanda and Burundi, Congo, East Timor, as well as in Bosnia, Kosovo, and Northern Ireland, and thousands, including children, were senselessly mutilated in civil wars in Sierra Leone and elsewhere. As the new millennium dawns, approximately 300,000 children serve as soldiers. Throughout many locations in the Third World, the violence of the twentieth century was a continuation of the violence and exploitation of colonialism, undertaken in many cases with the complicity of the church.

Serious theological reflection on issues of violence in the Third World began in the mid-1960s. Influenced both by the Second Vatican Council's attention to the social teaching of the Roman Catholic church and by the World Council of Churches' attention to racism, theologians paid greater attention to the call of Jesus Christ to act in life-giving ways against all forms of oppression, including violence. Their reflections took many different paths. In Latin America attention was given to the *institutionalized violence*, also known as structural sin, that occurs when unjust political, economic, and social systems are deliberately maintained even when they deprive the vast majority of people of their basic needs. One of the most significant figures in Latin American theology and the church, Dom Helder Camara, said it was the duty of all human beings and all Christians to help the children of God to escape from the "inhuman situation" in which they find themselves. Emphasis was given to the presence of the reign of God within human history, and theological reflection on violence often made use of the hermeneutical circle of "see, judge, act."

James H. Cone, and other African American theologians as well as theologians in South Africa, focused on the *violence and sinfulness of racism*, noting that the gospel demands that Christians take sides with the victims of injustice and not with the oppressors. As was true of Helder Camara, Cone pointed out that Christians cannot remain neutral: "God created us as one humanity, made for each other because we are God's children. But the condition of the poor is a blatant denial of our oneness."

The theological reflection of Engelbert Mveng, a Jesuit priest from Cameroon, took a different path. Mveng focused on the *violence of "anthropological annihilation,"* the systematic elimination of the humanity of a people, as occurred in Africa as a result of the slave trade and colonization. He also reflected on "anthropological impoverishment," which he saw as the destruction of the dignity of persons as daughters or sons of God. Those persons bereft of "their identity, their dignity, their freedom, their thought, their history, their language, their faith universe, . . . their hopes, their ambitions"—the legacy of centuries of slavery and colonization—challenge the church, the gospel, and the reign of God.

Asian theologians have identified a growing culture of violence in Asia, mainly as a result of economic globalization. Doing theology in the Asian context thus involves naming its violent effects, among which is the massive exploitation of Asian peoples and resources causing worsening and degrading poverty and irreversible ecological destruction. Through sophisticated media technology, globalization imposes an invasive monoculture and consumerism that threaten what Asians hold as good and noble and that wound the spiritual and religious attitudes of the people. The military is used as an arm of globalization. Although there has been a decrease in the number of military regimes, there has been a substantial increase in arms purchases, augmenting the incidences of violence in the region. In 1999, the ruthless intimidation and killings of thousands of East Timorese by anti-independence militias, armed and backed by Indonesia's military, epitomized the culture of violence in Asia.

During the last decade of the twentieth century, Third World women theologians reflected on *violence against women*, noting that wherever there is generalized violence, as in times of war, natural disasters, social upheavals, and ecological violence, women and children bear the brunt of the hardships. They have also concluded that most violence against women is rooted in the mutually reinforcing heirarchies of patriarchy and androcentrism in cultures, religions, and economic systems. A 1994 conference brought together women theologians from North and South to seek to transform the contexts that generate violence, to assert authority over their own bodies, and to develop a cultural hermeneutic to guide them in resisting death-dealing cultural demands and victimization, including the violence of economic dependence.

All theologians—men and women alike—must work together to promote human worth and dignity for all people. They must help people move from struggling to survive toward living life fully. This includes support for all peace-making efforts; advocacy of care for the global environment; and promotion of full economic, social, and human development, including employment, education, housing, and health care for all of God's people. As the new millennium begins, theology must open the eyes of people from all cultures and religious traditions so they see that *all* unjust use of power by human beings results in violence, violence that is most often manifested against the sectors of society that do not share or participate in the arena of power.

Mercy Amba Oduyoye

See also: CHILDREN, LIBERATION THEOLOGIES, OPPRESSION, PATRIARCHY/ HIERARCHY, POVERTY, SEXISM.

Bibliography
James H. Cone, *Speaking the Truth: Ecumenism, Liberation, and Black Theology* (Grand Rapids, Mich.: Eerdmans, 1986; Maryknoll, N.Y.: Orbis Books, 1999).
Mary John Mananzan et al., eds., *Women Resisting Violence: Spirituality for Life* (Maryknoll, N.Y.: Orbis Books, 1996).
Engelbert Mveng, *L'Afrique dans l'Eglise: Paroles d'un Croyant* (Paris: L'Harmattan, 1985).
Peruvian Bishops' Commission, *Between Honesty and Hope: Documents from and about the Church in Latin America Where the Crisis Deepens and Violence Threatens* (Maryknoll, N.Y.: Orbis Books, 1970).
Sergio Torres and Virginia Fabella, MM, eds., *The Emergent Gospel: Theology from the Underside of History* (Maryknoll, N.Y.: Orbis Books, 1978).

WOMANIST THEOLOGY

(See **Third World Women's Theologies: African American**)

WORSHIP/RITUALS

Worship is a world phenomenon whereby human beings express their relationship with the Supreme Being through signs, symbols, and gestures in homage, reverence, and adoration. In the Third World, worship ranges from indigenous rituals in open fields to Christian liturgies in churches. Each religion and cult has its own form and place of worship, such as a shrine, a temple, or a mosque.

Most indigenous communities in the Third World, maintaining that spirits are present everywhere, still perform the primordial ritual of revering the good spirits and appeasing the malevolent and angry ones. These rituals aspire to maintain harmonious relationships with the invisible cosmic forces (including spirits of dead ancestors) that are virtually regarded as gods and goddesses. They also seek favors of these deities. The Ifugao farmers in the Philippines, for instance, perform a ritual to the rice god for an abundant harvest. Rituals that celebrate the cosmic cycle of birth, death, and new life; the unity of the visible with the invisible world; the sacredness of the earth; and healing rituals form part not only of indigenous people's worship but of popular religiosity.

Third World Christians, while sharing one faith in the God of Jesus Christ, express their worship in various ways. Prior to Vatican Council II, Catholic liturgy, as the official public worship of the Roman Catholic Church, was characterized by uniformity cast in a "Roman" mold. Vatican II put an end to this monocultural rigidity by encouraging liturgical renewal to "foster the spiritual adornments and gifts of the various races" for "an ever-increasing vigor to the Christian life of the faithful." Since then, conscious efforts have been made to develop meaningful and creative liturgies that are pluriform. Some attempts to inculturate the liturgy have involved reclaiming worldviews and cultural traditions that incarnate or give expression to the Christian faith within local culture.

In Africa, inculturation of the liturgy means incorporating movement and gestures that derive their meaning from the community's experience of the universe. These actions include going barefoot, tapping the hands,

238

swaying the body in dance, and emitting strident cries. As one African liturgist claims, when adopted in the Christian liturgy (as in the Zairean liturgy), "they not only carry the ancestral memory of the African peoples but become carriers of the memory of Jesus the Christ."

In India, inculturation includes scriptures of other faiths. Indian eucharistic liturgies make use of *bhajan*, singing, and *arate* (waving a tray of light, flowers, and incense three times) taken from Brahminic Hindu customs. Folk and tribal dances also enrich the liturgy, creating an atmosphere in which the local people truly feel at home. In eastern Indonesia, too, liturgical dancing is generally part of a feast or celebration.

In Latin America, liturgical renewal seeks not only to "inculturate" but also to "historicize" the liturgy by the creative use of symbols wherein the people express their struggle for life. Initiated mostly by the Christian base communities, liturgical renewal includes fasts, vigils, non-violent movements, and popular liturgies such as those celebrating the memory of Latin American martyrs.

Although most Protestant churches in the Third World have maintained the form of worship service passed on to them from their parent churches in the West, many of them have contextualized their music and prayers. Some major innovations have been initiated by women members. In South Korea, for instance, an ecumenical "Women Church," however small, arose from women's struggle for full humanity. One of its important features is the drama worship, which, combining biblical texts with women's life stories, becomes a new message of God for Korean society. The rituals reflect the interconnectedness of women, their relationship to nature, the need of healing, and the promotion of justice, peace, and the unification of Korea. Unlike the Roman Catholic Church, which excludes women from its official priesthood, the Women Church is led by ordained women from different Protestant denominations. Worship that legitimizes classism, racism, casteism, and sexism is dehumanizing and alienating. True worship is that which liberates and calls people to wholeness.

Margaret Shanthi, ICM

See also: ECCLESIOLOGIES, INCULTURATION, INDIGENOUS THEOLOGIES.

Bibliography
Tissa Balasuriya, ed., *A Rainbow in an Unjust World. Voices from the Third World* XV/2, (Colombo, Sri Lanka: EATWOT, 1992).
Louis-Marie Chauvet and François Kabasele Lumbala, eds., *Liturgy and the Body, Concilium* 1995/3 (Maryknoll, N.Y.: Orbis Books, 1995; London: SCM Press, 1995).
Elochukwu E. Uzukwu, *Worship as Body Language: Introduction to Christian Worship: An African Orientation* (Collegeville, Minn.: Liturgical Press, 1997).

LIST OF CONTRIBUTORS

Carlos H. Abesamis, SJ, a Filipino theologian, is a professor of scripture at the Ateneo de Manila University in the Philippines.

Joe Aldred, a Jamaican theologian, serves as bishop of the Church of God of Prophecy, a world-wide Pentecostal church, and is director of The Centre for Black and White Christian Partnership at Selly Oak Colleges, Birmingham, England.

Kalarikkal Poulose Aleaz, an Indian theologian, is a professor of religions at Bishop's College, Calcutta.

Marcella Althaus-Reid, an Argentinian feminist theologian, is a lecturer in Christian ethics and practical theology in the Faculty of Divinity at The University of Edinburgh.

Michael Amaladoss, SJ, an Indian Jesuit priest/theologian, is a professor of theology at Vidyajyoti College of Theology, Delhi, India.

Elizabeth Amoah, a Ghanaian Methodist, is a professor and chair of the Department for the Study of Religion at the University of Ghana, Legon.

María Pilar Aquino, a Mexican feminist theologian, is an associate professor of theology and religious studies and associate director of the Center for the Study of Latino Catholicism at the University of San Diego, California.

S. Wesley Ariarajah, a Sri Lankan theologian, is a professor of ecumenical theology at the Drew University School of Theology in Madison, New Jersey.

Maurice Assad, a member of the Coptic Orthodox Church in Egypt, is a former associate general secretary of the Middle East Council of Churches.

Naim Stefan Ateek, a Palestinian Episcopal priest and canon of St. George's Cathedral in Jerusalem and pastor of its Arab-speaking congregation, is also director of the Sabeel Ecumenical Liberation Theology Center in Jerusalem.

241

Leelamma Athyal, an Indian theologian, is a professor of theology at the Gurukul Lutheran Theological College and Research Institute in Kilpauk, India.

Tissa Balasuriya, OMI, a Sri Lankan priest and theologian, is director of the Centre for the Study of Society and Religion in Colombo, Sri Lanka.

J. B. Banawiratma, SJ, an Indonesian priest, teaches at the Faculty of Theology, Sanata Dharma University, Yogyakarta, Indonesia.

Nancy E. Bedford, an Argentinian Baptist theologian, is a professor of systematic theology at the Instituto Superior Evangélico de Estudios Teológicos (ISEDET) and the Seminario Internacional Teológica Bautista, Buenos Aires, Argentina.

María Clara Bingemer is professor of theology at the Pontifical Catholic University of Rio de Janeiro in Brazil.

Clodovis Boff, a Brazilian Servite priest, is a professor at the Catholic University of São Paulo, Brazil.

Leonardo Boff, a Brazilian theologian, is a professor emeritus of ethics and philosophy at the Universidade do Estado do Rio de Janeiro (UERJ) in Brazil.

Gerald M. Boodoo, a native of Trinidad and Tobago, is associate professor and chairman of the Department of Theology at Xavier University of Louisiana, New Orleans.

Katie G. Cannon, an African-American ordained Presbyterian minister, is associate professor of religion at Temple University, Philadelphia, Pennsylvania.

J. Russell Chandran, an Indian theologian, was formerly principal of the United Theological College, Bangalore, India.

Frank Chikane, an ordained minister of the Apostolic Faith Mission, is the director general in the office of the president of the South African Council of Churches.

Chung Hyun Kyung, a Korean feminist theologian, is a professor of theology at Union Theological Seminary in New York.

Sathianathan Clarke is an associate professor of theology at the United Theological College in Bangalore, India.

James H. Cone is a professor of systematic theology at Union Theological Seminary in New York.

J. Severino Croatto, a specialist in Semitic languages and biblical archeology, is professor of Old Testament Studies and Hebrew at the Instituto Superior Evangélico de Estudio Teológicos (ISEDET) in Buenos Aires, Argentina.

Kortright Davis, an Anglican priest from Antigua, is a professor of theology at the Howard University Divinity School, Washington, D.C.

Laura E. Donaldson, a Cherokee, is associate professor of English, Women's Studies and American Indian/Native Studies at the University of Iowa.

Kelly Brown Douglas, an Anglican priest, is an associate professor of systematic theology at the School of Divinity, Howard University, Washington, D.C.

Christopher Duraisingh, an Indian theologian, teaches applied theology at the Episcopal Divinity School, Cambridge, Massachusetts.

Virgilio P. Elizondo, a Mexican American priest, is director of archdiocesan television ministry in San Antonio, Texas, and a board member of *Concilium,* the international Catholic journal.

Simon P. K. Enno is a professor of ecumenics and world religions at the Myanmar Institute of Theology.

Virginia Fabella, MM, a Filipino Maryknoll sister, is on the faculty of the Institute of Formation and Religious Studies in Quezon City, Philippines.

Eleazar S. Fernandez, a Filipino theologian who is an ordained pastor in the United Church of Christ in the Philippines, is a professor of theology at the United Theological Seminary of the Twin Cities, New Brighton, Minnesota.

Mario Garcés, a lay Chilean theologian, is a professor of sociology at the Universidad de Santiago, the Universidad ARCIS and the Universidad Católica Card. Raúl Silva Henriquez, all in Santiago, Chile.

Ivone Gebara, a Brazilian Sister of Our Lady-Canonesses of Saint Augustine, is a visiting professor of feminist theology throughout Latin and North America and Europe.

Mary Getui, a Seventh-Day Adventist, is senior lecturer and chair of the Department of Religious Studies, Kenyatta University in Nairobi, Kenya.

Aruna Gnanadason, an Indian theologian, is presently coordinator of the Justice, Peace and Creation Team of the World Council of Churches and has special responsibility also for the WCC's Women's Programme.

Roberto S. Goizueta, a Cuban American, is a professor of systematic theology at Boston College.

Gustavo Gutiérrez is a Peruvian priest and theologian.

Diana L. Hayes, an African American theologian, is a professor of systematic theology at Georgetown University in Washington, D.C.

Sarojini Henry, an Indian theologian, is a visiting lecturer in systematic theology at the United Theological College, Bangalore, India.

Dwight N. Hopkins, an African American theologian, is a professor of theology at The Divinity School, The University of Chicago.

Huang Po Ho is a researcher and director of the Research and Development Center of the General Assembly of the Presbyterian Church in Taipei, Taiwan.

Simeon O. Ilesanmi, a Nigerian, is professor of Christian ethics at Wake Forest University, Winston-Salem, North Carolina.

Diego Irarrázaval, CSC, a Chilean priest and theologian, is director of the Instituto de Estudios Aymaras in Puno, Peru.

Ada María Isasi-Díaz, a Cuban American theologian, is a professor of systematic theology and ethics at Drew University in Madison, New Jersey.

Musimbi R. A. Kanyoro, a Kenyan theologian, is general secretary of the World Young Women's Christian Association.

Jung Ha Kim, a Korean American, is a sociologist at Georgia State University in Atlanta, Georgia.

Ninan Koshy, an Indian lay theologian, now retired, was director of the Commission on International Affairs of the World Council of Churches.

Teruo Kuribayashi, a Japanese Protestant theologian, is a professor of theology at Shikoku Gakuin University, Zentsuji, Japan.

Kwok Pui-lan, a Chinese feminist theologian, is a professor of Christian theology and spirituality at the Episcopal Divinity School, Cambridge, Massachusetts.

Emmanuel Yartekwei Lartey, a Ghanaian theologian, is a senior lecturer in pastoral studies in the Department of Theology of the University of Birmingham in England.

Archie C. C. Lee, a Chinese theologian, teaches in the Religion Department of Chung Chi College at The Chinese University of Hong Kong and directs the Christianity in Asia Project located in the Faculty of Divinity, University of Cambridge, England.

João Batista Libânio, SJ, a Brazilian, is a professor of fundamental and systematic theology at the Centro de Estudos Superiores da Companhia de Jesus in Brazil.

Arche Ligo, a lay Filipino theologian, teaches theology and women's studies at St. Scholastica's College in Manila, Philippines.

Domingo Llanque Chana, an Aymara priest, serves a parish in the Altiplano of Peru in the Juli Prelature.

Eleazar López Hernández, a Zapoteca Catholic priest from Mexico, is a member of the Coordinating Board of the Centro Nacional de Ayuda a las Misiones Indigenas (CENAMI) in Mexico.

María López Vigil is a journalist and analyst who has written many books on the church in Central America.

Seree Lorgunpai, a Thai biblical scholar, is a professor of Old Testament studies at the Bangkok Institute of Theology and acting general secretary of the Thailand Bible Society.

Otto Maduro, a Venezuelan philosopher and sociologist of religion and a Roman Catholic parent and husband, is professor of world Christianity at the Drew University Theological School, Madison, New Jersey.

Laurenti Magesa, a Catholic priest serving a parish in Tanzania, is also a lecturer at the Maryknoll Institute of African Studies in Nairobi, Kenya.

Mary John Mananzan, OSB, a Filipino Benedictine sister, is president of St. Scholastica's College and executive director of the Institute of Women's Studies in Manila, Philippines.

Emmanuel Martey, a Ghanaian Presbyterian, is a lecturer in theology at Trinity Theological Seminary, Legon, Ghana.

Pedrito Maynard-Reid, a Jamaican theologian, is a professor of biblical studies and missiology in the School of Theology at Walla Walla College in Washington State.

Monica J. Melanchthon is a professor of Old Testament studies at Gurukul Lutheran Theological College and Research Institute, Chennai, India.

Néstor Oscar Míguez, an Argentinian biblical scholar, is professor of New Testament at the Instituto Superior Evangélico de Estudios Teológicos (ISEDET) in Buenos Aires, Argentina.

José Míguez Bonino, an ordained minister of the Argentine Methodist Church, is a professor emeritus of systematic theology and ethics at the Instituto Superior Evangélico de Estudios Teológicos (ISEDET) in Buenos Aires, Argentina.

Nirmal Minz, a retired bishop of the Gossner Evangelical Lutheran Church in India, now lives in Ranchi, India.

Aloo Osotsi Mojola, a Kenyan translation scholar who was formerly a lecturer in philosophy at the University of Nairobi, is a translation consultant for the United Bible Societies in the Africa region.

Ronaldo Muñoz, SSCC, a Chilean priest and theologian, lives and works in Rio Bueno in southern Chile.

Albert Nolan, OP, a South African priest and theologian, is the editor of *Challenge,* a bi-monthly magazine published by Contextual Publications in Johannesburg.

Mercy Amba Oduyoye, a Ghanaian theologian, is director of the Institute of Women in Religion and Culture at Trinity Theological Seminary in Legon, Ghana.

Teresa Okure, SHCJ, a Nigerian Sister of the Holy Child Jesus, is a professor of New Testament at the Catholic Institute in West Africa, Port Harcourt, Nigeria.

Manuel Ossa, a Chilean, is a professor of theology and sociology at the Centro Ecuménico Diego de Medellín in Santiago, Chile.

Andrew Sung Park, a Korean theologian, is a professor of theology at United Theological Seminary in Dayton, Ohio.

Luke Lungile Pato, an Anglican canon, is rector of The College of the Transfiguration, Grahamstown, South Africa.

Anne Pattel-Gray, an Australian aboriginal theologian, is chair of Mission and Ecumenics at the United Theological College, Bangalore, India.

Rienzie Perera, formerly general secretary of the National Council of Churches of Sri Lanka, is currently research director of the Life and Peace Institute in Uppsala, Sweden.

Peter C. Phan, a Vietnamese priest, is a professor of religion and culture at the Catholic University of America, Washington, D.C.

Isabel Apawo Phiri is an associate professor and director of the Centre for Constructive Theology, University of Durban, Westville, South Africa.

Aloysius Pieris, SJ, a Sri Lankan priest and theologian, directs the Tulana Research Centre in Kelaniya, Sri Lanka.

Samuel Rayan, SJ, an Indian priest, is a professor of theology at Vidyajyothi College of Theology in Delhi, India.

Pablo Richard, a Chilean priest/theologian, is a professor of scripture at the National University of Costa Rica in San José.

Mercedes Román, a lay missioner from Ecuador, is a representative at the United Nations for Maryknoll's Office of Global Concerns and is responsible for children's issues.

Fernando F. Segovia, a Cuban American, is a professor of New Testament and early Christianity at The Divinity School, Vanderbilt University, Nashville, Tennessee.

Juan E. Sepúlveda, a pastor of the Pentecostal Mission Church and director of the Department of History of the Evangelical Faculty of Theology in Santiago, Chile, is also responsible for Ecumenical Relations at SEPADE (Evangelical Service for Development) in Chile.

Anicet Setako, SJ, a Rwandan priest and educator, is an administrator in a Jesuit secondary school in Rwanda.

Margaret Shanthi, ICM, an Indian theologian who lectures in theology and religious formation and is active in human rights work, is based at St. Joseph's Hospital Community, Dindigul, Tamil Nadu, South India.

Silvia Regina de Lima Silva, a Brazilian theologian and Franciscan sister, is professor at the Universidad Biblico Latinoamericano in San José, Costa Rica.

R. S. Sugirtharajah, a Sri Lankan theologian, is a senior lecturer in biblical hermeneutics at the University of Birmingham, England.

David Kwang-sun Suh, professor emeritus of theology at Ewha Woman's University, Seoul, Korea, is a visiting professor of Asian theology at the Drew University Theological School in Madison, New Jersey.

Luis Antonio G. Tagle, a Filipino parish priest, is also rector of Tahanan Ng Mabuting Pastol, the major seminary of the diocese of Imus, Cavite, Philippines.

Masao Takenaka, a Japanese artist, is honorary president of the Asian Christian Art Association.

Elsa Tamez, a Mexican theologian, is president of the Universidad Biblico Latinoamericano in San José, Costa Rica.

Edmond Tang, a theologian from Hong Kong, directs the Research Unit for East Asian Christian Studies at the Department of Theology, University of Birmingham, and coordinates the China Desk at the Churches Together in Britain and Ireland (formerly the Council of Churches for Britain and Ireland).

Elizabeth S. Tapia, a Filipino theologian and ordained minister, is academic dean and a professor of theology at Union Theological Seminary, Cavite, Philippines.

Ana María Tepedino, a Brazilian theologian, teaches ecclesiology at the Pontifical Catholic University (PUC) in Rio de Janeiro, Brazil.

M. Thomas Thangaraj, an Indian theologian, is an associate professor of world Christianity at the Candler School of Theology, Emory University, Atlanta, Georgia.

(George) Tink Tinker, a member of the Osage, is professor of Native American cultures and religious traditions at the Iliff School of Theology in Denver, Colorado.

Sergio Torres González, a Chilean priest in a parish outside of Santiago, is also a professor of systematic theology at the Instituto Alfonsiano de Teología y Pastoral in Santiago, Chile.

Molefe Tsele, a South African theologian and ordained Lutheran pastor, is executive director of the Ecumenical Service for Socio-Economic Transformation in Johannesburg, South Africa.

Justin S. Ukpong, a Nigerian priest and scripture scholar, is dean of the Catholic Institute of West Africa in Port Harcourt, Nigeria.

Elochukwu Eugene Uzukwu, CSSP, a Nigerian Spiritan priest, is rector and lecturer at the Spiritan International School in Enugu, Nigeria, and a visiting lecturer at the Catholic Institute of West Africa and the Institut Catholique in Paris.

Laura Vargas is executive director of the Comisión Episcopal de Acción Social (CEAS) in Lima, Peru.

Albert Sundararaj Walters, a Malaysian theologian, is a lecturer at Seminari Theoloji Malaysia in Seremban, Malaysia.

Vincent L. Wimbush is a professor of New Testament and Christian origins at Union Theological Seminary and an adjunct professor of religion at Columbia University, both in New York.

Wong Wai Ching is an assistant professor of religion at the Chinese University of Hong Kong and an officer of the Congress of Asian Theologians.

SELECTED ENGLISH-LANGUAGE JOURNALS
ON ISSUES IN THIRD WORLD THEOLOGIES

AFER: African Ecclesial Review
AMECEA Gaba Publications
P.O. Box 4002
Eldoret
KENYA

Africa Journal of Evangelical Theology
P.O. Box 49
Machakos
KENYA

Africa Theological Journal
P.O. Box 314
Arusha
TANZANIA

African Journal of Biblical Studies
Nigerian Association of Biblical Studies
University of Ibadan
Ibadan
NIGERIA

Al-Mushir: Theological Journal of the Christian Study Centre
P.O. Box 529 126, Murree Road
Rawalpindi Cantt
PAKISTAN

AMECEA Documentation Service
P.O. Box 21400
Nairobi
KENYA

Arasaradi Journal of Theology
Tamil Nadu Theological Seminary
Arasaradi
Madurai, 625010
INDIA

Asia Journal of Theology
P.O. Box 4635
57, Miller's Road, Benson Town
Bangalore 560 046
INDIA

Bangalore Theological Forum
United Theological College
63, Miller's Road
Bangalore 560 046
INDIA

Bible Bhashyam
Vadavathoor
Kottayam 686 010
Kerala
INDIA

Bigard Theological Studies
Bigard Memorial Seminary
P.O. Box 327
Enugu
NIGERIA

Black Theology in Britain: A Journal of Contextual Praxis
Department of Theology
University of Birmingham
Birmingham
ENGLAND

Bodtja Journal
Seminary of Saint Peter and Paul
P.O. Box 5171
Ibadan
NIGERIA

Bulletin for Contextual Theology in Africa
School of Theology
Private Bag X01
Scottville 3209
REPUBLIC OF SOUTH AFRICA

Bulletin of Ecumenical Theology
Spiritan International School of Theology (S.I.S.T.)
P.O. Box 9696
Enugu
NIGERIA

Catalyst
The Melanesian Institute for Pastoral and Socio-Economic Service Inc.
P.O. Box 571
Goroka 44 1, E.H.P.
PAPUA NEW GUINEA

Catholic Theology and Thought
Catholic University
90-1, Hye Hwa Dong, Jong Ro Ku
Seoul 110-530
SOUTH KOREA

Catholic Thought Today
Catholic Bishops' Conference of Korea
C.P.O. Box 16
Seoul 100-600
SOUTH KOREA

China Study Journal
China Study Project
Interchurch House
35-41, Lower Marsh
London SE1 7RL
ENGLAND

Chinese Theological Review
Foundation for Theological
Education in Southeast Asia
313 Glengarry Court
Holland, Michigan 49423
USA

Ching Feng
Christian Study Centre on Chinese Religion and Culture
6/F Kiu Kin Mansion
566 Nathan Road
Kowloon
HONG KONG

Christian Orient
An Indian Journal of Eastern Churches for Creative Theological
  Thinking
Manganam P.O.
Kottayam 686 018
INDIA

Crossroads
Africa Synod House
29-31 Selous Avenue
Box CY2220
Causeway
Harare
ZIMBABWE

Crown with Thorns
Baraku Liberation Centre
2-23 Miamino 5 Chome
Shijonwate City
Osaka 575
JAPAN

CTC Bulletin
Bulletin of the Commission on Theological Concerns
Christian Conference of Asia
Pak Tin Village
Mei Tin Road
Shatin
HONG KONG

C.U.E.A. African Christian Studies
Journal of the Catholic University of Eastern Africa
P.O. Box 24205
Nairobi
KENYA

Dalit International Newsletter
P.O. Box 932
Waterfront, Connecticut 06385
USA

Dharma Deepika
P.O. Box 6188
55, Luz Avenue
Mylapore
Chennai 600 004
INDIA

Dialogue
The Ecumenical Institute for Study and Dialogue
490/5, Havelock Road
Colombo 6
SRI LANKA

DIWA
Graduate School of Divine Word Seminary
Tagaytay City 4120
PHILIPPINES

East Asian Pastoral Review
East Asian Pastoral Institute
P.O. Box 221/1J.P.Campus
Quezon City 1 1 0 1
PHILIPPINES

Ethiopian Review of Cultures
Capuchin Franciscan Institute of Philosophy and Theology
P.O. Box 21322
Addis Ababa
ETHIOPIA

Focus
Pastoral Institute
GPO Box 288
Multan
PAKISTAN

Grace and Truth
Journal of Catholic Reflection
P. Bag 6004
Hilton, 3245
REPUBLIC OF SOUTH AFRICA

The Harp
St. Ephrem Ecumenical Research Institute (SEERI)
Baker Hill
Kottayain 686 001
INDIA

In God's Image
Asian Women's Resource Centre for Culture and Theology
Lorong Anggor
Taman Shanghai
58100 Kuala Lumpur
MALAYSIA

Indian Church History Review
Vidya Jyoti
23 Raj Niwas Marg
Delhi 110054
INDIA

Indian Journal of Spirituality
Rajajinagar I Block
P.B. 5639
Bangalore 560 010
INDIA

Indian Missiological Review
Sacred Heart Theological College
Shillong 793 008
INDIA

Indian Theological Studies
St. Peter's Pontifical Seminary
Malleswaram West P.O.
Bangalore 560 055
INDIA

Ishvani Documentation and Mission Digest
Ishvani Kendra
P.O. Box 3003
Pune 411 014
INDIA

The Japan Christian Review
JNAC Office, Room 51
Japan Christian Center
2-3-18 Nishi Waseda
Shinjuku-ku
Tokyo 2169
JAPAN

The Japan Mission Journal
Oriens Institute for Religious Research
28-5, Matstbara 2 chome
Setagaya-ku
Tokyo 156
JAPAN

Japanese Religions
NCC Center for the Study of Japanese Religions
Karasuma Shimotachiuri
Kamikyo-ku
Kyoto 602
JAPAN

JCTR Bulletin
Jesuit Centre for Theological Reflection
P.O. Box 37774
10101 Lusaka
ZAMBIA

Jeevadhara: A Journal of Christian Interpretion
Theology Centre
Kottayam 686 04
INDIA

Jian Dao: A Journal of Bible
   and Theology
22 Peak Road
Cheung Chau
HONG KONG

Jnanadeepa: Pune Journal of Religious Studies
Jnana Deepa Vidyapeeth
Pune 411014
INDIA

Jos Studies
St. Augustine's Major Seminary
P.O. Box 182
Jos
Plateau State
NIGERIA

Journal of African Christian Thought
Akrofi-Christaller Memorial Centre for Mission Research and Applied
   Theology
P.O. Box 76
Akropong-Akuapem
GHANA

Journal of Asian and Asian American Theology
Center for Asian Studies
1325 North College Ave.
Claremont, California 91711-3199
USA

Journal of Black Theology in South Africa
Department of Systematic Theology
University of South Africa
P.O. Box 392
Pretoria
000001 Gauteng
REPUBLIC OF SOUTH AFRICA

Journal of Constructive Theology
Centre for Constructive Theology
Faculty of Theology
University of Durban-Westville
Private Bag X54001
Durban 4000
REPUBLIC OF SOUTH AFRICA

Journal of Dharma
Dharma Research Association
Centre for the Study of World Religions
Dharmaram Vidya Kshetram
Dharmaram College
Bangalore 560 029
INDIA

Journal of Hispanic/Latino Theology
The Liturgical Press
Collegeville, Minnesota 56321
USA

Journal of Inculturation Theology
Faculty of Theology
Catholic Institute of West Africa (CIWA)
P.O. Box 499
Port Harcourt
NIGERIA

The Journal of the Interdenominational Center
700 Martin Luther King, Jr. Drive, SW
Atlanta, Georgia 30314-4143
USA

Journal of Theology for Southern Africa
Department of Religious Studies
University of Cape Town
Rondebosch 7701
REPUBLIC OF SOUTH AFRICA

Kristu Jyoti
Kristu Jyoti College
Salesians of Don Bosco
Krishnarajapuram
Bangalore 560 036
INDIA

Landas
Loyola School of Theology
P.O. Box 4082
1000 Manila
PHILIPPINES

Leadership
P.O. Box 2522
Kampala
UGANDA

The Living Word
The Manager
Pontifical Institute
Alwaye 683 103
INDIA

Logos and Pneuma: Chinese Journal of Theology
Institute of Sino-Christian Studies
33, Tao Fong Shan Road
Shatin
New Territories
HONG KONG

Melanesian Journal of Theology
Christian Leaders' Training College
P.O. Box 382
Mt. Hagen (WHP)
PAPUA NEW GUINEA

Missionalia
P.O. Box 35704
Menlo Park 0102
REPUBLIC OF SOUTH AFRICA

Mission Today
Sacred Heart Theological College
Shillong 793008
INDIA

MST Review
Maryhill School of Theology
P.O. Box 1323
1099 Manila
PHILIPPINES

National Council of Churches Review
Christian Council Lodge
Post Bag No. 205
Civil Lines
Nagpur 440 001
INDIA

New People
Comboni Missionaries
P.O. Box 21681
Nairobi
KENYA

The Nigerian Journal of Theology
Seat of Wisdom Seminary
P.O. Box 2124
Owerri
NIGERIA

Orientation
Institute for Reformational Studies
Potchefstroom University for Christian Higher Education
Potchefstroom 2520
REPUBLIC OF SOUTH AFRICA

Pacific Journal of Theology
South Pacific Association of Theological Schools
P.O. Box 2426 GB
Suva
FIJI

Pacifica
The Manager
P.O. Box 271
Brunswick East
Victoria 3057
AUSTRALIA

PTCA Bulletin
McGilvary Faculty of Theology
Payap University
Chiang Mai 50000
THAILAND

Quest
University of Zambia
Department of Philosophy
c/o P.O. Box 9703
NL - LC Groningen
THE NETHERLANDS

The Reason and the Faith
Kwangju Catholic College
P.O. Box 30
Bukwangju 500-600
Kwangju
SOUTH KOREA

Religion and Society
Christian Institute for the Study of Religion and Society
    Publications Trust
P.O. Box 4600
73 Miller's Road
Bangalore 560 046
INDIA

Religion in Malawi
Department of Theology and Religious Studies
Chancellor College
P.O. Box 280
Zomba
MALAWI

Salaam
Islamic Studies Association
Flat No. 302, R- 1, Hauz Khas Enclave
New Delhi 110 016
INDIA

Scriptura: International Journal of Bible, Religion and Theology
    in Southern Africa
Department of Religion
Private Bag XI
Matieland 7602
REPUBLIC OF SOUTH AFRICA

Sevartham
St. Albert's College
P.O. Box 5
Ranchi 834 001
INDIA

Studies in World Christianity
Edinburgh University Press
22 George Square
Edinburgh EH8 9LF
SCOTLAND

Stulos: Theological Journal
Bandung Theological Seminary
105 Dr. Jununan
Bandung 40173
INDONESIA

TCNN
Theological College of Northern Nigeria
P.O. Box 64
Bukuru
Plateau State
NIGERIA

Theology and Life
Lutheran Theological Seminary
P.O. Box 20
Shatin
New Territories
HONG KONG

Theology Annual
Holy Spirit Seminary College
6, Welfare Road
Aberdeen
HONG KONG

Theology for Our Times
Ecumenical Christian Centre
Post Bag 11
Whitefield
Bangalore 560 066
INDIA

Theology in Context
Institute of Missiology
Missio
P.O. Box 1110
52012 Aachen
GERMANY

Third Millennium: Indian Journal of Evangelization
Bishop's House, P.B. No. 1
Kalavad Road
Rajkot 360 005
Gujarat
INDIA

Trinity Theological Journal
Trinity Theological College
7 Mt. Sophia
Singapore 228 458
SINGAPORE

Vidyajyoti
4A, Raj Niwas Marg
Delhi 110 054
INDIA

Voices from the Third World
P.O. Box 4635
57, Miller's Road
Bangalore 560 046
INDIA

Word and Worship
National Biblical, Catechetical and Liturgical Centre
Post Bag 8426
Hutchins Road 2nd Cross
Bangalore 560 084
INDIA